Third Edition

From Phonics to Fluency

Effective Teaching of Decoding and Reading Fluency in the Elementary School

Timothy V. Rasinski
Kent State University

Nancy D. Padak
Kent State University, Emerita

PEARSON

Boston   Columbus   Indianapolis   New York   San Francisco   Upper Saddle River
Amsterdam   Cape Town   Dubai   London   Madrid   Milan   Munich   Paris   Montreal   Toronto
Delhi   Mexico City   São Paulo   Sydney   Hong Kong   Seoul   Singapore   Taipei   Tokyo

Vice President, Editor-in-Chief: *Aurora Martínez Ramos*
Associate Sponsoring Editor: *Barbara Strickland*
Editorial Assistant: *Katherine Wiley*
Director of Marketing: *Christine Gatchell*
Executive Marketing Manager: *Krista Clark*
Production Project Manager: *Liz Napolitano*
Manager, Central Design: *Jayne Conte*
Cover Designer: *Karen Noferi*
Manager, Visual Research: *Mike Lackey*
Cover Image: © *Annie Fuller/Pearson*
Full-Service Project Management: *Pavithra Jayapaul, Jouve India*
Composition: *Jouve India*
Printer/Binder/Cover Printer: *R.R. Donnelley/Harrisonburg*
Text Font: *PalatinoLTStd Roman*

Credits and acknowledgments for material borrowed from other sources and reproduced, with permission, in this textbook appear on the appropriate page within the text.

10 9 8 7 6 5 4 3 2 1

ISBN-10: 0-13-285522-4
ISBN-13: 978-0-13-285522-8

Contents

CHAPTER 17

Teaching Phonics and Fluency: Making Critical Choices for Authentic and Effective Instruction   273

CHAPTER 18

Involving Parents in Word Study and Reading Fluency Instruction   286

Foreword

Richard T. Vacca, Ph.D.
Professor Emeritus,
Kent State University
Past President, International Reading Association

It took a war—The Reading Wars—to bring the teaching of reading
into balance. The Reading Wars were waged in the 1990s along several
battlefronts: in the media, in legislatures, in school districts, and among
colleagues. Media coverage, more often than not, dramatized The Reading
Wars as a do-or-die battle between the proponents of phonics or whole
language. Rather than view phonics and whole language on an instructional
continuum, newspaper and television accounts of The Reading Wars only
served to muddle the public's understanding of how to teach reading to
beginners. Although The Reading Wars pretty much ran its course as we
entered a new millennium, one of its unfortunate consequences is that
it reinforced, and perhaps even perpetuated, a false dichotomy in the
teaching of word-learning skills: Either teachers of beginning readers initiate
instruction by using letter-sound relationships (phonics) or by using "look-
say" methods to teach words as wholes (whole language). This dichotomy
not only mischaracterizes whole language as simply "teaching words as
wholes," but it also narrowly portrays phonics instruction as the rigid, rote
learning of letters and sounds. Neither characterization could be further
from the instructional realities of today's classrooms.

From Phonics to Fluency, fortunately, does much to repair the damage
created by simplistic either-or portrayals of word learning in reading.
Moreover, this important book underscores the relationships that exist
among word study, fluency, and reading comprehension. Reading is
about making sense. The only legitimate reason to teach word study to
children is that they will be able to use decoding skills and strategies to
better comprehend what they read. Children must be able to identify
words accurately and quickly while reading. Tim Rasinski and Nancy
Padak, the authors of *From Phonics to Fluency,* recognize that phonics

is a tool needed by all readers and writers of alphabetically written languages such as English. However, they are not proponents of isolated drill, overreliance on worksheets, or rote memorization of phonic rules. They view phonics in the broader context of word study and support the use of contemporary instructional strategies that teach children what they need to know and actually do to identify words accurately and quickly. These strategies need to be taught explicitly in well-planned lessons, many of which are explained and demonstrated in this book.

What I like about *From Phonics to Fluency* is that it provides a balanced treatment of word study and fluency that draws on both phonics and whole language perspectives. Phonics and whole language are grounded in knowledge and beliefs that can be supported by a body of research as well as common sense about the teaching of reading. Padak and Rasinski wisely avoid locking themselves into ideological shackles. Instead, they draw on what works based on research-supported practice on word learning. For example, they underscore the importance of authentic texts and the role of parental support in word study. Parents and teachers of beginners have mutually supportive roles to play in children's reading development. Both parents and teachers support and develop children's knowledge of words in early reading in numerous ways, including reading stories, poems, and songs and discussing letter-sound relationships and patterns of letters in words that rhyme; encouraging children to listen for and identify sounds in words; encouraging children to spell the sounds they hear in words as they write; and comparing and contrasting letter and sound patterns in children's names, high-interest words, and words drawn from the books children are reading and the stories they write.

The core chapters of *From Phonics to Fluency* move teachers through a logical sequence of instructional strategies that will make a difference in the literate lives of elementary students: from teaching beginners to become phonemically aware; to instruction in the recognition of onsets and rimes; to making discoveries about words through word-making activities; to the use of word walls, word sorts, and word banks; to context-based strategies that help children cross-check for meaning; to strategies designed to develop children's reading fluency. Throughout each chapter, there are strong theoretical underpinnings to the practical strategies offered in this book.

I am pleased for Tim Rasinski and Nancy Padak. They have taken an old, beleaguered topic in the teaching of reading and given it a fresh approach. They have brought together the best of what is known about phonics and authentic word-learning situations. Maybe The Reading Wars had some positive consequences after all.

Preface

The first sentence of our preface to the first edition to this book said, "One of the ongoing issues of twentieth century reading instruction has been the nature and role of word recognition instruction, or word study, in reading education." Now, from the vantage point of more than a decade into the twenty-first century, we acknowledge that some things have changed. The 2000 Report of the National Reading Panel and the federal Reading First legislation that followed have focused our attention, and rightly so, on five elements that should form the core of effective reading instruction: phonemic awareness, phonics and word study, fluency, vocabulary, and comprehension.

This book focuses on the first three of these elements, although we hope you will see the importance of vocabulary and comprehension "beneath" the strategies and activities we describe. You can find more information about vocabulary and comprehension, as well as the topics of this book—phonemic awareness, phonics and word decoding, and fluency—in a professional development series that we have written, along with colleagues Gay Fawcett, Maryann Mraz, Evangeline Newton, Robin Wisniewski, and Belinda Zimmerman. Information about this series, *Evidence-Based Instruction in Reading,* is found inside the front cover of this book.

We enter this word study milieu by stating up front that competency in word recognition is absolutely essential to proficient reading. Moreover, although we believe that contextual reading is perhaps the best way to develop and consolidate word recognition strategies and skills, we also feel that direct instruction and ongoing coaching by teachers in word recognition are essential to optimal growth in reading. Not any kind of direct instruction and coaching will do, however. Word study should be engaging and challenging for all students, it should be enjoyable and nurture a love of the written word among students, and it should be accomplished as authentically as possible so that students can see the application and importance of what they are learning.

One of the main purposes of this book, then, is to provide you, the aspiring or veteran teacher, with workable approaches to word study that students will find authentic, engaging, and enjoyable. The approaches that we share with you are based on solid literacy theory, reading research, and actual classroom application. In addition, you will find icons in this edition that spotlight technology- and research-based strategies. Material tagged by the technology icons will lead you to many helpful resources. We have included the research icons to mark teaching strategies that scholars have found successful.

From Phonics to Fluency does not stop with word study. Most word study books for teachers begin and end on the topic of words. Our book goes beyond words and explores effective fluency instruction. Indeed, our goal as teachers should not be readers who read accurately, regardless of whether meaning is constructed from the text. Rather, our goal should be fluent readers who read efficiently, expressively, and meaningfully so that they can easily construct meaning. Fluency is necessary for good comprehension, and fluency is more than accurate word recognition. In this book we share with you many proven and effective instructional strategies for teaching reading fluency— strategies that can be easily and authentically integrated into other areas of the school curriculum, strategies that can lead to improvements in word recognition and comprehension, as well as fluency.

These two issues—engaging and authentic word study, and effective fluency instruction—are the topics that differentiate this text from many others on word identification instruction. We have also tried to give you, the reader, a sense for how these strategies have actually played out in classrooms by including the voices of real teachers who struggle with designing and implementing instruction for children every day. These teacher voices provide a real-life context that helps even veteran teachers imagine how the instructional strategies may play out in their own classrooms.

New to This Edition

Those familiar with this book will find some significant changes in the third edition. The topic of this book is an old one. But our approach to the topic is fresh. The instruction described in this book, when examined and adapted by real teachers, new and experienced, for their own classrooms, will lead not only to improved word recognition, more fluent reading, and better reading comprehension, but also will help nurture in many students a lifelong fascination with words and reading.

- We have made some significant organizational changes in this third edition. Since what we teach should be dependent on what students need to know, the assessment chapter is now one of the first chapters. The chapter about instructional routines, which offers curriculum development guidance, is also near the beginning of the book. We believe that this change will help you frame your learning about phonics and fluency instruction.

- Significant content has also been changed. Readers will find an expanded focus on instruction for children who are learning English as a new language. In addition, instructional tips for English learners are marked with a marginal icon.

- In addition, we address Response to Intervention and offer ways to weave RTI principles into word study and fluency instruction.

- We also more fully attend to issues surrounding technology and authentic instruction in word recognition and fluency through use of multiple genres. This is especially relevant in the word pattern chapters.

- Easy access to supplementary material is available through the inclusion of many new websites.

- And, of course, research citations and book lists have been updated.

CourseSmart eBook and other eBook Options Available

CourseSmart is an exciting new choice for purchasing this book. As an alternative to purchasing the printed book, you may purchase an electronic version of the same content via CourseSmart for reading on PC, Mac, as well as Android devices, iPad, iPhone, and iPod Touch with CourseSmart Apps. With a CourseSmart eBook, readers can search the text, make notes online, and bookmark important passages for later review. For more information or to purchase access to the CourseSmart eBook, visit www.coursesmart.com. Also look for availability of this book on a number of other eBook devices and platforms.

Acknowledgments

We wish to acknowledge the many teachers we have met and worked with over the years who have shared with us their knowledge, their ideas, and their frustrations about word study and fluency instruction. We are particularly indebted to teachers who read the second edition and told us what they liked and what they would like to see added. Our gratitude also to reviewers of this third edition: Tracy Hendrix, Carnesville Elementary School (Carnesville, GA); Lillian M. Martin, West Chester University (West Chester, PA); Judith Mazur, Buena Vista Elementary School (Walnut Creek, CA); Melissa Olson, Eau Claire Area School District (Eau Claire, WI); and Sharon M. Pitcher, Towson University.

Finally, we thank Aurora Martínez for her ongoing support and considerable patience as we worked to complete this edition.

1

Word Study and Fluency

Two o'clock on a Saturday afternoon, and everyone was tired. We had just completed another Saturday reading diagnostic clinic at our university. We assess struggling readers from the surrounding area to determine their reading levels and specific areas of difficulty and then make instructional recommendations to parents and teachers to solve those areas of difficulty. After the children leave, the clinicians remain to score and examine the children's performances on the various assessments. Two clinicians, Sandi and Tom, seemed perplexed.

Sandi and Tom had worked with fifth-grader Ted. Ted's teachers and parents reported that his major area of difficulty was in comprehension. He simply did not have good recall for texts he had read in school or at home. Sandi and Tom had anticipated looking into Ted's reading recall, his ability to make inferences and connections from his reading, his understanding of words and concepts, and his study skills. They were surprised that these weren't the source of Ted's reading difficulties.

What we found was that Ted had trouble in word recognition. Even when we gave him a passage to read orally at the second-grade level, he made a significant number of errors or miscues; over 10 percent of the words he read were not what was written in the text. And, whether he read orally or silently, his reading was extremely slow and labored. Actually, when we asked him to retell what he had read, we were surprised that he was able to remember so much. His recall was affected by his word recognition problems, but it wasn't bad at all. In fact, when we looked at his comprehension of a text read to him, we had to conclude that his comprehension was a strength. It was his word recognition and fluency problems that made him appear to have poor comprehension.

This is common among the students we see in our reading clinic. They come with a significant reading problem, which is felt to lie in comprehension or general reading achievement. But often, the comprehension problem is really a side effect of more fundamental problems—problems at the root of many reading difficulties—difficulty in word recognition or decoding and struggles with fluency. Indeed, Duke, Pressley, and Hilden (2004) suggest that, based on current research, 80 to 90 percent of struggling readers (those who cannot comprehend grade-appropriate texts) have decoding difficulties. In our own work we have found that the major concern facing students referred for reading intervention services is difficulty in dealing with the words on the page—reading the words accurately and fluently (Rasinski and Padak 1998). This book concerns that very important part of learning to read—namely, how to recognize words one finds in text.

For years, scholars have argued whether decoding actually needs to be taught at all, and if so, what the best methods are for teaching it. Jeanne Chall's seminal book *Learning to Read: The Great Debate* (1967) focused on this question. Chall concluded that children must learn word decoding and that phonics instruction is the most productive method for doing so.

At about the same time that Chall's book was published, scholars began looking at reading from a new, psycholinguistic perspective (Goodman 1967; Smith 1973). One tenet of this approach, which evolved into reading instruction known as whole language, is that making meaning is the central act of reading. Furthermore, students can use the act of constructing meaning to help them figure out (decode) words that they don't know. Consider the following sentences:

I ate lunch at McDonald's. I had a B_____ M_____ , F_____ _____, and a st_____ sh_____.

Of the 16 words in the sentences, 7 cannot be decoded with certainty from the letters given. Phonics (sound-symbol) information is minimal. In this case, the overall meaning of the passage helps the reader determine that the unknown words are *Big, Mac, French, fries, a, strawberry,* and *shake.* Meaning is the most significant factor in determining these words, not phonics—since the letter information is minimal or nonexistent.

Whole language gained momentum throughout the '70s, '80s, and early '90s. Since the late '90s, whole language has been in decline. Many reading scholars acknowledge that in some whole language approaches, phonics and word recognition were taught too indirectly for some children. It was often left up to students to notice generalizations that existed in letter-sound relationships and other letter patterns in words. However, these same scholars recognized that whole language theory made exceptionally positive contributions to reading instruction—the focus on real books and other forms of authentic texts, the focus on students and their needs and interests rather than the text as the focus of instruction, the recognition that understanding is the intended result of reading, and the need to read for real purposes, not for contrived purposes defined by the teacher or the reading textbook. With these contributions in mind, many reading scholars have moved toward an orientation called *balanced reading*.

Balanced reading instruction retains the best of whole language—real reading for real purposes—and adds direct instruction in necessary reading strategies and skills. Among the most important reading strategies and skills are those related to word recognition or decoding, moving from the written form of a word to its oral representation.

In this book we approach reading instruction from a balanced perspective. We know that all reading instruction should be aimed at getting students to read independently in order to ultimately find satisfaction and meaning in reading. We also know that, for many children, reaching that point requires a considerable amount of direct instruction in words and how words work in texts. Thus, although we subscribe to the notion that learning to read requires attention to words and learning how words work, other principles guide our understanding of exemplary reading instruction. These guiding principles include:

- Teachers should maximize students' contextual reading. A large body of research indicates that reading achievement results from lots of reading. Thus, at the foundation of our approach to reading instruction is increasing the amount of real reading students do at school and at home.

- And it isn't just during those special times devoted to sustained silent reading. Think of all the missed opportunities for students to read something during the school day—waiting for the school day to begin; during the lunch period; while lining up to use the restrooms; while in art, music, and PE classes; when waiting for buses to arrive at the end of the school day. And, of course, think of trying to expand students' reading when school is not in session—not only during the evening hours and weekends during the school year, but also during the long breaks that occur in winter, spring, and summer. (It is a fact that many students lose ground in reading over these breaks because they stop reading.)

- In order to maximize students' reading as well as their satisfaction with and motivation for reading, teachers and parents should create conditions in the classroom and home that will inspire students to read for their own purposes, as well as those the teacher assigns. This means having plenty of engaging, authentic materials for reading in the classroom, creating a pleasant and safe environment for reading, talking about reading and writing often, reading to students regularly, encouraging students to read and write, recommending books, and celebrating students' reading and writing.

- Students need time for authentic reading. They also need time for instruction. This is especially true for students who find learning to read difficult, including our English language learners. An additional 15–20 minutes of focused instruction three to four days a week can make a huge difference in students' reading growth.

- Students need to read for their own purposes. As teachers, we need to help students see all the reasons for reading. By integrating literacy into the school curriculum and life in general, students come to see that reading is an instrument for solving problems; learning about their world on their own; and finding enjoyment through stories, poetry, and other aesthetic texts. Teachers should help students see how important reading and writing are for learning about science, social studies, art, music, sports, and health. Teachers must also help students make literacy connections to their personal, family, and community lives. Students need to see that they can learn about themselves by keeping a personal journal; learn about their families through oral histories; and learn about their communities through newspapers, local publications, public libraries, the Internet, and bookstores.

- Students need to read a wide variety of materials. Over the past decade we have become increasingly focused on informational texts and stories as the primary type of reading for students. Although we agree that these texts do form the core of any good reading program, we also want students to read poetry, song lyrics, readers, theater scripts, newspaper and magazine articles, essays, letters and journal entries, jokes, et cetera. Indeed, we want students to read material that they themselves compose—their own stories, essays, letters, and poems.

- Teachers and parents should be models of proficient, lifelong, and engaged readers for students. Children emulate adults. They are most likely to learn those things that they feel adults value.

Students need to see their teachers reading throughout the school day. Teachers should share with students what they are reading, why they read, and how they read, so students know that reading is something adults do for real purposes.

- Teachers and parents should read to students daily. This helps to *sell* reading to students and underscores the joy of reading. Teachers should use the read-aloud session to introduce students to genres they may not read on their own—poetry, biography, fantasy, historical fiction, science fiction, and so on.

- Regular read-alouds promote better comprehension skills and larger vocabularies. Teachers find that they can read more difficult texts to students than students can read on their own. Thus, through the read-aloud experience students negotiate more challenging texts with more sophisticated words and more complex plots than they would (or could) read on their own. In addition, read-alouds help students develop an appreciation and love for good stories and, if teachers read to students in fluent and expressive voices, they provide students with a direct model of what fluent oral reading should sound like.

- Teachers and parents should read with students daily. There are many texts that even the most beginning readers can read with the assistance of a teacher, parent, or classmate(s)—partners who will read with them as a duet, a trio, or even in a large group (such as a whole class reading chorally). Poems, nursery rhymes, song lyrics, and the like are easy to learn to read. By reading with others, students learn that reading is a communal act. They also learn that trying their best to read while listening to a more proficient partner or partners will eventually help them learn to read the text on their own without assistance.

- Students' reading needs to be wide and deep. Students need to read widely for sure. When students read widely, they read one text after another—much as we do as adults. However, they also need to read deeply. By deep reading we mean reading a text several times until it can be read well. Many students who struggle do not read a text well the first time. Rather than move on to a new text (which is also read in a less-than-fluent manner), these students need to practice reading that first text (or a portion of it) several times (deeply) until they can read it well. We need to allow even struggling readers to read texts to the point where they are able to read them like proficient readers. In this way they will eventually move to proficiency in their reading.

- Exemplary literacy instruction makes connections with students' homes. Reading growth is maximized when students read at home as well as in school. Perhaps the largest amount of time available for reading, assigned and pleasure, is at home in the evenings, on weekends, and during vacations. Reading at home is most likely to occur when teachers make connections between home and school, encourage parents to help their children in reading, and support parents in their quest to do so.

- Exemplary reading instruction is comprehensive—it covers all the important aspects of reading. Here's that notion of balanced reading again. Teachers should spend instructional time focused on reading comprehension, vocabulary (word meaning), spelling, word recognition, reading fluency, self-selected reading, and writing.

- Literacy teachers must be informed decision makers (Spiegel 1998). Although researchers have identified instructional practices that lead to reading growth, the informed teacher decides what is best for students at any given time. Moreover, the informed teacher decides how to weave together varied instructional activities into routines that meet students' needs in reading. Some routines focus on whole text reading; others focus on individual words and word parts. Sometimes teachers work with individuals; other times they work with small and large groups. Sometimes students read for their own purposes; other times the teacher offers direct instruction. All this is woven into a seamless whole that helps students keep sight of the end goal of reading instruction—lifelong and meaningful engagements with texts.

- Effective literacy teachers monitor their students' progress in reading. These teachers know that not all instructional practices work equally well with all students. Thus, teachers monitor students' growth to determine if they are responding appropriately to instruction or intervention (usually referred to as Response to Intervention, or RTI). If they are, then teachers are assured that their instructional practice is effective. If not, they know they need to change what they are doing.

Kathy subscribes to a balanced literacy approach. In her first-grade classroom students do plenty of reading and writing for their own purposes. But she also provides time for direct individual, small group, and some whole class instruction in reading. We asked Kathy to talk about her approach to reading instruction.

Real reading with real children's literature and real writing define my reading program. I read stories to my students two or three times a day. They read on their own for SQUIRT (super quiet uninterrupted independent reading time) every day for at least

20 minutes. We have whole class shared reading with big books and language experience stories, and we have literature discussion groups with books that small groups of readers read together. My students also write in their own personal journals and literature response journals, and they write their own stories during our writing workshop time.

But . . . I also spend some time, nearly each day, teaching my students what we used to call phonics, decoding, and other skills. Actually, I like to think of them as activities that promote reading strategies. I will spend up to a half hour a day teaching these skills or strategies to my students. My students keep word banks, and they practice their words with a partner daily. They also sort their words into categories I give them a couple of times each week. We keep new sight words that we are learning on our word wall, and we read the wall every day. We cover at least two word families a week, and the word family words that we make go on another wall in our room. We make words and we play word games too. The students don't mind these activities. In fact, I think they like them. I keep these lessons fast-paced and interesting. I think my students see that what they learn . . . helps them immediately in their real reading and writing.

This book is indeed about teaching word recognition, or word decoding, going from printed symbols to meaningful oral representations of words and reading fluency, reading with expression and meaning. In reading this book you will find that we subscribe to particular approaches to word recognition and reading fluency, sometimes to the exclusion of more traditional (and commercial) approaches. Nevertheless, the instruction you will read about in this book is based on research, informed opinion, and actual instructional practice with students. Underlying our approach to word recognition and fluency is the following set of instructional principles, aimed primarily at phonics, outlined by Steven Stahl and colleagues (Stahl, Duffy-Hester, and Stahl 1998). Exemplary word recognition instruction:

■ helps students understand the alphabetic principle—that letters in English represent sounds.

■ develops students' phonemic or phonological awareness—the awareness of sounds in spoken words, an essential precursor to employment of the alphabetic principle and success in phonics instruction.

- provides students with a thorough grounding in letter recognition. To exploit the alphabetic principle and succeed in phonics instruction, students must be able to overlay spoken sounds onto written letters. Letter recognition is necessary for this to happen.

- does not require the teaching of rules or the use of worksheets and workbooks, and absolutely does not have to be boring or tedious. Successful word recognition instruction depends on direct teacher instruction followed closely by student use in authentic reading of connected texts (e.g., stories).

- provides practice in reading words. This is done through (1) reading words in stories and other connected texts; (2) reading words in isolation through word bank activities, word games, and other word-oriented activities; and (3) writing words, through dictation and through invented or phonemic spelling. In dictated writing activities, students learn groups of words that have a common phonic or other pattern. In invented or phonemic spelling, students apply their emerging knowledge of sound-symbol relationships in their writing for their own purposes.

- leads to automatic word recognition, the ability to recognize words quickly and with minimal analysis—by sight. This is an important part of fluent reading and is achieved through extensive reading—reading stories, reading words, and practicing words in writing.

- is only one part of reading instruction. By now we're sure you've noticed that we have mentioned this critical point several times already, and this is only the first chapter! Even though this book exclusively focuses on word recognition and reading fluency, these are only two aspects of the total picture. Word recognition and reading fluency are absolutely important in reading, but alone, they are not a complete or sufficient reading or literacy program. As Spiegel (1998) has noted, in a balanced reading curriculum "reading is not just word identification, but word identification is a part of reading" (p. 117). Instruction in word identification and reading fluency needs to be balanced with and integrated into authentic reading experiences.

**Research-Based
Strategies**

The notion that learning to read requires mastery of several skills and strategies that need to be taught directly to students in a balanced manner received significant support with the 2000 publication of the report of the National Reading Panel (NRP). The federal government commissioned the NRP to review research on how children learn to read and to identify factors that, if taught, provide the greatest chance of success for all children. The NRP identified five specific factors that were supported by empirical research: phonemic awareness, phonics or word decoding, reading fluency, vocabulary, and comprehension. The logical implication that arises from the report is that a reading curriculum that includes these areas can be considered balanced and comprehensive.

One of the best examples of a balanced approach to literacy instruction in the elementary grades is known as the *Four Blocks approach* (Cunningham, Hall, and Defee 1991, 1998). The approach is simple yet powerful and effective. In the Four Blocks approach the reading and writing curriculum are combined and divided into four equal blocks of time. Normally, this means about 30 minutes per block, each of which focuses on some aspect of literacy. One block is used for self-selected reading; students spend this time block reading material of their own choosing and talking about their reading with each other and their teacher.

A second block focuses on guided reading. Here, groups of students read common books or other reading material the teacher selects. Younger students, as a group, orally read, reread, and perform predictable and big books with teacher support. Older students read independently and then gather to discuss their reading—their perceptions and understandings, important points, and questions about the reading. These can be stories from basal readers, trade books that are required for the reading curriculum, and/or texts that make connections to other areas of the curriculum. This type of reading may be guided by authentic literature circles, book clubs, or discussion groups (Raphael and McMahon 1994).

The third block is a writing block. Short mini-lessons are followed by student writing—journal writing, writing versions of favorite stories, writing their own original stories, writing essays, making lists, writing letters to friends, and so on. In many classrooms, this block is sometimes known as the writing workshop period.

The final block is called word study: students work on word recognition and reading fluency through a variety of instructional activities (many of which are described in this book). Essentially, this is the time in which students learn to decode words, expand their word knowledge, and apply their word skills to fluent reading.

**Research-Based
Strategies**

Cunningham and colleagues (1991, 1998) have applied this balanced format at the primary grades for several years with extraordinary results. For example, six years of implementation have demonstrated that 91 to 99 percent of students who participate in the Four Blocks curriculum during first and second grade read at or above their assigned grade level (Cunningham et al. 1998). Moreover, a majority of students maintain their excellent progress in reading through grade 5. We like the Four Blocks approach, especially for beginning reading teachers. It provides a clear, workable, and effective framework for literacy instruction. And, although Cunningham and associates have used the program in the primary grades, we have worked with upper elementary and middle school teachers who have successfully adapted the Four Blocks framework for their own classrooms. Some blocks may require more time, others less time. For example, as students move through the grade levels, the word study block moves from a primary focus on decoding to a greater focus on word meanings—vocabulary.

Given our recognition of the importance of reading fluency, however, we would add a fifth block to Cunningham's model—reading fluency. In this block students engage in authentic repeated and assisted reading of texts for the purpose of developing automaticity in their word recognition and expressiveness in their reading that reflects the meaning of the passage practiced. We are convinced that balance is one of the reasons for the success of the Four (Five) Blocks Model and other curriculum models like it; children have consistent opportunities to learn to be skilled and strategic readers and writers.

Certainly, other balanced approaches can be developed and employed at any grade level. Whatever approach you devise, remember that, especially in the elementary grades, word study, word recognition, and reading fluency are absolutely essential to the program's success. But equally important, word recognition and reading fluency should be balanced with instruction and practice in the other essential areas of reading.

In Conclusion

This book is aimed at helping teachers develop critical competencies in teaching words and reading fluency. Thus, you will find chapters devoted to instruction in word decoding (phonics), word meaning (vocabulary), and reading fluency. You will also find a chapter dealing with the precursor to phonics—phonemic awareness. Notice that throughout this book you will be learning about four of the five critical areas of reading. The only missing critical area, comprehension, is also of central importance in this book. In order to comprehend, readers need to decode the words in the text, know what the words mean, and do all this fluently or effortlessly. Thus, by helping students develop competency in words and fluency, you are setting the stage for their comprehension.

Word study and reading fluency are necessary but not sufficient competencies for proficient reading. This book, then, deals with only one important part of a larger literacy framework. Comprehension instruction is critical, and students need time to engage in authentic reading and writing. A balanced approach, one that provides instructional emphasis to all important areas of reading, is required. Still, through applying the ideas in this book, you will provide your students with state-of-the-art instruction in decoding words and reading with exceptional fluency. In other words, you will help them take one important step toward successful, lifelong, and meaningful reading.

References

Chall, J. S. (1967). *Learning to read: The great debate*. New York: McGraw-Hill.

Cunningham, P. M., Hall, D. P., and Defee, M. (1991). Non-ability grouped, multilevel instruction: A year in a first grade classroom. *The Reading Teacher, 44*, 566–571.

Cunningham, P. M., Hall, D. P., and Defee, M. (1998). Nonability-grouped, multilevel instruction: Eight years later. *The Reading Teacher, 51*, 652–664.

Duke, N. K., Pressley, M., and Hilden, K. (2004). Difficulties in reading comprehension. In C. A. Stone, E. R. Silliman, B. J. Ehren, and K. Apel (Eds.), *Handbook of language and literacy: Development and disorders* (pp. 501–520). New York: Guilford.

Goodman, K. S. (1967). Reading: A psycholinguistic guessing game. *Journal of the Reading Specialist, 6*, 126–135.

National Reading Panel. (2000). *Report of the National Reading Panel: An evidence-based assessment of the scientific research literature on reading and its implications for reading instruction*. Washington, DC: National Institute of Child Health and Human Development.

Raphael, T. E. and McMahon, S. I. (1994). Book club: An alternative framework for reading instruction. *The Reading Teacher, 48*, 102–116.

Rasinski, T. V. and Padak, N. D. (1998). How elementary students referred for compensatory reading instruction perform on school-based measures of word recognition, fluency, and comprehension. *Reading Psychology: An International Quarterly, 19,* 185–216.

Smith, F. (1973). *Psycholinguistics and reading.* New York: Holt, Rinehart and Winston.

Spiegel, D. L. (1998). Silver bullets, babies, and bath water: Literature response groups in a balanced literacy program. *The Reading Teacher, 52,* 114–124.

Stahl, S. A., Duffy-Hester, A. M., and Stahl, K. A. M. (1998). Theory and research into practice: Everything you wanted to know about phonics (but were afraid to ask). *Reading Research Quarterly, 33,* 338–355.

2

Basic Concepts and Terminology

"I have to admit, sometimes I get mixed up about all the jargon and terms surrounding reading and I know my fellow teachers do also," says Julia, a reading specialist in an elementary school. "Occasionally I will get into a conversation with some other teachers and the discussion will turn to some reading skill or element such as digraphs. Although digraphs is the topic, diphthongs and blends are provided as examples of digraphs. Boy! It's confusing. I don't think students need to know all this special vocabulary, but I think I should. How else can we talk about these things unless we agree on what they are and what they mean?"

Our colleague Julia is absolutely correct. Any discussion of issues related to phonics, word recognition, reading fluency, and reading instruction needs to begin with an understanding of the basic concepts and terminology that frame these skills and issues. Without this understanding, productive interchanges of ideas about issues related to phonics, word recognition, and reading fluency are difficult and often confusing. With this in mind, in this chapter we identify and define some essential concepts related to phonics, word recognition, and reading fluency using language understandable to teachers, parents, and other school audiences. A more comprehensive and technical presentation of definitions can be found in *The Literacy Dictionary* (Harris and Hodges 1995).

Affix   A meaningful combination of letters that can be added to a base word in order to alter the meaning or grammatical function. Prefixes and suffixes are types of affixes.

Prefix   An affix that is added in front of a base word to change the meaning (e.g., _predetermine_, _disallow_).

13

Suffix   An affix that is added to the end of a base word that changes the meaning of the base word (e.g., *instrumental, actor, containment*).

Alphabetic Principle   The notion that in certain languages, such as English, each speech sound or phoneme can be represented by a written symbol or set of written symbols.

Automaticity   In reading, automaticity refers to the ability to recognize words in print quickly and effortlessly. It is a component of fluent reading and is marked by word recognition that is accurate and at an appropriate rate.

Balanced Literacy Instruction   Literacy instruction that is marked by an equal emphasis on the nurturing of reading through authentic reading experiences with authentic reading materials and more direct instruction in strategies and skills needed for successful reading. It is a

> decision-making approach through which the teacher makes thoughtful choices each day about the best way to help each child become a better reader and writer. A balanced approach is not constrained by or reactive to a particular philosophy. It is responsive to new issues while maintaining what research and practice has already shown to be effective. (Spiegel, 1998, p. 116)

Consonants   Refers to both letters and sounds. Consonant sounds represent all the letters of the alphabet except the vowels, *a, e, i, o, u,* and sometimes *y* and *w*. The letters and letter combinations (blends and digraphs) that represent consonants do so with fairly good correspondence, especially at the beginning of words and syllables.

Consonant Blends   Two or more consonant letters grouped together in which the sound of each of the consonants is retained (e.g., *bl, cl, pr, tr, sm, st, scr, str*).

Consonant Digraphs   Two or more consonant letters grouped together that produce one sound. That sound can be a new sound not represented by any other letter or letter combination (*that*), a sound represented by one of the grouped letters (*gnome, back*), or a sound represented by a letter not present in the group (*phone*).

Context   The linguistic environment. The words or phrases surrounding a written word. For word recognition, context refers to the meaning that precedes and follows words that are analyzed. Context can aid in the recognition of words in texts.

Decode   To analyze graphic symbols (letters in written words and sentences) into their oral representation, which leads to meaning. Synonymous with word identification and word recognition.

Fluency   To read expressively, meaningfully, in appropriate syntactic units (phrases, clauses), at appropriate rates, and without word recognition difficulty. Fluency has two major components: word recognition automaticity and prosody. Word recognition automaticity refers to the ability to recognize words effortlessly or automatically so that readers can attend to meaning while reading. Prosody refers to reading with expression and phrasing that reflect the meaning of the passage read.

Grapheme   A written letter or combination of letters that represents a phoneme.

Homographs   Words that have the same spelling but different pronunciations and meanings (e.g., *sow*—a female pig; to plant seeds).

Homonyms   Words that have the same spelling and pronunciation but different meanings (e.g., *plain*—flat land; ordinary looking).

Homophones   Words that have the same pronunciation but different spellings and meanings (e.g., *bare/bear, do/dew*).

Morpheme   The smallest unit of meaning in oral and written language (e.g., the word *cars* contains two morphemes—*car*, an automobile, and *s*, meaning more than one).

Orthography   Refers to the symbols or letters in a writing system. Spelling is part of orthography.

Phoneme   The smallest unit of speech that affects meaning of words (e.g., *b* in book vs. *k* in cook).

Phonemic Awareness   The awareness of individual phonemes in spoken words; the ability to consciously manipulate (e.g., identify, segment, blend) individual phonemes in spoken language.

Phonics   A method of teaching word recognition or decoding that emphasizes the relationships between written symbols (letters) and sounds that exist in a language. Phonics is usually employed in the beginning stages of reading instruction.

>   **Analogical Phonics**   An approach to phonics in which learners are taught letter patterns found in words they recognize and apply that knowledge to new, unknown words. For example, if students know that *at* in *bat* has a particular sound, they can use that knowledge to help decode new words such as *sat, cat, rattle,*

and *Patrick*. Word families or rimes and affixes are the most common letter patterns used in analogical phonics instruction.

Analytic Phonics   An approach to phonics instruction that maintains a whole-to-part orientation. Students are initially taught a set of words by sight. Then, from these sight words, phonics generalizations (letter-sound relationships) are identified and then applied to other words.

Synthetic Phonics   In contrast to analytic phonics, synthetic phonics embodies a part-to-whole approach to phonics instruction. Students are directly taught specific individual sounds that are represented by letters and letter combinations. Students are then instructed in synthesizing or putting together multiple letters and sounds to decode or sound out a word.

Phonogram   Also known as a *rime* or *word family*. See syllable.

Prosody   The melodic qualities of oral language, including expression and phrasing during oral reading. A component of fluent reading.

Response to Intervention (RTI)   A method of academic inter- vention and instruction. RTI seeks to prevent academic failure through early intervention, frequent progress measurement, and the employment of graduated and intensive research-based instructional interventions for students who continue to have difficulty. Students who do not demonstrate a positive response to one level of intervention are referred for a more intensive intervention level.

Schwa   The sound "uh" made by vowel in the unaccented syllables in a multisyllabic word (e.g., the vowel sound in the second syllable of *secret,* the vowel sound in the first syllable of *about*). As with many technical elements of language and reading, knowledge of the schwa is not essential to reading success.

Semantics   The study of meaning in language (words, phrases, sentences, paragraphs, entire texts); semantic knowledge can aid readers in decoding unknown words in context.

Sight Word   A word that is recognized immediately as a whole with minimal effort and without detailed analysis. Sight words are recognized automatically. The collection of words recognized by sight is referred to as a person's *sight vocabulary*.

Syllable   A group of letters that are produced as a unit and contain one vowel sound (except in words containing vowel diphthongs). Some basic syllable patterns are described below (C = consonant, V = vowel):

CVC (also known as closed syllable)	Short vowel sound	cat, sit, shot, back, myth
CV (also known as open syllable)	Long vowel sound	be, because, she, try, total, label
CVVC	Often long vowel sound	beak, sail, coat
VCe	Long vowel sound	late, bite, tote
Cle	L controlled sound	maple, babble, stable

In addition to the information listed above, there are several patterns that guide readers in dividing longer words into individual syllables. These patterns include:

base word—base word (compound words)	cowboy	cow/boy
prefix—base word—suffix	unfit retool basement	un/fit re/tool base/ment
V/CV	bacon open baby	ba/con o/pen ba/by
VC/CV	temper carton ginger	tem/per car/ton gin/ger

Onset   The part of a syllable that contains any consonants that precede the vowel (e.g., *b* in bat, *sl* in slack, *t* and *p* in temper, *c* and *t* in carton). The sound-symbol relationship between onset letters and sounds is quite reliable.

Rime   Also known as a *phonogram* or *word family*. The part of a syllable that contains the vowel and any consonants that follow the vowel. Letter rimes are easily recognized and are consistent in the sound or sound combination they represent (*at* in cat and *ight* in sight are rimes).

Syntax   The pattern of word order in sentences, clauses, and phrases and the effect of word order on meaning. Syntactic knowledge can aid readers in decoding unknown words in context.

Vocabulary   The stock of words for which a person knows or understands the meaning.

Vowels   Refers to sounds and letters. The sounds represented by the letters *a, e, i, o, u*. The letter *y* can serve as a vowel when it is not in the initial position of a word (e.g., *why*). The *w* can function as a vowel when it follows a vowel (e.g., *cow*). Vowels are the most prominent sound in and defining feature of a syllable. Vowel letters typically represent more than one vowel sound. Vowel sounds can be represented by a variety of letter combinations (e.g., the long vowel *a* can also be represented by *ai* in bait, *eigh* in eight, and *ay* in day).

Long vowel sounds are associated with the letter name of a vowel. Long vowel sounds are often marked by a macron (ˉ):

make	broke
beak	unit
pie	

Short vowel sounds are another group of sounds associated with the vowel letters. The short vowel is marked by a brev (˘), and the sound of each vowel letter is found in the following words:

bad	body
bed	bud
bid	

L Controlled Vowels   Occurs when the letter form of a vowel is followed by the letter l, which alters the vowel sound (e.g., when the letter *a* is followed by an *l*, a particular sound is produced, as in *shallow* and *tall*.)

R Controlled Vowels   Occurs when a letter form of a vowel is followed by the letter *r*, which alters the sound of the vowel (e.g., *star, her, sir, for, burr*).

Vowel Digraphs   Two adjacent vowels that represent one sound, usually the long sound of one of the vowel letters (e.g., *bead, boat, beet, bay, sew, die, chief*).

Vowel Diphthongs   Also known as vowel blends. Diphthongs are sounds made up of the blending of two vowel sounds (e.g., *oi* as in boil, *oy* as in boy, *ou* as in ouch, *ow* as in how, and *aw* as in flaw).

Word Family   Also known as *phonogram* or *rime*. See syllable.

Word Recognition   The process of analyzing a word in print in order to determine its pronunciation. Same as *decoding* and *word identification*.

In Conclusion

These definitions are helpful to us because they establish meaning and a common language for terms we use throughout the book. The list is helpful for you because it focuses your thinking in instructionally productive ways. As with so many other areas of education, teachers need to know these terms and their underlying concepts, but students do not. Indeed, many people have probably become excellent readers despite lacking definitions for *macron, diphthong,* or *schwa* and many other technical terms. Teachers need the labels; readers need to read!

References

Harris, T. and Hodges, R. (Eds.). (1995). *The literacy dictionary.* Newark, DE: International Reading Association.

Spiegel, D. L. (1998). Silver bullets, babies, and bath water: Literature response groups in a balanced literacy program. *The Reading Teacher, 52,* 114–124.

3

Assessing Word Recognition and Reading Fluency

Carol works as a third-grade teacher in a school with high student turnover. "We are always getting students coming in and leaving the school. In my classroom alone last year I had 10 students leave and 13 new ones come in." When new students enter her classroom Carol needs to assess where they are in reading: "Rather than try some standardized test, I use some of the informal instruments I have learned about over the years. I ask students to read for me for a few minutes from a grade-level book. From that reading I can get a sense for their ability to decode words, I can estimate their reading efficiency or reading fluency, and by the students' recall of what they read, I can get a pretty good sense for how well they understand what they read."

Not only does Carol's informal assessment provide her with a starting point for how to work with new children, it also gives her data that she can use as a baseline against which to determine how well children are responding to instruction and progressing in reading. Actually, Carol's assessments aren't just for new students who come to her classroom during the school year. She observes: "I assess everyone in my classroom during the first week of school, and I do a quick assessment for all my children about every two or three months throughout the school year. The information from these quick assessments truly helps me see if I am doing my job and guides me in planning instruction that meets the needs of all my students."

No book on word recognition and reading fluency would be complete without providing guidance about assessment. In this chapter, then, we provide several approaches for assessing students' word recognition and fluency. We divide our discussion of assessment into three portions: initial assessment, measuring continuous progress and making initial diagnoses, and diagnostic assessment. There is considerable overlap among these areas. Diagnostic assessment, for example, should include information about students' initial assessments as well as progress-monitoring information gathered periodically. Moreover, the diagnostic assessments can also be used to measure students' progress.

Initial Assessment

Before beginning instruction in phonics, word recognition, and vocabulary with young students, it is important to know just where students are in terms of some basic understandings with print and how it works. Fortunately, it's fairly easy to obtain this information.

Phonemic Awareness

Phonemic awareness, an important predictor of early and continual success in reading, is discussed in Chapter 6. There we present an adaptation of the Yopp-Singer Test of Phonemic Awareness. This test of 22 items, which can be administered in minutes, provides teachers with a good understanding of individual students' ability to perceive and manipulate speech sounds in words.

Letter-Name Knowledge

Letter-name knowledge is important in early reading instruction simply because teachers make reference to letters using their names. If students do not know letter names, they have a much greater chance of experiencing difficulty in word recognition instruction. Letter-name knowledge is easily assessed by printing the letters, uppercase and lowercase, on index cards, shuffling the deck, and asking students individually to name the letters.

Letter-Sound Knowledge

Letter-sound knowledge is also an important part of early word recognition instruction. Phonics instruction usually begins with the sounds associated with individual letters. As with letter names, letter sounds can be assessed by presenting individual children with letter cards (primarily consonants) and asking them to identify the sounds associated with the letters.

Another way to assess students' knowledge of letters and sounds is to examine their unaided writing or writing from dictation. Especially when students invent spellings for words, we can see much about their letter-sound knowledge in their efforts.

For any of the preceding assessments, if a child has little or no knowledge of the concepts being tested, halt the assessment. If a child misses several items in a row, you can safely conclude that those concepts need to be taught. It's important to limit the child's frustration. You do not need to go through every letter name to conclude that letter-name knowledge is largely present or absent.

Word Meanings—Vocabulary

Readers who can decode words but who do not know their meanings are often referred to as *word callers*; they are seldom successful comprehenders. Therefore, you need to get a sense of students' vocabulary or knowledge of word meanings.

A simple way to do this is to select 10 representative words from your grade-level textbooks. Then present the words individually to each student, orally and in print, and ask the students to give the meaning of the word or use it appropriately in a sentence. Give full credit for words that are thoroughly defined or described, half credit for words that are partially defined or described, and no credit for words for which students have minimal or no understanding. A score of 9 or better indicates a strong vocabulary. A score of 5 or below indicates that vocabulary may hinder the student's reading development, so he or she will need additional support and instruction in vocabulary.

Basic Print Concepts

Basic print concepts refer to ideas that are essential to reading and reading instruction. They are the stuff around which reading instruction revolves. Ideas such as *letter, word, sentence, beginning,* and *end* are concepts that can easily be assessed in individual students.

To begin an assessment of basic print concepts, have individual students dictate a brief story (two to four sentences) to you. The story could simply be about what the child did earlier in the day or the previous day. Print the story verbatim on a blank sheet of paper as it is dictated. Then, read it back to the student, pointing to individual words as they are read. Now ask the student questions about basic print concepts:

- Point to the *beginning* of the story or line of text.
- Point to the *end* of the story or line of text.
- Point to the *top* of the story.
- Point to the *bottom* of the story.
- Circle *one letter* in the story. Circle *two letters* together in the story.
- Circle a *capital* or *uppercase* letter in the story.
- Circle *one word* in the story. Circle *two words* together in the story.
- Point to a period; ask the child if she or he knows its name and purpose.
- Ask the child to point to and say any words he or she may know in the story.

If the child is not reading conventionally yet, you may also want to check the child's knowledge of one-to-one correspondence between words spoken and written as well as his or her ability to learn words on sight. Rewrite the first sentence from the story and read it several times to the child with the child looking at the text. Point to the words as you read. After reading the sentence several times slowly, invite the child to read the text to you, pointing to the words as they are read. Does the child make a one-to-one match between the written and spoken words? Ask him or her to find certain words from the sentence. Is the child able to do so? Does the child find the words by immediate recognition or by rereading the sentence from the beginning? Write one of the words from the sentence on a card or another sheet of paper. Ask the child to identify the word. If the child is unable to do so, can she or he match it with the same word in the sentence? If the child can match the written word in isolation with the word in context, can he or she then say the word?

You will find these procedures helpful for English language learner (ELL) students as well as those whose first language is English. In

English Language Learners

case studies of twelve 4- and 5-year-old biliterate (Spanish/English) children, Reyes and Azuara (2008) found that children developed metalinguistic knowledge and knowledge about print in both languages. They observed: "We learned that young bilingual children are beginning to understand that Spanish and English are written in distinct ways" (p. 390).

Book Awareness

Since so much of reading and other content area instruction centers on books, it is critical that even young students have some basic understandings about books and how they work. An easy way to assess book knowledge is to have a child examine a picture book and answer specific questions about it. For example, hand the picture book to the child so that the child receives it with the back cover facing up and the spine facing the child. The child's responses to the following directives and questions should provide you with a good idea of book awareness:

- Show me the front of the book.
- Open the book up to where you start to read.
- (With the book open) On what page should you start to read?
- (Looking at one page) Where do you start reading on this page?
- What do you do when you come to the end of each line?
- What do you do when you come to the end of the page?
- (After looking at both pages of an open book) Now where do you go next in this book?

Although complete mastery is not necessary, some knowledge of letter names, letter sounds, sound segmentation and manipulation, and basic print concepts will surely facilitate students' word recognition learning. Those students who experience severe difficulty in these assessments may need some extra help, in the classroom and at home, in these important early stages of reading and word recognition. These quick assessments may also be administered periodically to those individual students who have difficulty in order to chart their progress.

Measuring Continuous Progress and Making Initial Diagnoses

Instruction benefits students at different rates and in different ways. In this age of increased accountability, teachers must document students' progress periodically throughout the school year. This provides evidence of student progress and clear and quick indications of children who may need more or different instruction.

A simple way to document progress and make preliminary diagnoses of reading problems in word recognition and fluency is to take periodic samples of students' oral reading of authentic reading from trade books or textbooks. This approach, called *curriculum-based assessment* (Deno 1985; Deno, Mirkin, and Chiang 1982; Salvia and Hughes 1990), is a valid, effective, and efficient way to monitor progress and identify potential trouble spots in students' reading.

We have developed a simple and quick approach for measuring students' progress in word recognition that is based on curriculum-based assessment and on more traditional but time-consuming informal reading inventories. We call it *Three Minute Reading Assessments* (Rasinski and Padak 2005a, 2005b). Although *Three Minute Reading Assessments* is available commercially, teachers can easily create their own version of the assessment using their own materials. Here is how it works:

- Find several grade-level passages of about 200 to 400 words from textbooks or trade books appropriate to your assigned grade level.

- Ask individual students to read one passage in their best voice and at their normal reading rate. Remind them that you will be asking them to recall what they have read after reading the passage.

- As each individual student reads, keep a copy of the passage in front of you and mark any uncorrected errors he or she makes. Also mark where the student is at the end of one minute.

- When the student has read the passage, remove it from his or her sight and ask the child to retell what he or she read. If the child is unable to provide any summary or response to the passage, you may wish to offer prompts. At this point the assessment is finished. It should take approximately three to five minutes to complete.

- Do this assessment at the beginning of the school year to get baseline data and then monthly or quarterly to determine whether students are responding well to your instruction and are making progress over the course of the school year.

You may wish to record each student's reading to document and analyze his or her performance. You can also document students' reading errors, one-minute reading location, and comprehension while they are reading and recalling what they have read. Here is how you can use students' performance to measure word recognition, fluency, and comprehension.

Word Recognition

Determine the percentage of words students read correctly. This can be done by dividing the number of words read correctly by the total number of words read in the passage. For example, if the passage had 210 words and a student mispronounced 6 of the words, he or she would have read 204 words correctly. Divide 204 by 210 to get a percentage of words read correctly: 97 percent. In other words, this student read 97 percent of the words correctly in the passage.

A score of 98 percent or better indicates that the student has strong word recognition skills for material at his or her grade level. Scores between 93 and 97 percent are indicative of adequate word recognition, and scores at 92 percent or below indicate marginal or weak word recognition skills.

Used as a measure of continuous progress, this portion of the *Three Minute Reading Assessment* can help you to track a student's word recognition skills; in this case, you will want the percentage of words a student reads correctly to increase as the school year progresses. Used diagnostically, it will enable you to determine which students need additional focused instruction in phonics and word recognition; in this case, you will want to identify those students who score at the 92 percent or below level and then to provide them with additional assessments (see the next major section in this chapter) to verify their difficulty in word recognition.

Fluency

Fluency has two components: automaticity in word recognition and prosody, or expressiveness while reading. *Automaticity* refers to the ability to recognize words with minimal cognitive effort. This is significant because readers who minimize the amount of cognitive energy needed for word recognition can employ that energy for the more important goal in reading—comprehension.

Figure 3.1 Target Reading Rates for Automaticity by Grade Level

Grade	Fall	Winter	Spring
1	0–10 wcpm	10–50 wcpm	30–90 wcpm
2	20–80	40–100	60–130
3	60–110	70–120	80–140
4	70–120	80–130	90–150
5	80–130	90–140	100–160
6	90–140	100–150	110–170
7	100–150	110–160	120–180
8	110–160	120–180	130–190

Automaticity is very easy to assess using the curriculum-based assessment/*Three Minute Reading Assessment* format. The number of words students read correctly in the initial minute of reading (wcpm) is the measure of automaticity in word recognition. When you use this format as a measure of continuous progress, you will want to see students' reading rates increase over the course of the school year. When you use it diagnostically, compare students' performance against the reading rates for the appropriate grade level and time of year (see Figure 3.1). Students who score near the low end of the grade-level range or below may need additional instruction and support in fluency automaticity.

Prosodic, expressive reading involves readers using their voices (whether reading orally or silently [internal voices]) to add meaning to the words. Meaning can be expressed through phrasing, emphasis, pausing, volume, rate, and pitch, as well as the words. So when readers read with expression, they are reading with meaning. In our *Three Minute Reading Assessments,* expressive reading is assessed by simply listening to students read and asking ourselves if the reading sounds like real language—Is the student reading with good phrasing, appropriate volume, and pace? Does it sound smooth or does it tend to be choppy? A scoring rubric (see Figure 3.2), adapted from Zutell and Rasinski (1991), is divided into four distinct aspects of expressive reading. Simply listen to students read and score them for each of the four dimensions of fluency.

Figure 3.2 Multidimensional Fluency Scale

Score	Expression & Volume	Phrasing	Smoothness	Pace
1.	Reads words as if simply to get them out. Little sense of trying to make text sound like natural language. Tends to read in a quiet voice.	Reads in monotone with little sense of phrase boundaries; frequently reads word-by-word.	Makes frequent extended pauses, hesitations, false starts, sound-outs, repetitions, and/or multiple attempts.	Reads slowly and laboriously.
2.	Begins to use voice to make text sound like natural language in some areas but not in others. Focus remains largely on pronouncing the words. Still reads in a quiet voice.	Frequently reads in two- and three-word phrases, giving the impression of choppy reading; improper stress and intonation; fails to mark ends of sentences and clauses.	Experiences several "rough spots" in text where extended pauses or hesitations are more frequent and disruptive.	Reads moderately slowly.
3.	Makes text sound like natural language throughout the better part of the passage. Occasionally slips into expressionless reading. Voice volume is generally appropriate throughout the text.	Reads with a mixture of run-ons, midsentence pauses for breath, and some choppiness; reasonable stress and intonation.	Occasionally breaks smooth rhythm because of difficulties with specific words and/or structures.	Reads with an uneven mixture of fast and slow pace.
4.	Reads with good expression and enthusiasm throughout the text. Varies expression and volume to match his or her interpretation of the passage.	Generally reads with good phrasing, mostly in clause and sentence units, with adequate attention to expression.	Generally reads smoothly with some breaks, but resolves word and structure difficulties quickly, usually through self-correction.	Consistently reads at conversational pace; appropriate rate throughout reading.

Source: Adapted from Zutell and Rasinski (1991).

Over the course of a school year you should see continual improvement in students' expressive reading. Diagnostically, students whose total score is 8 or below on grade-level texts demonstrate inadequate expressiveness in their reading, which may be related to difficulty in comprehension. These students may need additional and focused instruction on reading with appropriate expression and meaning.

Comprehension

Comprehension is the goal of reading. Although comprehension is not the main focus of this book, we need to realize that we teach word recognition and fluency so that students can comprehend what they read. When it is possible to gain information about students' comprehension, we need to take advantage of it.

The *Three Minute Reading Assessments,* or an adaptation you may wish to develop for your own use, allows you to assess students' global reading comprehension using the retelling they provide after they have finished reading. Rate the retelling according to the rubric presented in Figure 3.3.

Figure 3.3 Comprehension Rubric

1. The student has no recall or minimal recall of only a fact or two from the passage.
2. The student recalls a number of unrelated facts of varied importance.
3. The student recalls the main idea of the passage with a few supporting details.
4. The student recalls the main idea along with a fairly robust set of supporting details, although not necessarily organized logically or sequentially as presented in the passage.
5. The student's recall is a comprehensive summary of the passage, presented in a logical order, with a robust set of details, and includes a statement of main idea.
6. The student's recall is a comprehensive summary of the passage, presented in a logical order, with a robust set of details, and includes a statement of main idea. The student also makes reasonable connections beyond the text to his or her own personal life, another text.

When you use this rubric as a measure of ongoing progress in reading comprehension, you will want to see higher scores and more elaborate retellings over the course of the school year. As a diagnostic tool, scores that fall in the lower half of the rubric may suggest the need for further assessment and direct instruction in comprehension skills and strategies.

As the name implies, this assessment procedure takes only a matter of minutes per student to administer and score. When your students' reading is sampled in this way every month or so and charted (see Figure 3.4), you should get a good picture of each student's progress in several important reading competencies over time. As you analyze the trends in your students' reading development, it will become evident—either through the initial assessment or over time—which students are experiencing

Figure 3.4   Student Reading Progress Chart

Date	Text Source and Grade Level	Percentage of Words Read Correctly	Reading Rate (wcpm)	Prosody: 4–16	Comprehension: 1–6

difficulty in word recognition, fluency, or comprehension. These students may require more detailed and diagnostic analyses of their reading in order to identify specific areas for corrective instruction.

Diagnostic Assessment

Word Recognition

Diagnostic assessment provides further information about individual students' word recognition and fluency so teachers can tailor needs-based instruction. Moreover, these assessments can also be used to measure ongoing progress in these areas.

Sight vocabulary words are words that readers recognize instantly and automatically. One way to measure growth in this area is to keep a running tally of the contents of students' word banks (see Chapter 11). As we mentioned earlier, the best words to have in one's sight vocabulary are those that appear with the greatest frequency in reading. The Fry Instant Words are high-frequency words that are good candidates for any reader's sight vocabulary. The first 300 of these words make up approximately two-thirds of all the words elementary school readers will encounter.

High-frequency words can also be used diagnostically. We have created a diagnostic sight word assessment by identifying words that should be learned by sight in grades 1 through 4 (see Figure 3.5). Put these words on index cards, one per card, and present them to individual students. Students should read the words accurately and quickly in order to be given credit. Since this assessment measures sight vocabulary, accurate but slow recognition should not be counted correct. First-grade students should have the first group of 20 mastered (90 percent immediate accuracy, or 18 of 20) by the end of first grade; second-graders should have the first two groups of 20 mastered by the end of second grade; third-grade students should have the first three groups mastered as sight words by the end of third grade; and fourth-graders and above should have all four groups of 20 mastered by the end of grade four. Students who fall below these thresholds can benefit from sight vocabulary instruction of high-frequency and other common words.

Phonograms, Word Families, and Rimes

In Chapter 7 we note that word patterns, particularly rimes or phonograms, are an excellent focus for teaching phonics. In addition, we share the 38 most common rimes (Fry 1998) that should be initially

Figure 3.5 High-Frequency and Common Words for Sight Word Assessment

Group 1	Group 2	Group 3	Group 4
some	bread	city	bicycle
have	sound	country	remember
was	work	earth	certain
you	sentence	laugh	transport
they	know	thought	encourage
were	where	few	covered
your	through	group	measure
their	around	might	midnight
each	follow	always	carefully
said	apple	important	language
would	another	children	government
about	large	myself	thousands
them	because	river	attraction
time	went	carry	understand
write	please	second	building
people	picture	enough	machine
water	play	birthday	weather
yellow	animal	mountain	rearrange
down	mother	young	instruments
over	America	family	continuing

Students should have, by the end of first grade, automatic mastery (instant recognition of 90 percent or more) of Group 1 words, automatic mastery of Group 2 words by the end of second grade, automatic mastery of Group 3 words by the end of third grade, and automatic mastery of Group 4 words by the end of fourth grade.

Source: Based on Fry (1998).

taught. In order to assess students' mastery of the most common rimes, we have developed an informal word list test (see Figure 3.6) that contains the 38 rimes in one-syllable and multi-syllable words. Asking students to read the words in the lists should provide an indication

Figure 3.6 Rasinski–Padak Common Phonogram Assessment

Ask students to pronounce each of the following words in Groups 1 and 2. Make note of any errors or patterns of errors that occur.

Group 1	Group 2	Group 1	Group 2
say	playmate	bug	dugout
spill	willful	stop	popcorn
ship	skipping	chin	tinsel
bat	satisfy	Stan	flannel
slam	hamster	nest	Chester
brag	shaggy	think	trinket
stack	packer	grow	snowplow
crank	blanket	chew	newest
quick	cricket	score	adore
yell	shellfish	red	bedtime
got	hotcake	crab	dabble
king	stacking	knob	robber
clap	kidnap	block	jockey
junk	bunker	brake	remake
nail	railroad	shine	porcupine
chain	mainstay	light	sighted
weed	seedling	brim	swimming
try	myself	stuck	truckload
spout	without	chum	drummer

of students who have mastered these rimes and those who are still in the process of learning and may need more thorough instruction on particular rimes.

The Common Phonogram Assessment provides information on the phonograms or rimes students know and may not yet have mastered; however, neither it nor the Fry Instant Word List Sample provides information on students' developmental level in word recognition or their mastery of some of the more traditional phonics concepts.

The cloze procedure can assess students' use of meaningful context to decode words in text. Cloze assessments are created with a few more rules than cloze texts for instruction, as described in Chapter 12. To create one, find a text of at least 150 words from students' reading curriculum. Retype the passage leaving the first sentence intact. Then delete every fifth word, leaving a blank space where the word was deleted. After at least 25 deletions, add a final sentence with no deletions. Then ask students to write in the words they believe fit the deletions. If students find the text too difficult to read on their own, you may wish to read it to them, making sure you don't read the deleted words.

An alternative (and easier) construction involves making a copy of the target passage, deleting every appropriate word by lining through it with a marker, and numbering each deletion by hand. Then make sufficient copies for use. Provide students with the cloze text and a numbered answer sheet on which to write the deleted words.

Scoring is fairly simple. Any word that closely fits the context should be counted correct. A score in the range of 40 to 60 percent correct indicates that the text will be useful for instruction. Less than 40 percent correct may suggest that the student has difficulty in using context to determine unknown words.

Reading Fluency

Fluency is the ability to read expressively, meaningfully, with appropriate phrasing, and with appropriate speed. Given that assessing expressiveness, meaningfulness, and phrasing may involve a bit of a judgment call, assessing fluency may seem somewhat enigmatic.

Nevertheless, since it is an important part of reading, we need ways to assess it.

Perhaps the easiest way of assessing the automatic word recognition component of fluency is through reading rate. Although this may seem a rather gross measure, several studies have indicated that rate is a predictor of overall reading proficiency. At the very least, reading rates provide some indication of the degree to which students can decode words by sight or at least through efficient analysis. As you may recall from earlier in this chapter, we built reading rate into our *Three Minute Reading Assessments*. If the reading rate from the *Three Minute Reading Assessments* appears to demonstrate a concern with word recognition automaticity, you can verify this determination by having students orally read additional passages at or slightly below their assigned grade level. When students read in order to measure rate, be sure to ask them to read in their normal manner. You should probably make several rate calculations over a couple of days to determine each student's average reading rate.

Students' average reading rates can be compared to grade and time-of-year norm ranges (see Figure 3.1). Students scoring below or at the lower end of the norm range may require more intensive and targeted instruction.

$$\text{Reading rate in words per minute} = \frac{\#\ \text{words in passage}}{\#\ \text{seconds to read}} \times 60$$

A second method for assessing fluency involves listening to students read a text at their instructional levels and rating the expressiveness of their oral performance against some standards. Several studies (Daane et al. 2005; Pinnell et al. 1995; Rasinski 1985) have found a robust relationship between elementary students' expressiveness in their oral reading and their silent reading comprehension and overall reading proficiency.

A procedure and rubric for measuring expressiveness in our *Three Minute Reading Assessments* is presented earlier in this chapter. If this assessment indicates concerns, gather several additional samples by asking the student to read several other grade-appropriate passages from trade books and textbooks and rating their performance using the rubric in Figure 3.2. When listening to students read for expressiveness, don't read the text. Rather attend to their oral expressiveness (phrasing, volume, pitch, stress, rate, etc.). Students who consistently score on the lower half of the rubric (10 or below) likely need corrective instruction on reading with appropriate expression and meaning.

Some method of summarizing results and keeping track of students' growth over time is desirable. Many teachers we know use continuum or summary forms like those depicted in Figure 3.7 and Figure 3.8. Periodically, say every month or grading period, evaluate the accumulated assessment information and mark each child's progress on a copy of the continuum or summary form. Assessment data regularly recorded on a continuum or summary form provides an easy and understandable way to track progress over time. The forms are useful for conferences with students and parents as well.

In Conclusion

Assessment should provide us with measures of students' progress as well as directions for further instruction. Certainly other measures of word recognition and reading fluency are available; if you find some that work especially well for you and your students, we recommend that you use them.

**Research-Based
Strategies**

However, we urge caution. A recent large-scale study compared results from two commonly used assessments, the Dynamic Indicators of Basic Early Literacy Skills (DIBELS) and the Observation Survey (OS) (Clay 2006). Doyle et al. (2008) compared scores on these two assessments for more than 6,000 first-graders. They found that the assessments yielded similar results for letter identification, phonemic awareness, the alphabetic principle, and oral reading. "A problematic finding was the divergence in the identification of learner at-riskness revealed by the alternative measures. Specifically, applying the DIBELS criteria to the sample studied resulted in identification of a substantially reduced number of at-risk learners" (p. 157). The authors speculate that this discrepancy is due to differing theories about reading: "While DIBELS appears to assume that the acquisition of discrete skills causes later success, the OS is constructed to allow assessment of the complexity of literacy behaviors" (p. 157). As we mention throughout this book, use your professional judgment to interpret the results of any assessment, the ones we have described or any other.

Figure 3.7 Continuum for Word Recognition and Fluency Assessment

Child's Name_____ School Year_____

Teacher's Name_____

	No Evidence	In Process	Well Developed
Letter-Name Knowledge			
Letter-Sound Knowledge			
Basic Print Concepts			
One-to-One Correspondence			
Word Recognition			
Sight Vocabulary			
Phonograms			
Context (Cloze)			
Fluency			

Figure 3.8   Student Reading Summary

Student Name:_____

Grade:_____

School Year:_____

Date	Sight Vocab.	Phono-grams	Word Rec.	Cloze	Text Read	Fluency Rating	Fluency Rate (wcpm)	Compre-hension

The assessment instruments and approaches in this chapter provide you with some of the measures we have found useful in our own practice for determining progress and identifying areas for further instruction. For the most part, the assessments are quick, informal, easy to learn and administer, controlled and informed by the teacher or examiner (not some disembodied test manual), and can be analyzed in a variety of ways to get a better understanding of readers' word recognition and fluency. This combination of attributes provides you with an assessment foundation that will help you better understand your students' word recognition and fluency and design instruction that most effectively meets their needs.

References

Clay, M. (2006). *An observation survey of early literacy achievement.* Portsmouth, NH: Heinemann.

Daane, M. C., Campbell, J. R., Grigg, W. S., Goodman, M. J., and Oranje, A. (2005). *Fourth-grade students reading aloud: 2002 NAEP special study of oral reading.* Washington, DC: National Center for Education Statistics.

Deno, S. L. (1985). Curriculum-based measurement: The emerging alternative. *Exceptional Children, 52,* 219–232.

Deno, S. L., Mirkin, P., and Chiang, B. (1982). Identifying valid measures of reading. *Exceptional Children, 49,* 36–45.

Doyle, M., Gibson, S., Gomez-Bellenge, F., Kelly, P., and Tang, M. (2008). Assessment and identification of first-grade students at risk: Correlating the Dynamic Indicators of Basic Early Literacy Skills and an Observation Survey of Early Literacy Achievement. In Y. Kim and V. Risko (Eds.), *57th Yearbook of the National Reading Conference* (pp. 144–159). Oak Creek, WI: National Reading Conference.

Fry, E. (1998). The most common phonograms. *The Reading Teacher, 51,* 620–622.

Pinnell, G. S., Pikulski, J., Wixon, K., Campbell, J., Gough, P., and Beatty, S. (1995). *Listening to children read aloud: Data from NAEP's integrated reading performance record at grade 4.* Washington, DC: U.S. Department of Education, Office of Educational Research and Improvement.

Rasinski, T. V. (1985). *A study of factors involved in reader-text interactions that contribute to fluency in reading* (Unpublished doctoral dissertation). Columbus, OH: The Ohio State University.

Rasinski, T. V. and Padak, N. (2005a). *Three Minute Reading Assessments: Word recognition, fluency, and comprehension for grades 1–4.* New York: Scholastic.

Rasinski, T. V. and Padak, N. (2005b). *Three Minute Reading Assessments: Word recognition, fluency, and comprehension for grades 5–8.* New York: Scholastic.

Reyes, I. and Azuara, P. (2008). Emergent biliteracy in young Mexican American immigrant children. *Reading Research Quarterly, 43*, 374–398.

Salvia, J. and Hughes, C. (1990). *Curriculum-based assessment: Testing what is taught.* New York: Macmillan.

Zutell, J. B. and Rasinski, T. V. (1991). Training teachers to attend to their students' oral reading fluency. *Theory into Practice, 30*, 211–217.

4

Instructional Routines
for Word Study
and Fluency

Throughout this book, we describe instructional strategies that help young readers develop fluency, learn words, and learn how to solve problems related to words. These are fine strategies. They work. But effective instruction is more than simply the sum of all these ideas; teachers must also consider how they fit together into a coherent and effective curriculum. In this chapter we offer some suggestions for planning a word-learning, fluency-building curriculum.

Teaching styles, learning needs, and teachers' and students' preferences differ from classroom to classroom, even at the same grade level in the same school building. Because of these differences, teaching must involve planning curriculum. Nobody knows the situation and children's learning needs better than the teacher who interacts daily with children.

Planning a Word-Learning Curriculum

The curriculum planning process begins with careful thought about broad aims for literacy learning. Teachers might consider such questions as:

- What do I believe about literacy learning?
- What do I believe about children as learners?
- What is the role of the teacher?

- What sort of physical and psychological environment best promotes learning?
- How would I characterize an excellent learning activity?
- What role should word learning play within an overall literacy program?

Questions like these help teachers articulate their philosophies of teaching, learning, and literacy. We recommend making notes about beliefs because they are useful for guiding curriculum planning, selecting instructional activities, and evaluating the impact of programs on children as learners. Moreover, the beliefs can be used to double-check existing programs—to see if children have sufficient opportunities to learn what's important.

The next stage in curriculum planning is to establish a few broad instructional goals. These goals, which reflect the teacher's beliefs, articulate expectations for children in a particular grade. Goals provide the foundation for a reading program; they describe the general areas within which literacy instruction occurs. Here, for example, are Lyndell's goals for his kindergarten students:

- To develop interest in and appreciation for books and reading
- To develop and extend understanding of stories and informative text
- To learn concepts of print and gain an awareness of key features of books and printed language
- To develop phonemic awareness

In contrast, June's goals for her second-graders include:

- To develop interest in and appreciation for books and reading
- To develop and extend comprehension abilities with a variety of genres
- To read fluently
- To solve word-related reading problems successfully

Note that both sets of goals are comprehensive. Lyndell and June develop their entire reading programs based on these goals by ensuring that children have daily opportunities to develop proficiency in the targeted areas. Note, too, that their first and second goals are similar. Indeed, teachers throughout their school have similar goals. This makes sense because positive attitudes about reading and the continued focus on comprehension are all teachers' responsibilities.

The next stage in the curriculum planning process involves selecting or developing instructional routines. A routine is a regular block of time during which students engage in a predictable set of instructional activities related to a particular goal or set of goals. Teacher read-aloud and Making and Writing Words (see Chapter 10) are instructional routines, for example. Routines are helpful in curriculum planning—together they constitute the reading program. Routines also help students behave independently—they know what to expect. Our focus in this book is on fluency development and word learning, so our discussion of routines will focus on these important aspects of reading programs.

Principles for Routines

Some routines, like teacher read-aloud, are features of most classrooms. Others may be unique to the teacher or particular group of children. A few years ago in our summer reading program, for example, one child wanted to write a riddle on the chalkboard one day. This idea quickly caught on—soon everybody was looking for riddles, and the chalkboard was covered with a new set each morning. So finding, writing, reading, and solving riddles became a much-anticipated routine for this group of children. This riddle mania happened quite by accident and probably wouldn't have been as effective if teachers had planned it. Despite the occasional serendipity, effective routines for promoting word learning are generally based on several important principles. In this section we comment briefly on each.

Base Routines on What Children Need

Base routines on what children need, not on a skills list or sequence of lessons in materials. Think back on your own early years in school. Were you taught things you already knew? Boring, wasn't it? How about times when the lesson was not beneficial—too abstract, say, or not immediately useful? If you can't think of anything, try rules for determining accents in words or using semicolons. How many times did well-meaning teachers try to help you learn these rules? And when—if ever—did you finally figure the rules out so that you could use them in your reading and writing? Our point here is not to criticize past educational practices; rather, we wish to underscore the importance of basing instructional routines on what children need.

Planning needs-based instruction begins with determining needs. Observing students, listening to them read, and even analyzing their invented spellings are good ways to do this. Talking to children can also offer useful insights. We frequently ask children, "What do you do when you come to a word that you don't know?" "What do you do if that doesn't work?" "What does good reading sound like?" Children's answers, especially when considered along with samples of their oral reading, often provide on-target direction for instruction.

Next, classroom management issues must be resolved. The odds are slim that all children will have the same needs, so teachers must think about how to coordinate several classroom activities simultaneously. We offer two pieces of advice here. First, remember that the predictable nature of routines enables children to behave independently as learners. Second, remember that the best way to practice reading, frequently what the rest of the children do while the teacher works with some, is to read.

An effective record-keeping system is also necessary. Some teachers make notes on index cards or large computer labels. Others keep charts with children's names down one side and skills or strategies across the top. Another alternative is to keep lists of words or skills in children's reading portfolios and to indicate the dates on which children demonstrate proficiency. The format of the records is a matter of personal preference, but their existence is not. Teachers need a way to keep track of what children know and what instruction can promote word-learning growth.

Is all this effort worth it? We believe that it is, for two major reasons. First, for decades scholars have searched in vain for the single best way to teach all children to read. Nothing works for everyone, so attention to individual readers' needs is warranted. The second reason is, most likely, related to the first: children are different. Here's how Cunningham and Allington (1999) put it:

> Anyone who has ever observed how different children from the same family behave knows that all children do not learn, respond, and think in the same manner. Successful parents recognize the differences in their children and adjust their rules, routines, and interactions accordingly, in order to maximize the potential of each of their children. (p. 15)

We believe that teachers can take a lesson from parents in this regard. Providing effective instruction depends on the teacher's ability to determine both what children need to know and how they can best learn. No predetermined list of skills or sequence of instructional material can provide this insight.

Maximize Time on Task

It almost goes without saying that children need time to read in order to become readers. We say *almost* because sometimes instructional time is spent doing lots of reading-related and reading-like activities but very little reading. Surely responding to reading and working with words or even parts of words are important, but most important is time on task—reading connected text. Time spent reading is related to achievement in reading (Anderson, Wilson, and Fielding 1988; Postlethwaite and Ross 1992; Rupley, Wise, and Logan 1986).

The focus of children's attention during instruction is another issue related to time. This is especially true for children who struggle as readers. Descriptions of instruction for struggling readers show lack of opportunity for and emphasis on meaningful reading (Allington 1977, 1980; McDermott 1978). Instead, less able readers were asked to focus almost exclusively on decoding. As Allington (1977) has asked, "If they don't read much, how they ever gonna get good?"

Sometimes we're so busy teaching that we ignore this critical issue of time on the task of reading. Observing three readers for a couple of days is one way to begin to understand how much time students spend reading. A high-achieving reader, an average reader, and a low-achieving reader might be selected, and the teacher might tally minutes spent reading—not engaging in reading-related activity, but actually reading. This quick check is sometimes a real eye-opener.

Word-learning activities are important, but children need plentiful and daily opportunities to read and listen to texts read aloud. After all, that's what all the word learning is for. Besides that, both reading and listening foster fluency development.

Make It Engaging, Varied, and Fun

Many of the word-learning activities we describe in this book have a game-like feel to them. This is purposeful. Children learn best when they are successful and enjoy what they are doing.

We want students to be readers, to see the value in reading for their lives in and out of school, and to feel confident in their abilities to solve the inevitable problems readers encounter. Enjoyable, success-oriented word-learning activities can support the achievement of these goals.

What makes an activity enjoyable for children? Competition can be enjoyable, but only for the winners. Struggling readers, particularly, may not enjoy competitions that they regularly lose. Opportunities to win small prizes or other forms of external motivation can also be enjoyable; however, unlike internal motivation—doing something for personal reasons—external motivation ceases when the particular task is concluded (Sweet and Guthrie 1996). Too many competitions or activities dependent solely on external motivation, then, are probably not advisable. Aside from these general guidelines, each teacher will probably have to decide what makes an activity enjoyable. But remember, a teacher's enthusiasm for an activity contributes to its allure.

**Research-Based
Strategies**

Opportunities to be successful are also important. The repeated readings characteristic of fluency practice have success built in. Also, divergent thinking activities like open word sorts (see Chapter 11) invite success because of the many ways to complete them. One way to ensure success, then, is to provide frequent opportunities for children to engage in open-ended word-learning activities. Divergent thinking activities that pose problems for children to solve will engage them actively as learners. The level of difficulty of an activity also affects the likelihood of success. Here, teachers should strive for activities that are challenging but not frustrating, neither too easy nor too difficult.

Choice is motivating for students. For diverse students, such as English language learners (ELLs) or students with special needs in reading, motivation is linked to learner empowerment (see, e.g., Guthrie and Humenick 2004; Guthrie, Rueda, Gambrell and Morrison 2009). That is, when a student has an individual goal that has an immediate value, the student is more likely to be engaged.

**English Language
Learners**

Note that choice is not about whether or not to do something. It is a choice between two competing options. A parent may say, "Would you like broccoli or beans?" rather than, "Would you like a vegetable?" While you plan your curriculum, think about choice. You could list several word-sorting activities, for example, and request that each student complete two. Likewise, fluency instruction can feature choice of texts.

Make It Consistent

Whether the instructional routine is a daily event or a series of activities that take place over the course of a week, try to keep the general structure of the routine as consistent and transparent as possible. If a routine changes markedly from one day to the next, precious time will be spent in explaining and implementing the change. Many teachers' daily sustained silent reading (SSR) periods provide a good example of this principle. When done well, SSR takes place at the same time each day. Activities are consistent—students select a book or two to read, choose a location for reading, and engage in independent silent reading for 15 to 20 minutes. The teacher might put on some classical music to set the mood and to mask distractions. A noise may mark the end of each session, after which students spend three minutes writing summaries or responses to their reading. Finally, the teacher may ask students to discuss their reading in some brief way. With the final response, the routine ends.

Develop Home-School Connections

One clear conclusion from five years of research supported by the National Reading Research Center relates to this principle: "Literacy learning occurs both at school and home, and connections between home and school enhance children's learning in both environments" (Baumann and Duffy 1997, p. 21). Effective teachers realize the importance of inviting the home and community into the classroom. They know that reading is not just for school; it's for life.

Research is clear about the uniformly positive effects of promoting home-school partnerships. In one multinational study, parental involvement and support was the most important characteristic of schools where children achieved exceptionally well as readers (Postlethwaite and Ross 1992). Another research project looked at the relationships among classroom support, home support, and low-income children's achievement in reading (Snow 1991). Results show the enormous impact of both of these factors on children's achievement (see Figure 4.1). Chapter 18 offers many ways to nurture home-school partnerships.

Research-Based Strategies

Figure 4.1 Home Support, Classroom Support, and the Percentage of Children Who Achieve Success

Classroom Support	Home Support	
	High	Low
High	100%	100%
Mixed	100%	25%
Low	60%	0%

Source: Based on Snow (1991); adapted from Cunningham and Allington (1999), p. 2.

Use a Whole-to-Part-to-Whole Model for Teaching Skills and Strategies

Learning about words and parts of words is most successful and meaningful if students first focus on whole text. A narrower highlight on words or word parts follows, after which teachers and students explore the usefulness of new knowledge—how knowing about the -*it* family, for example, can help students solve word-related problems in reading. This focus on problem solving for authentic purposes seems natural to children because it mirrors the way they learned oral language:

> Babies use a variety of strategies to discover relationships about language and thinking. . . . They find ways to distinguish the sounds of language from the sounds of cars, cats, and fire engines. In order to learn they do not have to isolate these sounds. . . . As a consequence of using language and thought authentically children have learned to sample, infer, predict, confirm, and integrate new information into their existing linguistic and pragmatic schema. These same strategies are used by students learning to read if they are permitted to capitalize on them in the classroom and if significant written context is available. (Goodman, Watson, and Burke 1996, p. 53)

A skill becomes a strategy with purposeful use. In the final analysis word-learning skills are useful only if students can apply them when they need to, as in the case of an unknown word. Routines designed to foster word learning should seek to develop both skills and strategies. The best way to accomplish this is to begin an instructional routine within an authentic reading context, pull from that context the skills and content to be taught, and end by returning the focus to meaningful and authentic context.

Enhancement of children's sight vocabularies—those words they recognize immediately without thought—is another goal of word-learning activities. Essentially this memorization process happens as a result of many meaningful encounters with words. We do not foster sight vocabulary growth by solely and extensively asking children to look at words in isolation, as on flash cards; instead, words become known by sight because children have seen and used them successfully in multiple contexts. Also, teachers should look for opportunities to focus children's attention on the visual features of the words. Here are several ways to do this (also see word bank activities listed in Chapter 11):

Ask children to locate and circle all examples of a sight word in a story they are reading.

Place the words on word walls and practice reading the words (see Chapter 9).

Record the words in personal or class dictionaries or add them to students' word banks.

Make word collages—cut the words out of old magazines and paste on construction paper.

Construct the words with magnetic letters; write the words in the sand tray, in finger paint, or in shaving cream.

Play word games with the words (see Chapter 14).

Remember the Overall Goal: Grow Readers

The final principle for establishing word-learning routines reminds us to keep word learning in perspective, not to lose the forest for the trees. As Baumann and Duffy (1997) note, "Reading skills and strategies can be taught effectively and efficiently when instruction is systematic and integrated with quality children's literature" (p. 17). In other words, although important, instruction in words and word learning should not be the focus of the reading program. Reading aloud to children, guiding children to read texts themselves, and encouraging students to read and write independently and with one another are also essential. Next we explore some ways to plan instruction so that all these features receive the emphasis they deserve.

Types of Routines

Designing a classroom reading program involves making some decisions about using space. For example, some teachers create centers, such as a book nook for independent reading, a writing center filled with writing tools (including computers), and a words center where children can complete word-related activities either independently or with partners. Others prefer for children to work at their tables or desks. In either case, the classroom should be organized to promote independent learning. Daily lists of things to do or simply written charts posted around the classroom can save lots of time. Children won't have to wait for instructions; they will be able to get about the business of learning.

Teachers must also decide how to break up the larger block of reading time. In part, this decision may involve thinking about how large the instructional group will be—Whole class? Small groups? Individual activity? Many of the activities we describe in this book can work well within any of these formats. We offer a word of caution, however, about whole-group instruction—for this organizational scheme to work effectively, all children must be appropriately engaged all the time. This is a time-on-task issue.

The Four Blocks design, developed by Pat Cunningham and her colleagues, is a particularly promising curriculum framework. (See Chapter 1 for a description of Four Blocks.) Over a decade of research has shown its effectiveness with all young learners, particularly those who struggle with learning to read (Cunningham 2006; Cunningham, Hall, and Defee 1998). We find the model useful for teachers at all grade levels. Devoting approximately equal time (Cunningham and colleagues suggest about 30 minutes each day) to each of the four blocks—self-selected reading, guided reading, working with words, and writing—ensures a balanced reading and writing program that gives children ample opportunities to achieve the goals that the teacher has set.

Within each of the four blocks, teachers design smaller-scale routines of related activities. For example, in one classroom the daily self-selected reading routine may consist of 10 minutes of teacher read-aloud, 15 minutes of student silent reading, and 5 minutes of writing in response journals. In another classroom, the same block may involve student silent reading for 20 minutes followed by 10 minutes of oral sharing and response.

The routines for the working with words block might consist of activities described in this book. Here's one example:

Monday	Tuesday	Wednesday	Thursday	Friday
1. Read word wall	**1.** Read word family poems	**1.** Read word wall	**1.** Poetry festival	**1.** Word games
2. Mini-lesson	**2.** Student word family poems	**2.** Mini-lesson	**2.** Word sorts	
3. Making and Writing Words	**3.** Word sorts	**3.** Making and Writing Words		
4. Cloze		**4.** Cloze		

Teachers do not need to march children through the blocks each day. Indeed, some effective lessons involve several of the blocks simultaneously. The Fluency Development Lesson (see Chapter 16) is an example, since children participate in both guided reading and word-related activities in a brief 10- to 15-minute period. Books and poetry (see Chapter 5) can be used for word family instruction, word sorts, word walls, repeated readings, and paired readings. So the point is not to shift reading-related gears every 30 minutes; rather, when thinking about children's learning opportunities in a day or a week, teachers should see that the various areas receive appropriate emphasis.

Over several years fourth-grade teacher Lorraine Griffith has created a very successful 20- to 30-minute daily fluency routine (Griffith and Rasinski 2004). Each week a new passage (poem, speech, readers theater script, monologue, dialogue, etc.) is introduced to small groups of students or individuals. Early in the week Lorraine models fluent readings of the texts as students follow along. As the week progresses, students read and practice the texts with partners and on their own, in school and at home, with the teacher (and parents) coaching and giving feedback and plenty of praise. On Fridays students perform their texts for the teacher, fellow students, parents, and others. The following week the routine begins again.

Research-Based Strategies

Griffith and Rasinski (2004) report remarkable yearly gains in reading fluency and overall reading achievement as a result of this instructional routine. Analyses of three years of data revealed that struggling fourth-grade readers made, on average, close to three years' growth in reading achievement in their year with her!

When Readers Struggle

Young children struggle with the learning-to-read process for many reasons. Some have language barriers; others have special needs. Some may have had little exposure to books and print prior to school entrance. Still others may simply be late bloomers—children who are not yet developmentally ready to learn what the school system has designated for them. Regardless of the reasons, these children need all the support we can provide. Here, we offer several guidelines and adaptations that may help struggling readers to succeed (Cunningham and Allington 1999; Five and Dionisio 1999).

Chief among the guidelines is, we believe, to forget about the child's age or what other children are doing and to focus instead on the struggling reader's needs. Successful learning experiences, important for all, are doubly important for struggling readers. Teachers must focus on students' strengths, not their weaknesses, and must plan many daily opportunities for children to succeed with reading and reading-related activity. Sometimes this involves slowing down, allowing children time to grow and progress at their own rates. Often, teachers must find texts the child can read successfully. Other times, instructional adaptations may be necessary. For example, children might listen to an audio version of a book the class is using while reading the book. Or a buddy or tutor may read to or with the child. These strategies allow the child to be an active and successful participant in classroom activities.

Another general principle for working with struggling readers is this: keep it real. Sometimes we think that breaking reading down into minute skills or subskills will make it easier for children to learn. Not so. Some instructional programs for struggling readers even focus on shapes, pictures, or nonsense words. These are not effective: "Numerous studies have shown that matching shapes and pictures as preliminary instruction for letter and word discrimination is useless. . . . If we want students to visually identify the distinguishing features of letters and words, [lessons] should include letters and words, not nonword forms" (McCormick 1999, p. 477).

So what might a routine for struggling readers look like? First, it's essential that children can successfully read most materials. More invitations to read familiar books may accomplish this goal. Moreover, careful observation, including numerous opportunities to listen to and analyze the child's reading, will help determine the focus for instruction, which may differ from other students' mini-lessons. Multiple opportunities to read successfully coupled with needs-based instruction (and frequent celebrations of success) will go a long way toward ensuring that struggling readers achieve.

Coordination is another guideline. Coordinating with other teachers, whether Title I, special education, ELL/bilingual education, or Reading Recovery, is absolutely essential. Without joint planning, what begins as an effort to provide additional assistance may result in a "confusing and unhelpful conglomeration of reading lessons and activities" (Cunningham and Allington 1999, p. 202). Some teachers accomplish coordinated instruction by team-teaching; others plan jointly. All keep in close contact about the child's needs and what's happening in the child's classroom. This close coordination pays off:

> What is common among the very best programs is that children spend most of their time actually reading and writing in a way that supports classroom success. The support children receive from the specialist teacher provides immediate returns in improved reading and writing during classroom instruction. (Cunningham and Allington 1999, p. 203)

Volunteers, such as parent helpers, tutors, older students, or senior citizens, can also provide extra support for struggling readers. Before eliciting tutors' assistance, however, teachers should decide what tutors might do and how to teach them what they need to know to work successfully with children. Many of the activities we describe in this book can easily and successfully be adapted for tutoring. For example, tutors and children can play word games, or the tutor can listen to the child read a poem, dictated account, or pattern book. Most children can make considerable progress in reading if their strong classroom program is supplemented with the extra opportunities that one-on-one tutoring can provide. The time it takes to plan these tutoring opportunities and to help tutors learn about their roles is well worth it in the long run.

Teaching a young child who struggles with reading is sometimes a challenge, but it can also be very rewarding because doing so gives a child the gift of literacy. Although we have no easy answers for assisting struggling readers, we agree with Five and Dionisio (1999), who note that nearly all children "can succeed when we include them as valued members of [the classroom], enable them to work and learn collaboratively with peers, build on their strengths and knowledge, and meet their individual needs through explicit instruction" (p. 5).

Response to Intervention—RTI

In recent years a new concept called *Response to Intervention* (RTI) has captured the interest of educators and educational policy makers (Fuchs, Fuchs, and Vaughn 2008). Actually, RTI is not new at all; it is what good teachers have always done with students—make needs-based decisions about instruction. Essentially, RTI is an overarching, formalized instructional routine that aims to ensure that the instructional needs of all students are being met.

RTI assumes various levels and types of instruction to meet students' needs. Usually this takes the form of three tiers of instruction. Tier 1 instruction is the common core curriculum provided to all students. In any given classroom most students (e.g., 80 percent) should make good progress as a result of Tier 1 instruction. Regular assessments allow teachers to determine the students who are progressing well and those who are not. Students who are not progressing move to Tier 2 instruction, which is additional targeted instruction that supplements but does not supplant Tier 1. Tier 3 adds another layer of instruction and instructional intensity for those students who are not making sufficient progress in Tier 2. Special education personnel are ordinarily involved in Tier 3 instruction.

Molly teaches third-graders. She assesses students early in the year by asking them to read several grade-level passages. She notices that about a third of her students appear to have word recognition and/or fluency difficulties. These students are placed in Tier 2 intervention in addition to the reading curriculum she offers to all students. In her Tier 2 instruction, children receive 15 extra instructional minutes each day. They do word sorts with high-frequency words and engage in word-building activities (e.g., Making and Writing Words). Molly's home-involvement program asks parents to do paired and repeated reading with students (*Fast Start*; see Chapter 18) nightly for 15 minutes. After several weeks, Molly reassesses students and adjusts instruction as needed. She finds that one or two students need Tier 3 support each year, but she notes: "Nearly all students achieve their goals. One of the things I like about RTI is that everyone gets the same curriculum. It only differs in intensity and time. I think that's better for the children."

In Conclusion

Michael Pressley (2002) reviewed several studies of classrooms of highly effective reading teachers, looking for commonalities. He found that these teachers:

- Had excellent classroom management

- Communicated a positive tone

- Taught skills explicitly in the context of real reading and writing

- Had lots of books available; provided lots of time for children to read real books

- Taught in very academically busy classrooms

- Used an assess—plan—teach model; children did what they needed to do; teachers used assessment results to make instructional decisions

- Scaffolded, monitored, and provided just the right amount of support

- Encouraged self-regulation

- Fostered strong connections across curriculum

Teacher decision making is central to the creation of such a classroom: "There are no quick fixes with regard to improving children's literacy. There's no reform package that a school can buy that delivers improved achievement with certainty. The influences of packaged reforms are often uneven or small" (Pressley 2002, p. 180).

Children will learn what they have the opportunity to learn. Moreover, no one knows children's needs and interests as readers better than their classroom teacher. For these reasons, curriculum planning must be part of the teacher's responsibility. Effective instruction in word learning is more than just the sum of interesting and engaging activities. To plan effective instruction, the teacher must first look at the big picture—think about beliefs and establish instructional goals. These ideas are used to develop complete programs, which are designed to make the best use of children's time and to help them achieve the goal of proficient reading.

References

Allington, R. L. (1977). If they don't read much, how they ever gonna get good? *Journal of Reading, 21,* 57–61.

Allington, R. L. (1980). Teacher interruption behaviors during primary grade oral reading. *Journal of Educational Psychology, 72,* 371–377.

Anderson, R., Wilson, P., and Fielding, L. (1988). Growth in reading and how children spend their time outside of school. *Reading Research Quarterly, 23,* 285–303.

Baumann, J. and Duffy, A. (1997). *Engaged reading for pleasure and learning: A report from the National Reading Research Center.* Athens, GA: National Reading Research Center.

Cunningham, P. (2006). High-poverty schools that beat the odds. *The Reading Teacher, 60,* 382–385.

Cunningham, P. and Allington, R. (1999). *Classrooms that work* (2nd ed.). New York: Longman.

Cunningham, P. M., Hall, D. P., and Defee, M. (1998). Nonability-grouped, multilevel instruction: Eight years later. *The Reading Teacher, 51,* 652–664.

Five, C. and Dionisio, M. (1999). Teaching the struggling reader and writer. *School Talk, 4*(2).

Fuchs, D., Fuchs, L. S., and Vaughn, S. (2008). *Response to intervention: A framework for reading educators.* Newark, DE: International Reading Association.

Goodman, Y., Watson, D., and Burke, C. (1996). *Reading strategies: Focus on comprehension* (2nd ed.). Katonah, NY: Richard C. Owen.

Griffith, L. W. and Rasinski, T. V. (2004). A focus on fluency: How one teacher incorporated fluency with her reading curriculum. *The Reading Teacher, 58,* 126–137.

Guthrie, J. T. and Humenick, N. M. (2004). Motivating students to read: Evidence for classroom practices that increase reading motivation and achievement. In P. McCardle and V. Chhabra (Eds.), *The voice of evidence in reading research* (pp. 329–354). Baltimore: Brookes.

Guthrie, J. T., Rueda, R. S., Gambrell, L. B., and Morrison, D. A. (2009). Roles of engagement, valuing, and identification in reading development of students from diverse backgrounds. In L. Morrow and R. S. Rueda (Eds.), *Handbook of reading and literacy among students from diverse backgrounds* (pp. 195–215). New York: Guilford Press.

McCormick, S. (1999). *Instructing students who have literacy problems* (3rd ed.). Upper Saddle River, NJ: Prentice-Hall.

McDermott, R. (1978). Pirandello in the classroom: On the possibility of equal educational opportunity in American culture. In M. Reynolds (Ed.), *Futures for exceptional children: Emerging structure* (pp. 41–64). Reston, VA: Council for Exceptional Children.

Postlethwaite, T. N. and Ross, K. N. (1992). *Effective schools in reading: Implications for educational planners*. The Hague: International Association for the Evaluation of Educational Achievement.

Pressley, M. (2002). Effective beginning reading instruction. *Journal of Literacy Research, 34,* 165–188.

Rupley, W., Wise, B., and Logan, J. (1986). Research in effective teaching: An overview of its development. In J. Hoffman (Ed.), *Effective teaching of reading: Research and practice* (pp. 3–36). Newark, DE: International Reading Association.

Snow, C. (1991). *Unfulfilled expectations*. Cambridge, MA: Harvard University Press.

Sweet, A. and Guthrie, J. (1996). How children's motivations relate to literacy development and instruction. *The Reading Teacher, 49,* 660–662.

5

Using Authentic Texts to Learn New Words and Develop Fluency

It was a rainy vacation day at the beach. Three-year-old Annie took a nap; her mom and her Aunt Nancy each grabbed a book and were engrossed in their reading when Annie awoke. After she rubbed the sleep from her eyes, she began trying to find a playmate. She asked her mom to play dolls; her mom said, "Sure. Just let me finish this chapter." She asked Nancy to do watercolors with her; Nancy's reply was the same. Annie looked around at the adults reading, went to her room, and came back with Bill Martin's *Brown Bear, Brown Bear, What Do You See?* (2010). She hopped up on the couch, opened her book, and began reading aloud.

Annie had heard *Brown Bear* many times and had read it along with her mother. The story's pattern was easy for her to recall, so she read the words by remembering previous readings and by looking at the pictures for clues. For Annie, *Brown Bear* was a supportive and encouraging text. *Support* and *encouragement* are important concepts for all readers, but particularly for those who are just beginning to learn to read or who struggle with reading. They describe the instructional environment, the teacher's role, and especially materials. Effective materials for beginners or struggling readers support and encourage them in their quest for meaning. Authentic texts that are predictable, like *Brown Bear*, work well because they enable even a beginning reader to predict, sample, and confirm—in short, do all the things a mature reader does. For our purposes in this book, an added benefit of authentic predictable text is that its familiar, dependable context provides a rich resource for word learning. Moreover, because predictable books are easy for children to read, they often read them repeatedly, which enhances fluency development.

Materials are predictable when children can easily determine what will come next—both what the author will say and how it will be said. Language-experience texts (see Chapter 13) are predictable because they reflect children's own experiences in their own words. We describe many other sources of predictable text in this chapter, and we also offer some suggestions for using predictable texts to foster word learning. First, however, we explore some conceptions (and misconceptions) about what makes material easy to read.

What Is Easy to Read?

We can all agree that beginning and struggling readers need access to texts that they can easily read (Allington 2005). We may disagree, however, about what makes something easy to read. Is a highly structured text with controlled vocabulary easier to read than one that relies on natural language patterns? Some believe structure and control facilitate learning. Others, however (and we include ourselves here), see faults with this "go, Spot, go" type of writing. Simple language patterns are usually unfamiliar to children because they do not represent the natural oral language they hear in daily life; moreover, the vocabulary repetition is unnatural (when was the last time you said, "Look. Oh look, look, look" in conversation?). Stories written to fit a formula with certain words and restricted sentence patterns usually lack literary merit.

Heidi Mesmer (2006) surveyed 300 primary-level teachers who were members of the International Reading Association about the materials they used for beginning reading instruction. Most chose not to use decodable texts or controlled vocabulary readers (14 percent and 15 percent, respectively). Teachers said decodable text was "stilted, boring, and flat" (p. 411). Mesmer (2010) also explored the influence of text type (decodable vs. more natural language patterns) on first-grade children's word recognition and fluency. Three times over the school year she assessed children who regularly read each type of text. Decoding results were inconclusive, but children who read texts with

Research-Based Strategies

more natural language patterns read more fluently than their peers who read decodable texts.

For these reasons, among others, many educators rely on pattern books and other authentic, predictable texts for reading instruction. These texts contain distinct language patterns—naturally repetitive language, cumulating events, and/or use of rhythm or rhyme—all of which support children's reading success. Moreover, the repetitive and predictable language patterns are an enjoyable way for children to play with sounds, words, phrases, and sentences.

Types of Authentic Text

In addition to dictated texts (see Chapter 13), several other types of authentic texts provide the support that beginning and struggling readers need to learn words—indeed, to learn to read. Following are a variety of suggestions we recommend for use with these readers.

Pattern Books

Many wonderful, new children's pattern books are published each year. And because teachers continue to be interested in using pattern books for instruction, many old favorite titles are still available as well. These predictable books are easy for children to read because they quickly catch on to the pattern that the author used to write the book. Patterns usually involve repetitive language and/or repeating or cumulative episodes (as in *The House That Jack Built*). Rhyme may also be used. Figure 5.1 provides titles of dozens of pattern books. Many titles are appropriate for older struggling readers and English language learner (ELL) students as well as beginning readers. Rereading pattern books, first with support and later independently, is important for all three groups of readers (Barone 1996; Helman and Burns 2008; Rasinski, Padak, and Fawcett 2010).

Many pattern books are available from children's book clubs in big book format, so teachers might strive to collect sets of children's favorites that include both a big book version and several copies of little books. After the whole group works with the big book version, copies of the little books are eagerly sought for independent reading.

English Language
Learners

Adams, P. (2007). *This old man*. New York: Grosset and Dunlap.

Aliki. (1991). *My five senses*. New York: Crowell.

Allenberg, J. and Allenberg, A. (1986). *Each peach, pear, plum*. New York: Viking Press.

Baer, G. (1994). *Thump, thump, rat-a-tat-tat*. New York: Harper and Row.

Barton, B. (1993). *Dinosaurs, dinosaurs*. New York: Crowell.

Brown, M. W. (1947). *Goodnight moon*. New York: Harper and Row.

Brown, M. W. (1949/1999). *The important book*. New York: HarperCollins.

Brown, R. (1992). *A dark, dark tale*. New York: Dial.

Campbell, R. (2007). *Dear zoo*. New York: Four Winds.

Carle, E. (1996). *The grouchy ladybug*. New York: Crowell.

Carle, E. (1997). *Today is Monday*. New York: Putnam.

Carle, E. (2009). *The very hungry caterpillar*. New York: Philomel.

Carle, E. and Iwamura, K (2003). *Where are you going? To see my friend!* New York: Orchard Books.

Chaconas, D. (2007). *One little mouse*. Glenview, IL: Pearson Scott Foresman.

Cowley, J. (2006). *Mrs. Wishy-Washy*. Bothell, WA: Wright Group.

Dillon, L. (2002). *Rap a tap tap: Here's Bojangles*. New York: Blue Sky Press.

Dougherty, T. (2006). *Days of the week*. Minneapolis, MN: Picture Window Books.

Fox, M. (1992). *Hattie and the fox*. New York: Bradbury.

Galdone, P. (1986). *The teeny tiny woman*. New York: Clarion.

Galdone, P. (2006). *The little red hen*. New York: Scholastic.

Guarino, D. (1989). *Is your mama a llama?* New York: Scholastic.

Hayles, M. (2005). *Pajamas anytime*. New York: G.P. Putnam's Sons.

(Continued)

Figure 5.1 (Continued)

Hennessy, B. G. (1992). *Jake baked the cake.* New York: Viking.

Hoberman, M. (2000). *The seven silly eaters.* New York: Voyager.

Hoberman, M. (2007). *A house is a house for me.* New York: Puffin.

Hutchins, P. (1971). *Rosie's walk.* New York: Macmillan.

Hutchins, P. (1989). *The doorbell rang.* New York: Greenwillow.

Hutchins, P. (1993). *Titch.* New York: Aladdin.

Janovitz, M. (2007). *Look out, bird!* New York: North-South.

Jonas, A. (1989). *Color dance.* New York: Greenwillow.

Jones, C. (1998). *Old MacDonald had a farm.* New York: Sandpiper.

Keats, E. J. (1999). *Over in the meadow.* New York: Scholastic.

Kraus, R. (2000). *Whose mouse are you?* New York: Macmillan.

Langstaff, J. (1991). *Oh, a-hunting we will go.* New York: Atheneum.

Leuck, L. (1996). *Sun is falling, night is calling.* New York: Simon and Schuster.

Lies, B. (2006). *Bats at the beach.* Boston: Houghton Mifflin.

Martin, B. (2010). *Brown bear, brown bear, what do you see?* New York: Holt.

Martin, B. (2009). *Chicka chicka boom boom.* New York: Aladdin.

McKissack, F. (1986). *Who is coming?* Chicago: Children's Press.

Neitzel, S. (1998). *The bag I'm taking to Grandma's.* New York: Harper Trophy.

Numeroff, L. (1985). *If you give a mouse a cookie.* New York: Harper and Row.

Numeroff, L. (1994). *If you give a moose a muffin.* New York: HarperCollins.

Peek, M. (2006). *Mary wore her red dress.* New York: Clarion.

Raffi. (1988). *Down by the bay.* New York: Crown.

Ricci, C. (2004). *Say "cheese"!* New York: Simon Spotlight.

Sadler, M. (2006). *Money, money, honey, bunny.* New York: Random House.

Sendak, M. (1994). *Chicken soup with rice.* New York: Williams.

Seuss, Dr. (1960). *Green eggs and ham.* New York: Random House.

Seuss, Dr. (2005). *Wet pet, dry pet, your pet, my pet.* New York: Random House.

Shaw, N. (1992). *Sheep on a ship.* Boston: Houghton Mifflin.

Shaw, N. (2006). *Sheep in a jeep.* Boston: Houghton Mifflin.

Strickland, P. (2002). *One bear, one dog.* San Francisco: Chronicle Books.

Wescott, N. (1980). *I know an old lady who swallowed a fly.* Boston: Houghton Mifflin.

Williams, S. (2000). *I went walking.* Orlando, FL: Harcourt Brace Jovanovich.

Wood, A. (1991). *The napping house.* New York: Harcourt Brace Jovanovich.

Wood, A. (2007). *Silly Sally.* San Diego: Harcourt.

Yolen, J. (2000). *How do dinosaurs say goodnight?* New York: Blue Sky Press.

Zelinsky, P. (1990). *The wheels on the bus.* New York: Dutton.

Some teachers also make their own big books. Materials needed for making a big book include chart paper (18" × 20" or larger) for the pages, stiff cardboard such as poster board for covers, a wide felt-tip marker for printing the text, materials for illustrations, and something, such as metal shower rings, to bind the finished product together. Individual pages might be laminated so that they will withstand repeated readings. Print should be large and legible from at least 15 feet.

Children can prepare illustrations for class-made big books. The first step in this process is for the teacher and students to read the story several times in order to decide where the page breaks should be. Pairs of learners can then read a portion of the text to be illustrated, talk about illustration possibilities, decide, and illustrate. All this activity involves reading and rereading the text—excellent fluency practice and a wonderful opportunity for word learning; children must also comprehend their individual pages in order to create appropriate illustrations. Moreover, children's pride of ownership and accomplishment are a joy to see.

Songs, Finger Plays, and Other Rhymes

These are already staples in most primary classrooms. To make them into material for reading instruction, the teacher simply needs to make text copies of them, make the copies available for children to see, and use them instructionally. Since children already know the words, these items are particularly useful for developing concepts about print (e.g., What is a word?) and for learning sight words.

Some songs are used repeatedly throughout the school year, such as *"Happy Birthday to You."* The teacher can make a copy of this song, leaving a blank where the child's name is to be sung. The birthday child can create a name card to be affixed at the appropriate spot. After the class sings to the birthday child, the teacher can use the text of the song to help children learn new words.

Because of the repetitive nature of the language and the accompanying actions, children likewise learn finger plays rapidly. These, too, become reading material as soon as the teacher creates a large version of the rhyme for children to read. Some finger plays and other childhood rhymes have many stanzas, but they tend to be highly repetitive. A generic chart containing most of the stanza can be prepared, and word cards can be used to differentiate the stanzas. In the rhyme below, for example, the beginning blank is completed with word cards containing the numbers ten through one:

> _____ little monkeys jumping on the bed.
> One fell off and bumped its head.
> Mama called the doctor, and the doctor said,
> "No more monkeys jumping on the bed!"

As children chant the verse, they need to read the number cards to decide which goes next. In this way, they learn the number words by sight.

Jump rope rhymes and other childhood chants are likewise helpful for word learning. Teachers should keep their ears open while children are on the playground; opportunities for reading material will abound!

Nursery Rhymes and Poems

Many Mother Goose rhymes and other childhood poems are excellent choices for authentic, predictable texts. These short poems with strong rhythms and clear rhymes are easy for children to learn. As we note in Chapters 7 and 16, these texts are also quite useful for building students' competencies in both phonics and fluency. Easy-to-read poems are located in most children's poetry anthologies. Moreover, teachers and students can write their own rhymes and poems. Poetry reading should be a daily routine in classrooms.

Environmental Print

Children learn a great deal from their surroundings. Print in the environment, both outside of school and in the classroom, is a great source for incidental word learning. Children begin to recognize print in real-life contexts, such as road signs, fast-food logos, and the packaging on their favorite toys, at a very early age, as anyone who lives with a preschooler knows. To recognize environmental print, children appear to attend to shapes, colors, and logos, as well as print. Recognition of decontextualized print comes later, usually when children enter school (Lomax and McGee 1987). Nevertheless, children's strong interest in environmental print makes it a good choice for reading material.

Research-Based Strategies

Although simply seeing environmental print and other predictable texts may be too indirect to foster precise word learning (Stahl and Murray 1993), teachers can focus children's attention on the words in environmental print messages fairly easily. For example, children can look through old newspapers, magazines, and junk mail to find material to put into theme books about environmental print (Christie, Enz, and Vukelich 1997). Theme books can be created for such topics as soft drinks, sneakers, pizza, fast food, cereal, cookies, and professional sports teams. To encourage focus on the words and not just the logos, teachers can insert pages into the theme books that contain the words alone in standard print or type format. Many children enjoy guessing which words belong with which logos.

Labels, lists, schedules, directions, messages, and other forms of environmental print inside the classroom can also foster word learning. In general, we recommend using as much functional print as possible in the classroom. Children see and often must use these words daily, so they naturally learn them. Moreover, such a print-rich classroom shows children rather directly about the functions of writing and the value of the written word.

Using Authentic Text

Probably the best way to introduce authentic, predictable texts to children is through what Holdaway (1979) calls the "Shared Book Experience," an idea inspired by parents and children reading bedtime stories in a comfortable, relaxed manner. Translating this experience into classroom practice involves preparing an enlarged version of the text, since it is critical for the children to see the words as the teacher reads them. Teachers may use chart paper to make these enlarged texts; electronic versions can be projected using an LCD projector. We recommend that teachers prepare smaller versions of the texts, perhaps with room for children's illustrations, so that each child can have an individual copy.

In general, pattern books or other types of authentic text should be read to children several times to allow children to learn them thoroughly. The next stage is to read the text with children in choral or antiphonal fashion (see Chapter 16). Many teachers pause before reading repetitive portions of the text; the children chime in, usually with gusto, to say the parts they know. Finally, children are invited to read the text alone. (See Chapter 16 for other ideas for repeated readings.) All this can be done over several days, if needed. This overall pattern, "I'll read it to you. You read it with me. Now you read it alone," provides the support that children need to decode the text successfully.

After children have learned the text, the teacher can begin to direct their attention to individual sentences, phrases, words, letters, and letter combinations. This natural progression from whole to part, which we have also described in other chapters, allows children to discover how smaller units of language work without distorting or disrupting the process of reading and enjoying the entire text. Moreover, it's easy to help children see the value of what they learn about words and sounds because the new knowledge can be easily related back to the text. Thus, transfer, a critical element in word recognition instruction, is facilitated.

Guessing Games

Texts can be used for instruction that focuses on the conventions of print and other aspects of word learning in a guessing-game format. For example, the teacher can ask questions like these:

- Where's the title? How many words are in the title? Where's the first word in the title? Where's the last word? Who can circle all the words in the title?

- Where's the first word in the story? Where's the last word? Where's the first word in line _____? How many words are in the first sentence? How many words are in the last line?

- Where does the first sentence begin? Where does it end? How can we tell where a sentence begins and where one ends? How many sentences are in our text? How many lines?

- Who can find a [letter] in the text? Are there more [letter]s? Who can find a capital [letter]? A lowercase [letter]?

- Who can find the word [a word with a featured word family]? How many words that contain the _____ family are in our text? What are they?

- Who can find a word that has a [phonic element]? How many words that contain [phonic element] are in our text? What are they?

- Who can find a two-syllable word? How many two-syllable words are there in our text?

Lessons like this focus children's attention on the parts of written language—lines, sentences, words, letters, and phonic elements. Note too the variation in difficulty of the guessing-game questions. Some focus on very beginning print concepts (e.g., Who can circle all the words in the title? Who can find a lowercase [letter]?), and others are more advanced (e.g., How many words that contain [phonic element] are in our text? Who can find a two-syllable word?). Children enjoy this sort of guessing game; it's also an easy way to differentiate instruction to accommodate different ability levels among individual children.

Children can use markers to circle or underline their responses to these questions on a second copy of the text. They can point with their fingers or use a pointer or flashlight. Some teachers use *word whoppers*, which are fly swatters with rectangles cut in them. Words of interest to children (or the teacher) can also be added to each student's word bank (see Chapter 11). However children respond, working with familiar and meaningful text provides support and allows them to discover relationships between the parts and the whole. And the multiple readings that occur naturally support both word learning and fluency development.

Word Sorts

Word sort activities (see Chapter 11) can also be used to direct children's attention to the language of the texts. Consider, for example, the following Mother Goose rhyme:

Jelly on a plate, jelly on a plate
Wibble, wobble, wibble, wobble
Jelly on a plate.

Sausage in a pan, sausage in a pan
Frizzle, frazzle, frizzle, frazzle
Sausage in a pan

Baby on the floor, baby on the floor
Pick him up, pick him up
Baby on the floor.

After the poem is enjoyed for its own sake, its words can be used to focus children's attention on the sounds of long and short A. The teacher can ask children to circle all the words containing the letter A in the poem. Next, in pairs or groups of three, they can complete a closed word sort in which they put each A word into a category, as shown here:

Long A	Short A	Other Sounds of A
plate	pan	sausage
baby	frazzle	

Copy Change

Individuals or small groups can make their own versions of authentic, predictable texts, especially pattern books and poems. This writing activity is often called *copy change* because children use the author's copy as a framework, but change it to reflect their own ideas. Simple pattern books, like *Brown Bear*, work well for introducing children to copy change. The teacher can simply read the book several times to children, eventually asking them to identify what the author "does over and over." Some teachers write children's ideas on the chalkboard so that they can refer to them later. Others prepare sheets with some of the text provided for children.

> Little mouse, little mouse, what do you see?
> I see a hungry cat looking at me.
>
> Pitcher, pitcher, what do you see?
> I see the batter looking at me.

Students thought about rhyming words and syllables as they wrote their own books. They also practiced writing sight words. Most important, they enjoyed the entire lesson and celebrated their authorship.

Songs can also be used for copy change activities. Here's a version of "Yankee Doodle" that a struggling first-grader recently wrote (and performed) in our reading clinic.

> Yankee Doodle went to town
> Riding on a doggy
> They got lost on their way
> Because it was so foggy.

In this case the student used the original text as a scaffold, but at the same time had to attend to rhythm, rhyme, and meaning as she created her own version of this simple text.

Copy change activities encourage careful reading and listening so that children can discover, appreciate, and use the author's words and language patterns. Children must also analyze the structure of the original text (Leu and Kinzer 1999). Best of all, students find it fun and satisfying to write stories or poems that are similar to those they have read and to share these new stories or poems with their classmates and families. All this practice promotes fluent, expressive reading.

One, two, three, four, five

Once I caught a fish alive.

Figure 5.2 Kevin's
Mother Goose Page

Other Independent Activities

Children can illustrate their copy change texts; they can also type their texts, one sentence per page, to make their own books. Figure 5.2 shows an example of an individual book Kevin made of the Mother Goose rhyme "One, two, three, four, five." Cloze exercises (see Chapter 12) are also effective.

All instructional texts should be available for children to reread independently. Because of the support they have received during the repeated reading and study of the texts, children can usually read them alone or with peers. They take great pride in this accomplishment and are generally interested in reading the texts again and again. This success fosters positive attitudes toward reading and helps children develop good concepts of themselves as readers. Children also learn about the conventions of print, acquire sight vocabulary, practice word recognition strategies, and develop fluency as they practice with the texts; these findings hold for both beginning readers and ELL students (Barone 1996; Helman and Burns 2008; Kuhn 2004).

English Language
Learners

Just Good Books

Finally, we recommend good stories and lots of reading for students. Not only do good stories provide students with great opportunities for practicing their word recognition skills and strategies, they also make

Research-Based
Strategies

reading satisfying and exciting for students—they help to get students hooked on reading and hooked on books. We know that students who are voracious readers tend to be our best readers. Indeed, the National Assessment of Educational Progress results from 1992, 1994, 1998, and 2000 showed that fourth-graders who read the most at school and at home had the highest levels of reading achievement (National Center for Educational Statistics 2001). Thus, teachers need to know the very best reading materials available for students, even when the instructional focus is phonics and word recognition.

With the thousands of children's books published every year, it's difficult for teachers to become experts in instruction and experts in children's literature at the same time. Fortunately, teachers can use several resources to help find great books for students to read. The primary resources, we think, are media specialists or librarians and other veteran teachers. These professionals are filled with knowledge about the very best books for students, books they know will turn kids on to reading. Media specialists and librarians, in particular, are trained to find books that students will enjoy. They read the professional materials that review, rate, and recommend books for children. If you are a new teacher, be sure to ask your school librarian and teacher colleagues to recommend books and other reading material, including online resources, for your students. You will find them most accommodating.

Book awards are another good resource for finding good books for children. The American Library Association (ALA) sponsors several awards for children's literature each year, including the prestigious Caldecott (for illustrations in books) and Newbery (for best story) medals. But don't limit yourself only to the winners. Caldecott and Newbery Honor Books didn't win the awards but are still of exceptional merit. Other important annual awards include the Batchelder Award for best books translated into English and the Coretta Scott King Awards for African American authors, illustrators, and "new talent"; both of these are also sponsored by the ALA. Current and past winners and Honor Books for all of these awards are located at the ALA website: http://www.ala.org/awardsgrants/. The Orbis Pictus Award for nonfiction books for children is sponsored by the National Council of Teachers of English (http://ncte.org). Many states also sponsor book awards. Children love reading books that have been recognized by others in their state.

Professional journals are also a valuable resource for teachers in search of good books. *The Reading Teacher (RT)*, published by the International Reading Association (IRA) (1-800-336-READ, www. reading.org), is one of the best. Many elementary and middle schools receive it. (If yours doesn't, ask your principal to get a subscription or two for your school.) Published monthly during the school year, *RT* frequently features review columns, written by children's literature and reading experts, on recently published books for students. *RT* also publishes *Children's Choices* (October issue) and *Teachers' Choices* (November issue). *Children's Choices* reports on recently published books that children across the country rated as their favorites. *Teachers' Choices* reports on favorite books of recent vintage from the teachers' point of view. The IRA newspaper, *Reading Today*, also publishes book reviews. The Web is another outstanding resource for learning about children's books.

Online bookstores such as barnesandnoble.com and amazon.com offer synopses and sometimes book reviews of selected titles. In fact, children can write and publish reviews of books they have read on these websites. The following list shows other handy Web resources for children's book lists:

Association for Library Service to Children
www.ala.org/alsc/

Carol Hurst's Children's Literature Site
http://www.carolhurst.com

Children's Literature Web Guide
www.ucalgary.ca/~dkbrown/index.html

The Internet Public Library (also includes many online texts for children to read)
http://www.ipl.org/div/kidspace/

Recommended Trade Books at the Ohio Literacy Resource Center
http://literacy.kent.edu/eureka/

Technology

Texts and Phonics

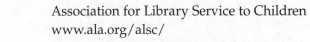

**Research-Based
Strategies**

Our main reason for selecting or recommending books for children should be their literary quality. Is the book a good read? Will the reader find the text engaging? Will the material lead students to want to read more? As students read books of exceptional merit, they exercise their phonics and word study strategies in real life and satisfying contexts.

This issue of providing children with authentic practice opportunities is very important. In their discussion of phonics research, for example, the National Reading Panel (2000) concluded:

> Programs that focus too much on the teaching of letter-sound relations and not enough on putting them to use are not likely to be very effective. In implementing systematic phonics instruction, educators must keep the *end* in mind and ensure that children understand the purpose of learning letter-sounds and are able to apply their skills in their daily reading and writing activities. (p. 2–96)

Authentic texts especially effective for providing this needed practice are a critical tool. Listed in Figure 5.3 (adapted from Trachtenburg 1990) are books that highlight particular vowel sounds. Figures 5.4 and 5.5 offer some resources for working with ELLs. Figure 5.4 mentions several easy bilingual series books, and Figure 5.5 lists single titles. After providing students with instruction in a particular vowel sound, introducing them to books associated with the relevant vowel will give them immediate practice in using their newfound knowledge in real reading.

English Language Learners

Figure 5.3 Trade Books That Repeat Phonic Elements

Short *a*

Flack, M. (1997). *Angus and the cat*. New York: Doubleday.

Griffith, H. (1982). *Alex and the cat*. New York: Greenwillow.

Kent, J. (1971). *The fat cat*. New York: Scholastic.

Most, B. (1992). *There's an ant in Anthony*. New York: William Morrow.

Robins, J. (1988). *Addie meets Max*. New York: Harper and Row.

Schmidt, K. (1985). *The gingerbread man*. New York: Scholastic.

Seuss, Dr. (1957). *The cat in the hat*. New York: Random House.

(Continued)

Figure 5.3 (*Continued*)

Long *a*

Aaredema, V. (1992). *Bringing the rain to Kapiti Plain*. New York: Dial.

Bang, M. (1987). *The paper crane*. New York: Greenwillow.

Byars, B. (1975). *The lace snail*. New York: Viking.

Henkes, K. (1996). *Sheila Rae, the brave*. New York: Greenwillow.

Hines, A. (1983). *Taste the raindrops*. New York: Greenwillow.

Short *e*

Aliki. (1996). *Hello! Good-bye*. New York: Greenwillow.

Ets, M. (1972). *Elephant in a well*. New York: Viking.

Galdone, P. (2006). *The little red hen*. New York: Scholastic.

Ness, E. (1974). *Yeck eck*. New York: Dutton.

Shecter, B. (1977). *Hester the jester*. New York: Harper and Row.

Thayer, J. (1975). *I don't believe in elves*. New York: William Morrow.

Long *e*

Brown, M. W. (1996). *Four fur feet*. Mt. Pleasant, SC: Dell.

Keller, H. (1983). *Ten sleepy sheep*. New York: Greenwillow.

Martin, B. (2010). *Brown bear, brown bear, what do you see?*
New York: Holt.

Oppenheim, J. (1967). *Have you seen trees?* New York: Young Scott
Books.

Reiser, L. (1996). *Beachfeet*. New York: Greenwillow.

Shaw, N. (1995). *Sheep out to eat*. Boston: Houghton Mifflin.

Shaw, N. (2006). *Sheep in a jeep*. Boston: Houghton Mifflin.

Short *i*

Hutchins, P. (1993). *Titch*. New York: Aladdin.

Kessler, C. (1997). *Konte Chameleon: Fine, fine, fine*. Honesdale, PA: Boyds Mills.

Lewis T. (1981). *Call for Mr. Sniff*. New York: Harper and Row.

Lobel, A. (1988). *Small pig*. New York: Harper and Row.

McPhail, D. (1992). *Fix-it*. New York: Dutton.

Robins, J. (1986). *My brother, Will*. New York: Greenwillow.

Long *i*

Cameron, J. (1979). *If mice could fly*. New York: Atheneum.

Cole, S. (1985). *When the tide is low*. New York: Lothrop, Lee and Shepard.

Gelman, R. (1976). *Why can't I fly?* New York: Scholastic.

Hazen, B. (1983). *Tight times*. New York: Viking.

Short *o*

Dunrea, O. (1985). *Mogwogs on the march!* New York: Holiday House.

Emberley, B. (1972). *Drummer Hoff*. New York: Prentice-Hall.

McKissack, P. (1986). *Flossie & the fox*. New York: Dial.

Seuss, Dr. (1965). *Fox in socks*. New York: Random House.

Long *o*

Cole, B. (2001). *The giant's toe*. New York: Farrar, Straus and Giroux.

Gerstein, M. (1984). *Roll over!* New York: Crown.

Johnston, T. (1972). *The adventures of Mole and Troll*. New York: Putman.

Johnston, T. (1977). *Night noises and other Mole and Troll stories*. New York: Putnam.

Hamanaka, S. (1997). *The hokey pokey*. New York: Simon and Schuster.

(*Continued*)

Figure 5.3 (*Continued*)

Pinczes, E. (1997). *One hundred hungry ants*. Boston: Houghton Mifflin.

Short *u*

Cooney, N. (1987). *Donald says thumbs down*. New York: Putnam.

Lorenz, L. (1982). *Big Gus and little Gus*. New York: Prentice-Hall.

Marshall, J. (2001). *The cut-ups at Camp Custer*. New York: Puffin.

Udry, J. (2001). *Thump and plunk*. New York: Harper and Row.

Long *u*

Lobel, A. (1966). *The troll music*. New York: Harper and Row.

Medearis, A. (1997). *Rum-a-tum-tum*. New York: Holiday House.

Segal, L. (1977). *Tell me a Trudy*. New York: Farrar, Straus and Giroux.

Books and Poetry Anthologies That Feature Several Vowel and Consonant Sounds

Carle, E. (1999). *Eric Carle's animals animals*. New York: Philomel.

de Regniers, B. S., et al. (1988). *Sing a song of popcorn: Every child's book of poems*. New York: Scholastic.

Lansky, B. (1996). *Poetry party*. Deephaven, MN: Meadowbrook.

Lansky, B. (1999). *The new adventures of Mother Goose: Gentle rhymes for happy times*. New York: Atheneum.

Lobel, A. (Ed). (2003). *The Arnold Lobel book of Mother Goose*. New York: Knopf.

Moss, L. (2000). *Zin! Zin! Zin! A violin*. New York: Simon and Schuster.

Slier, D. (Ed.). (2003). *Make a joyful sound: Poems for children by African-American poets*. New York: Checkerboard Press.

Source: Adapted from P. Trachtenburg (1990). Using children's literature to enhance phonics instruction. *The Reading Teacher, 43,* 648–654.

Figure 5.4 Spanish-English Bilingual Series Books

Barron's I Can Read Spanish series (also available in French): *George the Goldfish; Get Dressed, Robbie; Goodnight Everyone; Happy Birthday; Hurry Up, Molly; I Want My Bandana; I'm Too Big; Puppy Finds a Friend; Space Postman; What's for Supper?*

DK Publishing, *My First Spanish . . .* (board books): *Animals, Words, Farms, Numbers, Trucks*

Houghton Mifflin's Good Beginnings series, written by P. Zagarenski: *How Do I Feel? / Como Me Siento; What Color Is It? / Que Color Es Este?*

Little, Brown's Concept Books, written by R. Emberley: *My Animals, My Food, My Numbers, My Shapes, My Toys, My Clothes, My Day, My House, My Opposites*

Figure 5.5 Bilingual and Multilingual Books for Early Readers

Ada, A. and Zubizarreta, R. (Trans.). (1999). *The lizard and the sun: A folktale in English and Spanish / La lagarija y el sol*. New York: Dell.

Chin, C. (1997). *China's bravest girl: The Legend of Hua Mu Lan / Chin Kuo Ying Hsiung Hua Mulan*. Emeryville, CA: Children's Book Press.

De Zutter, H. (1997). *Who says a dog goes bow-wow?* New York: Doubleday.

Ehlert, L. (2003). *Moon rope / Un lazo a la luna*. San Diego: Harcourt.

Elya, S. (1997). *Say hola to Spanish, otra vez (again!)*. New York: Lee and Low Books.

Griego, M., Bucks, B., Gilbert, S., Kimball, L., and Cooney, B. (1988). *Tortillas para Mama and other nursery rhymes* (bilingual edition). New York: Holt.

Heiman, S. (2003). *Mexico ABCs*. Minneapolis, MN: Picture Window Books.

Hinojosa, T. (2004). *Cada niño / Every child: A bilingual songbook*. El Paso, TX: Conco Punto Press.

(Continued)

Figure 5.5 *(Continued)*

Jaramillo, N. (Comp.). (1996). *Las nanas de abuelita /
Grandmother's nursery rhymes*. New York: Holt.

Johnston, T. (1996). *My Mexico-México mío*. New York: G.P.
Putnam's Sons.

Morales, Y. (2003). *Just a minute: A trickster tale and counting
book*. San Francisco: Chronicle Books.

Reiser, L. (1998). *Tortillas and lullabies / Tortillas y cancioncitas*.
New York: Greenwillow.

Rohmer, H. (1997). *Uncle Nacho's hat / El sombrero del Tío
Nacho*. Emeryville, CA: Children's Book Press.

Soto, G. (1995). *Chato's kitchen*. New York: G.P. Putnam's Sons.

Dictated Texts

We are great believers in the potential of language-experience activities for nurturing students' reading development. Language experience for young readers begins with an experience, individual or shared (see Chapter 13), that is discussed with classmates and the teacher. Next, the child or children dictate a text about the experience to the teacher, who immediately transcribes the oral text onto paper that all participants can see or onto a computer screen using large fonts that enable easy viewing.

The dictated and written text then becomes instructional material. Students can read these texts because they are familiar. Moreover, children come to see themselves as writers as well as readers.

Dictated texts contain a variety of phonic and structural word patterns because they are derived from natural language. For this reason dictated texts are useful for focused instruction and practice in decoding skills and strategies. For example, after instruction about a particular beginning consonant (onset) or structural element, students can search their dictated texts for words that contain that element. The additional and repeated readings that occur when students read their dictated stories for targeted elements or patterns will also build their sight vocabulary and proficiency in reading fluency.

Texts and Reading Fluency

Fluency is the bridge between word recognition and comprehension.
It is marked by quick, accurate, and expressive oral reading that the
reader understands well. Fluency is a relative concept—all readers are
more or less fluent depending on the nature and difficulty of the text
being read. Although you are probably a fairly good reader, we could
easily make you a disfluent reader by asking you to read something
highly technical for which you have little background, perhaps an essay
on nuclear physics or a legal contract.

Thus, when teaching reading fluency, we recommend that the
texts students read not be overly difficult. For building reading
fluency, we recommend predictable stories and texts, stories drawn
out of a series (e.g., Cynthia Rylant's *Henry and Mudge* series or
Barbara Park's *Junie B. Jones* series), stories around a given theme,
stories with a minimum of difficult words or grammar, and stories
that are not too long. Once students become familiar with a book that
is part of a series, for example, their familiarity with the author's style,
the book's characters and setting, and the general plots will enable
them to read succeeding books in the series with greater fluency and
understanding.

Difficult texts may require teacher support. The teacher may read
the text once or repeatedly, for example, or ask students to read with
partners. Stahl and Heubach (2005) found that under these conditions
students can benefit from working with more challenging texts.

Among the instructional strategies we have advocated for fluency
development is repeated readings (Samuels 1979/1997). Because
repeated readings, by its very nature, requires students to read a passage
more than once, texts used in repeated readings should be relatively
short (50 to 250 words in length). Where do you find such texts? One
way is to break a story into 250-word segments. Another and preferred
approach is to use poetry for students. Poetry is short, highly patterned,
and predictable, and it contains letter patterns that can be adapted to
phonics instruction. Perhaps most importantly, poetry is meant to be
performed, to be read aloud to an audience. If a text is meant to be
performed orally, the reader has a real reason to practice so that reading
to the audience will be flawless and meaningful. Thus, poetry, the same
poetry that we mentioned earlier in this chapter for phonics and word
study instruction, is ideal for building students' fluency.

Research-Based
Strategies

With current reading programs' emphasis on prose reading, poetry is sometimes ignored in the reading curriculum (Perfect 2005). Using poetry for fluency instruction will certainly improve students' fluency. Of equal or greater importance, integrating poetry and poetry performance into the classroom will add variety and help students develop greater appreciation for this most aesthetic of reading texts.

In Conclusion

Predictable materials offer beginning readers the support and encouragement they need to grow as readers, and to grow in their belief in themselves as readers. Benefits are similar for children learning English and for those who struggle in reading. One study that compared children's learning with predictable literature to their learning with basal reading materials concluded that "using predictable materials with beginning readers spurs their acquisition of sight vocabulary, encourages them to use context clues when encountering unfamiliar words, and creates more positive feelings about reading aloud" (Bridge, Winograd, and Haley 1983, p. 890). This conclusion is a strong endorsement for using authentic, predictable materials, and one with which we concur.

References

Allington, R. L. (2005). *What really matters for struggling readers: Designing research-based programs* (2nd ed.). Boston: Allyn and Bacon.

Barone, D. (1996). Whose language? Learning from bilingual learners in a developmental first-grade classroom. In D. Leu, C. Kinzer, and K. Hinchman (Eds.), *Literacies for the 21st century: Research and practice* (pp. 170–182). Chicago: National Reading Conference.

Bridge, C., Winograd, P., and Haley, D. (1983). Using predictable materials versus preprimers to teach beginning sight words. *The Reading Teacher, 36,* 884–891.

Christie, J., Enz, B., and Vukelich, C. (1997). *Teaching language and literacy.* New York: Longman.

Helman, L. and Burns, M. (2008). What does oral language have to do with it? Helping young English language learners acquire a sight word vocabulary. *The Reading Teacher, 62,* 14–19.

Holdaway, D. (1979). *The foundations of literacy.* Sydney: Ashton Scholastic.

Kuhn, M. (2004). Helping students become accurate, expressive readers: Fluency instruction for small groups. *The Reading Teacher, 58*, 338–344.

Leu, D. and Kinzer, C. (1999). *Effective literacy instruction* (4th ed.). Upper Saddle River, NJ: Prentice Hall.

Lomax, R. and McGee, L. (1987). Young children's concepts about print and reading: Toward a model of word reading acquisition. *Reading Research Quarterly, 22*, 237–256.

Mesmer, H. (2006). Beginning reading materials: A national survey of primary teachers' reported uses and beliefs. *Journal of Literacy Research, 38*, 389–425.

Mesmer, H. (2010). Textual scaffolds for developing fluency in beginning readers: Accuracy and reading rate in qualitatively leveled and decodable text. *Literacy Research and Instruction, 49*, 20–39.

National Center for Educational Statistics. (2001). *Fourth grade reading highlights 2000.* Washington, DC: U.S. Department of Education, Office of Educational Research and Improvement.

National Reading Panel. (2000). *Report of the National Reading Panel: An evidence-based assessment of the scientific research literature on reading and its implications for reading instruction.* Washington, DC: National Institute of Child Health and Human Development.

Perfect, K. (2005). *Poetry lessons.* New York: Scholastic.

Rasinski, T., Padak, N., and Fawcett, G. (2010). *Teaching children who find reading difficult* (4th ed.). Boston: Allyn and Bacon.

Samuels, S. J. (1997). The method of repeated readings. *The Reading Teacher, 50*, 376–381. (Reprinted from *The Reading Teacher*, 1979, 32, 403–408.)

Stahl, S. and Heubach, K. (2005). Fluency-oriented reading instruction. *Journal of Literacy Research, 37*, 25–60.

Stahl, S. and Murray, B. (1993). Environmental print, phonemic awareness, letter recognition, and word recognition. In D. Leu and C. Kinzer (Eds.), *Examining central issues in literacy research, theory, and practice* (pp. 227–233). Chicago: National Reading Conference.

Trachtenburg, P. (1990). Using children's literature to enhance phonics instruction. *The Reading Teacher, 43*, 648–654.

6

Teaching Phonemic Awareness

Walk into Juanita's kindergarten classroom at the beginning of any school day, and you will find a lot of singing and choral reading going on. Children sing favorite songs and reread familiar and favorite rhyming poems. Sometimes Juanita asks children to change the refrain of a song to emphasize different sounds. For example, in "Row, Row, Row Your Boat," the refrain "Merrily, merrily, merrily, merrily" becomes "verrily . . ." or "cherrily. . . ." After reading the poems, Juanita asks children to name rhyming words from them and then to add other rhyming words. She also says individual sounds from a significant word from the poem and asks the children to name the word: "What is this word—*j, a, k*?"

Juanita's students love the songs and poetry, but Juanita also understands that in order to be successful in phonics and reading, children need to learn how sounds work, so she extends her music and poetry activities into natural opportunities for children to play with and manipulate sounds.

> It's no problem to move from the singing of a lyric into drawing students' attention to the sounds in the lyrics. In fact, I think it's kind of fun, and I know the children enjoy it too. . . . At the beginning of the school year, I am amazed by the number of children who have trouble with sounds. But as we make playing with songs, rhymes, and sounds a part of our day, it's not long before they all begin to hear the individual sounds in words. Kindergarten is a place for children to become ready for school and ready to learn to read. I think our work with sounds is really helping prepare them by showing them that words have sounds and that those sounds can be moved and changed.

Phonemic awareness, or what Juanita calls sound knowledge and sound play, refers to a person's awareness of speech sounds smaller than a syllable and the ability to manipulate them through such tasks as blending and segmenting. Phonemic awareness is a key element in learning word recognition through phonics and overall reading. Literacy scholar Keith Stanovich (1994) calls phonemic awareness a superb predictor of early reading acquisition, "better than anything else that we know of, including IQ" (p. 284).

**Research-Based
Strategies**

Phonemic awareness provides the foundation for learning phonics, the knowledge of letter-sound correspondences, which readers use to decode unknown words. Since readers must recognize, segment, and blend sounds that are represented by letters, *phonemic awareness* is a very important precondition for learning phonics as well as reading (Adams 1990; Ball and Blachman 1991; Bradley and Bryant 1983, 1985; Fielding-Barnsley 1997; Lundberg, Frost, and Peterson 1988; National Reading Panel 2000; Perfetti, Beck, Bell, and Hughes 1987; Stanovich 1986; Yopp 1992, 1995a, 1995b). Students who lack phonemic awareness are most at risk to experience difficulty in learning phonics and, more importantly, learning to read (Catts 1991; Maclean, Bryant, and Bradley 1987). Thus, success in phonics requires some degree of phonemic awareness. Indeed, the report of the prestigious Committee on the Prevention of Reading Difficulties in Young Children recommends that, among other instructional activities, "beginning readers need explicit instruction and practice that lead to an appreciation that spoken words are made up of small units of sound" (Snow, Burns, and Griffin 1998, p. 7). Similarly, in its position statement on phonemic awareness, the International Reading Association (1998), the leading professional literacy organization in the world, notes the importance of phonemic awareness and how it can easily be nurtured at home and school:

**Research-Based
Strategies**

> It is critical that teachers are familiar with the concept of phonemic awareness and that they know that there is a body of evidence pointing to a significant relation between phonemic awareness and reading acquisition. . . . Many researchers suggest that the logical translation of the research to practice is for teachers of young children to provide an environment that encourages play with spoken language as part of the broader literacy program. Nursery rhymes, riddles, songs, poems, and read-aloud books that manipulate sounds may be used purposefully to draw young learners' attention to the sounds of spoken language. (p. 6)[*]

*Reprinted with the permission of the International Reading Association.

However, the Association's statement further notes that 20 percent of young children have not attained sufficient phonemic awareness to profit from phonics instruction by the middle of first grade. For these children we need to go beyond the "natural." As the Association notes, we must

> promote action that is direct, explicit, and meaningful. . . . We feel we can reduce this 20% figure by more systematic instruction and engagement with language early in students' home, preschool, and kindergarten classes. We . . . can reduce this figure even further through early identification of students who are outside the norms of progress in phonemic awareness development, and through the offering of intensive programs of instruction. (p. 6)

The National Reading Panel (2000) reviewed research about the importance of phonemic awareness and about ways to teach it productively. With regard to importance, the NRP report says, "Correlational studies have identified phonemic awareness and letter knowledge as the two best school-entry predictors of how well children will learn to read during their first two years in school" (p. 2-1). This makes sense. Children who come to school with well-developed phonemic awareness and knowledge of letter names have probably had lots of preschool language and literacy experiences, which provide a firm foundation for subsequent reading achievement. The NRP also found that phonemic awareness instruction helped students learn to decode unfamiliar words, also logical given the relationship between phonemic awareness and phonics.

Research-Based Strategies

Several instructional guidelines can be derived from the National Reading Panel:

- Focus on one or two types of phoneme manipulation at one time.
- Assess before teaching; many children may not need instruction.
- Teach children in small groups.
- Keep sessions brief (only a total of 20 hours over an entire year).

Research-Based Strategies

- Make activities as "relevant and exciting as possible so that the instruction engages children's interest and attention in a way that promotes optimal learning" (p. 2-7).

Most children develop phonemic awareness naturally through everyday play with language sounds, from reciting nursery rhymes and childhood poems, from chanting and creating jump rope rhymes, from singing songs (e.g., "I've been working on the railroad; fee, fi, fiddly, I, oh"), and from simply talking with family members and friends. Through these opportunities to make and manipulate the sounds of language, children gradually develop phonemic awareness. By the time they enter kindergarten, this awareness of language sounds allows them to connect specific sounds with individual letters and letter patterns (i.e., phonics).

A significant number of children, however, enter school with insufficient awareness of language sounds. Some may have been plagued with chronic ear problems that make sound perception and manipulation difficult. Others may have had few opportunities to play with language through childhood rhymes and songs. For whatever reason, a fairly significant minority of young children entering school may not have sufficiently developed phonemic awareness to find success in phonics instruction. Difficulty perceiving sounds makes learning letter-sound correspondence and blending sounds into words—phonics—overwhelming and an early frustration in learning to read.

Assessing Phonemic Awareness

Because children's levels of phonemic awareness vary at school entrance, assessment is critical. Fortunately an easy-to-use phonemic awareness assessment is available. The *Yopp-Singer Test* of Phonemic Segmentation (Yopp 1995b) is a set of 22 words that students segment into constituent sounds (see Figure 6.1 for our variation of the *Yopp-Singer Test*). For example, the teacher says *back*, and the student says the three separate sounds that make up *back*: b, a, k.

The assessment takes only minutes to administer, yet the child's performance can provide an indication of his or her current awareness of language sounds, later success in reading, and important information to guide instruction. Phonemic awareness, as measured by the Yopp-Singer Test, is significantly correlated with students' reading and spelling achievement through grade 6 (Yopp 1995b). Clearly, this and related research (National Reading Panel 2000; Stanovich 1994) suggest that phonemic awareness must be considered when assessing young children and struggling readers.

Yopp reported that second-semester kindergarten students obtained a mean score of 12 on the test. Kindergartners who fall significantly below this threshold, say a score of 5 or below, should be provided additional opportunities to develop phonemic awareness, opportunities that fit well within a normal kindergarten classroom.

Research-Based
Strategies

Figure 6.1   Test for Assessing Phonemic Awareness

Test of Phonemic Segmentation

Student's name _____ Date _____

Student's age _____

Score (number correct) _____ Examiner _____

Directions: I'd like to play a sound game with you. I will say a word and I want you to break the word apart into its sounds. You need to tell me each sound in the word. For example, if I say "old," you should say "/o/-/l/-/d/." (*Administrator: Be sure to say the sounds in the word distinctly. Do not say the letters.*) Let's try a few practice words.

Practice items: (Assist the child in segmenting these items as necessary. You may wish to use blocks to help demonstrate the segmentation of sounds.) kite, so, fat

Test items: (Circle those items that the student correctly segments; incorrect responses may be recorded on the blank line following the item.)

1. to _____
2. me _____
3. fight _____
4. low _____
5. he _____
6. vain _____
7. is _____
8. am _____
9. be _____
10. meet _____
11. jack _____
12. dock _____
13. lace _____
14. mop _____
15. this _____
16. jot _____
17. grow _____
18. nice _____
19. cat _____
20. shoe _____
21. bed _____
22. stay _____

Source: Adapted from Yopp (1995b).

The *Yopp-Singer Test* has implications beyond kindergarten as well. We routinely administer it in our reading center to elementary-level struggling readers, many of whom have difficulty with the assessment. We expect students at second grade or beyond to score 20 or better. And yet it is not unusual to find fifth- and sixth-grade students, frustrated in reading, who score between 10 and 15. We wonder if these older students' struggles in reading began when they were asked to master phonics before they were developmentally ready to do so. Rather than being provided an alternative route to reading or the chance to develop phonemic awareness, they may have been forced down a road that they were unable to negotiate to begin with—more phonics, more intensive phonics. It is easy to imagine how these students became turned off to reading. While others read for pleasure and information, these students were stuck reading less and drilling more (Allington 1977, 1984, 1994), which in turn led to even less self-selected reading and further frustration in reading.

The *Yopp-Singer Test* of Phonemic Segmentation and our variation published here are valuable tools. Identifying students who lack phonemic awareness as early as possible may save them from years of frustration in reading.

Teaching and Nurturing Phonemic Awareness through Text Play and Writing

For most students, phonemic awareness is nurtured more than it is taught. Children learn language sounds as they talk, sing, and play at home. Informed teachers can nurture phonemic awareness in enjoyable, playful, and engaging ways at school, as well. Perhaps one of the most useful is simply to use rhymes, chants, and songs that feature play with language sounds. Children can read and reread nursery rhymes, jump rope chants, poetry, and songs. For example, playing with nursery rhyme lines such as the following will help children grasp the concept of the sound of *d*.

Dickery dickery dare, the pig flew up in the air . . .
Hey diddle diddle, the cat and the fiddle . . .
Diddle diddle dumpling, my son John . . .

And the tongue-twisting rhyme "Peter Piper picked a peck of pickled peppers . . ." will help children develop an awareness of *p*.

Jump rope chants, poems, and song lyrics can serve the same purpose as nursery rhymes. Griffith and Olson (1992) recommend that teachers read rhyming texts and other texts that play with sounds to students daily and help develop students' sensitivity to sounds. (See Figure 6.2 for a list of texts for developing phonemic awareness.) Moreover, these texts can be altered to feature different language sounds (Yopp 1992). For example, the familiar refrain of "Ee-igh, ee-igh, oh" in "Old MacDonald Had a Farm" can become "Dee-igh, dee-igh, doh" to emphasize *d*.

Older students can accomplish the same tasks with more sophisticated texts. Poems, tongue twisters, popular song lyrics, and raps can be learned, altered, rewritten, and ultimately performed to emphasize language sounds.

Figure 6.2   Texts for Developing Phonemic Awareness

Adams, P. (2007). *There was an old lady.* Auburn, ME: Child's Play International.

Anastasio, D. (1999). *Pass the peas, please.* Los Angeles: Lowell House.

Anderson, P. F. (1995). *The Mother Goose pages.* Dreamhouse Nursery Bookcase. http://www-personal.umich.edu/~pfa/dreamhouse/nursery/sources.html

Baer, G. (1994). *Thump, thump, rat-a-tat-tat.* New York: Harper and Row.

Barrett, J. (2001). *Which witch is which?* New York: Atheneum.

Bayor, J. (1984). *A: My name is Alice.* New York: Dial.

Benjamin, A. (1987). *Rat-a-tat, pitter pat.* New York: Cromwell.

Berger, S. (2001). *Honk! Toot! Beep!* New York: Scholastic.

Brown, M. W. (1996). *Four fur feet.* Mt. Pleasant, SC: Dell.

Buller, J. (1990). *I love you, good night.* New York: Simon and Schuster.

Butterworth, N. (1990). *Nick Butterworth's book of nursery rhymes.* New York: Viking.

Bynum, J. (2002). *Altoona Baboona.* Orlando: Harcourt.

Cameron, P. (1961). *"I can't," said the ant.* New York: Coward-McCann.

Figure 6.2 *(Continued)*

89

Teaching Phonemic
Awareness

Capucilli, A. (2001). *Mrs. McTats and her houseful of cats.* New York: Simon and Schuster.

Carter, D. (1990). *More bugs in boxes.* New York: Simon and Schuster.

Cole, J. (1993). *Six sick sheep.* New York: HarperCollins.

DePaola, T. (1985). *Tomie DePaola's Mother Goose.* New York: Putnam.

Dodd, L. (2000). *A dragon in a wagon.* Milwaukee, WI: Gareth Stevens.

Eagle, K. (2002). *Rub a dub dub.* Watertown, MA: Charlesbridge.

Ehlert, L. (2001). *Top cat.* Orlando: Harcourt.

Eichenberg, F. (1988). *Ape in a cape.* San Diego, CA: Harcourt.

Enderle, J. (2001). *Six creepy sheep.* Honesdale, PA: Boyds Mill.

Galdone, P. (1968). *Henny penny.* New York: Scholastic.

Gordon, J. (1991). *Six sleepy sheep.* New York: Puffin.

Hawkins, C. and Hawkins, J. (1986). *Top the dog.* New York: Putnam.

Hennessey, B. G. (1990). *Jake baked the cake.* New York: Viking.

Hoberman, M. (2004). *The eensy-weensy spider.* New York: Little, Brown.

Hymes, L. and Hymes, J. (1964). *Oodles of noodles.* New York: Young Scott Books.

Kellogg, S. (1985). *Chicken Little.* New York: Mulberry Books.

Krauss, R. (1985). *I can fly.* New York: Golden Press.

Kuskin, K. (1990). *Roar and more.* New York: Harper Trophy.

Langstaff, J. (1985). *Frog went a-courting.* New York: Scholastic.

Lansky, B. (1993). *The new adventures of Mother Goose.* Deerhaven, MN: Meadowbrook.

Lee, D. (1983). *Jelly belly.* Toronto, ON: Macmillan.

Leedy, L. (1989). *Pingo the plaid panda.* New York: Holiday House.

Lewis, K. (1999). *Chugga-chugga choo-choo.* New York: Hyperion.

Lewison, W. (1992). *Buzz said the bee.* New York: Scholastic.

Low, J. (1986). *Mice twice.* New York: Simon and Schuster.

Martin, B., Jr. and Archambault, J. (1989). *Chicka chicka boom boom.* New York: Simon and Schuster.

(Continued)

Figure 6.2 *(Continued)*

Marzollo, J. (1989). *The teddy bear book.* New York: Dial.

Marzollo, J. (1990). *Pretend you're a cat.* New York: Dial.

O'Connor, J. (1986). *The teeny tiny woman.* New York: Random House.

Obligado, L. (1983). *Faint frogs feeling feverish and other terrifically tantalizing tongue twisters.* New York: Viking.

Ochs, C. P. (1991). *Moose on the loose.* Minneapolis, MN: Carolrhoda Books.

Patz, N. (1983). *Moses supposes his toeses are roses.* San Diego, CA: Harcourt Brace Jovanovich.

Pearson, M. (1999). *Pickles in my soup.* New York: Children's Press.

Perez-Mercado, M. M. (2000). *Splat!* New York: Children's Press.

Pomerantz, C. (1974). *The piggy in the puddle.* New York: Macmillan.

Pomerantz, C. (1987). *How many trucks can a tow truck tow?* New York: Random House.

Prelutsky, J. (1986). *Read-aloud rhymes for the very young.* New York: Knopf.

Provenson, A. and Provenson, M. (1977). *Old Mother Hubbard.* New York: Random House.

Purviance, S. and O'Shell, M. (1988). *Alphabet Annie announces an all-American album.* Boston: Houghton Mifflin.

Raffi. (1988). *Down by the bay.* New York: Crown.

Salisbury, K. (1997). *My nose is a rose.* Cleveland, OH: Learning Horizons.

Salisbury, K. (1997). *There's a bug in my mug.* Cleveland, OH: Learning Horizons.

Scarry, R. (1970). *Richard Scarry's best Mother Goose ever.* New York: Western.

Schwartz, A. (1972). *Busy buzzing bumblebees and other tongue twisters.* New York: HarperCollins.

Sendak, M. (1962). *Chicken soup with rice.* New York: HarperCollins.

Figure 6.2 *(Continued)*

91

Teaching Phonemic
Awareness

Serfozo, M. K. (1988). *Who said red?* New York: Macmillan.

Seuss, Dr. (1957). *The cat in the hat.* New York: Random House.

Seuss, Dr. (1960). *Green eggs and ham.* New York: Random House.

Seuss, Dr. (1965). *Fox in socks.* New York: Random House.

Seuss, Dr. (1965). *Hop on pop.* New York: Random House.

Seuss, Dr. (1972). *Marvin K. Mooney, will you please go now!* New York: Random House.

Seuss, Dr. (1974). *There's a wocket in my pocket.* New York: Random House.

Shaw, N. (1986). *Sheep on a ship.* Boston: Houghton Mifflin.

Shaw, N. (2006). *Sheep in a jeep.* Boston: Houghton Mifflin.

Showers, P. (1991). *The listening walk.* New York: Harper Trophy.

Slepian, J. and Seidler, A. (1988). *The hungry thing.* New York: Scholastic.

Trapani, I. (2006). *Shoo fly.* Watertown, MA: Charlesbridge.

Wadsworth, O. A. (1985). *Over in the meadow.* New York: Penguin.

Winthrop, E. (1986). *Shoes.* New York: Harper Trophy.

Yektai, N. (1987). *Bears in pairs.* New York: Macmillan.

Zemach, M. (1976). *Hush, little baby.* New York: E. P. Dutton.

For other texts for developing phonemic awareness see Griffith and Olson (1992), Ericson and Juliebo (1998), and Yopp (1995a).

Hinky Pinkies are a playful way to develop sound awareness. Hinky Pinkies are simply riddles with answers that are two or more rhyming words. To make one, begin with the rhyming word pair answer and then think of a riddle that describes it. For example, *duck's truck* could be the answer to the riddle *What vehicle does a quacker drive?* Students love making and figuring out Hinky Pinkies. The Hinky Pinky idea can also focus on two or more words with the same initial sounds (alliterations). A wet pup, then, is a *soggy doggy* when the answer rhymes, but becomes a *drenched dog* when the game is changed to alliterations.

To succeed in these activities, students must attend to the sounds of language. Playing with language in this way develops sensitivity to sounds. In addition to songs and poems, many books feature sounds. Although the texts listed in Figure 6.2 are most appropriate for younger children, older students needing help in phonemic awareness could learn to read the books to younger buddies, thus developing their own and their younger partners' phonemic awareness. Students can also write their own versions of the books simply by changing the emphasized sounds.

**Research-Based
Strategies**

Writing in which students use their knowledge of sound-symbol correspondence, also known as invented or phonemic spelling, is a powerful way to develop both phonemic awareness and basic phonics knowledge (Clay 1985; Griffith and Klesius 1990; Morris 1998). When students attempt to write words using their knowledge of language sounds and corresponding letters, they segment, order, and blend sounds to make real words. Even if the words are not spelled conventionally, this type of writing provides students with unequaled practice in employing their understanding of sounds.

Invented spelling is not an end state in learning to write. Just as children move from babbling and incorrect pronunciation to full and correct pronunciation when learning to talk, children move rapidly from invented spelling to conventional spelling. By the late primary grades there is little if any difference in spelling errors of children taught to spell in a highly rigid and disciplined system and other children who are encouraged to invent spelling. In fact, one study showed that first-grade children encouraged to invent spellings were more fluent writers and better word recognizers than children who experienced a traditional spelling curriculum (Clarke 1988). Considering all the sound-symbol thinking that occurs when children invent their spelling, such results are to be expected.

**Research-Based
Strategies**

Teaching and Nurturing Phonemic Awareness through More Focused Activities

For those 20 percent of children who have not yet developed sufficient phonemic awareness skills to benefit from phonics instruction, more specific instruction is needed. Yopp (1992) and the National Reading

Panel (2000) have identified these conceptual levels of activity to develop phonemic awareness:

- Sound matching
- Sound isolation
- Sound blending
- Sound substitution
- Sound segmentation

These levels provide a conceptual framework for planning and designing instruction that treats phonemic awareness comprehensively, in an easy-to-more-complex order that eventually leads to learning phonics.

Most of the activities can be presented as simple games for children to play with their teacher and with one another. They can be effective for English language learners (ELLs) who are developing phonemic awareness in English, especially if teachers offer the time and support that children need. As Daniel Meier (2004) says, "In learning aspects of phonology in a new language, children experience all over again the journey of developing an ear for the particular rhymes and intonation of words in a language, a process that takes time, discovery, and practice" (p. 23). Understanding common phonological differences between the child's first language and English is also essential. For example, Spanish vowels, unlike their English counterparts, have single sounds (Helman 2005). Moreover, saying English sounds in isolation (e.g., *duh*, *ah*, *guh*) misrepresents the same sounds used in a word (e.g., *dog*), which may lead to additional confusion for ELL students (Meier 2004). So basic knowledge of language differences along with patience and support can assist teachers in helping ELL children develop phonemic awareness.

**English Language
Learners**

Sound Matching

Sound matching simply requires students to match a word or words to a particular sound. When a teacher asks students to think of words that begin with *p*, students are challenged to find words that match that sound. Having students think of the way they form their mouths to articulate individual sounds may help them form a more lasting concept of the sound. Sound matching can be extended to middle vowel sounds, ending sounds, rhyming words, and syllables. Familiar written words can be placed on a word wall (see Chapter 9) according to their beginning, middle, ending, or word family sounds.

Another sound-matching activity involves presenting students with three words, two of which have the same beginning sound—for example, *bat*, *back*, *rack*. Students must determine which two words have the same initial sound. This activity can also be played with middle and ending sounds, rhyming words, and words with differing numbers of syllables.

Sound Isolation

Sound isolation activities require students to determine the beginning, middle, or ending sounds in words. For example, the teacher may provide three words that begin with the same sound, *pig*, *pot*, *pet*, and ask students to tell the beginning sound (Yopp 1992). The same procedure can be done for middle and ending sounds, as well as for word families or rimes. After students develop proficiency in determining initial sounds from similar words, they can isolate sounds from different words. For example, the teacher may ask, "What is the beginning [middle, ending] sound you hear in these words: *bake*, *swim*, *dog*, *pin*, *that*?"

Sound Blending

In sound-blending activities, students synthesize sounds in order to make a word—this is required when decoding words using phonics. Using a game-like or sing-song format, the teacher simply presents students with individual sounds and asks them to blend the sounds together to form a word. The teacher might, for example, say to the class, "I am thinking of a kind of bird and here are the sounds in its name: *d*, *u*, *k*" (Yopp 1992). Of course, the children should say *duck*. Teachers can make this task easier by presenting three pictures of birds and asking students to pick the one that represents the sounds. Students can eventually create their own questions and present their own sounds and riddles to classmates.

Sound Substitution

Sound substitution requires students to subtract, add, and substitute sounds from existing words. A question such as "What word do you get when you take the *w* off *win*?" requires students to segment sounds from words and then re-blend using the remaining sounds. Similarly, sounds can be added to existing words to make up new words: "Add *b* to the beginning of *us* and what do you get?"

After adding and subtracting sounds from given words, students can try substituting sounds. Ask students to think what the names of their classmates might be if all their names began with a particular sound (Yopp 1992). If *t* were used as the new sound, Billy's name would become Tilly, and Mary and Gary would have the same name—Tary. Substituting middle and ending sounds is also possible.

Sound Segmentation

Sound segmentation requires students to determine all the constituent sounds in a word. This may begin with simply segmenting words into onsets (the sounds that precede the vowel in a syllable) and rimes (the vowel and consonants beyond the vowel in a syllable; another name for word family). So *stack* would be segmented into *st* and *ak*. Later, students can segment words into their individual sounds. This time *stack* would be segmented into *s, t, a, k*. Be sure to begin with short, two-sound words at first (e.g., *us, in, at*).

The generic activities we describe here can easily be transformed into a variety of games, performances, and playful activities. Teachers should try to make these activities engaging and enjoyable for students. We've found that several short game-like sessions throughout the day keep children's interest better than longer, more involved sessions. The activities can be shared with parents, even parents of preschoolers, so that they too may participate in their children's development of phonemic awareness.

Turtle Talk

As children are developing phonemic awareness, they may find that individual language sounds are not readily apparent. They cannot see, touch, feel, or smell them. Although language sounds can be heard, our normal speech is generally fast—so fast that children may have difficulty identifying individual sounds in normal speech.

One way to help children hear language sounds more distinctly is to slow down our speech. This is what happens in the game called Turtle Talk (Nicholson 2006). During a 10-minute Turtle Talk session the teacher explains that turtles are slow creatures. They move slowly and if they could speak they would likely speak slowly as well. Then the teacher demonstrates how a turtle might talk—for example, she says the word *c-a-t* in a slow, drawn-out fashion, asking students to look at how she uses her mouth to make the words. She asks students if they are able to determine the word that she is saying. Then she asks students to say the word in the same way, paying attention to how they have to move their mouths to go from one sound to another. This routine continues through several words—*m-ou-se*, *sh-ou-t*, *c-l-a-p*, and so on. These quick lessons (games) done on a regular basis will help students become aware that words are made up of individual sounds (sound isolation and segmenting) and that those sounds need to be blended (sound blending) together to make words.

A Routine that Adds Meaning

**Research-Based
Strategies**

By the time children are in first grade, nearly all have developed sufficient phonemic awareness to benefit from phonics and decoding instruction. Those who continue to struggle, however, need additional instruction. With such students in mind, Smith, Walker, and Yellin (2004) have developed and tested an instructional routine that combines attention to whole, meaningful texts and phonemic awareness. The routine has six key steps:

1. Hold a shared reading of a predictable rhyming book (such as one listed in Figure 6.2).

2. Highlight rhyming words from the book. Write a few on a chart, and provide children with small cards containing the words.

3. Select several rime patterns or word families that appear in the rhyming words, and draw children's attention to these. Provide small cards containing the rimes/word families, and ask children to spread these cards (and the rhyming words) out on their tables.

4. Reread the predictable book, drawing children's attention to the rhymes and rimes. Ask them to hold their cards up when they hear words or word families.

5. Ask students to create new rhymes and rimes that fit the pattern from the book. Write their contributions on the board or chart paper.

6. Reread this newly generated book in small groups.

Smith (2002) tested this strategy with 76 struggling second-graders and found that it led to significant improvement on a standardized reading achievement test. Smith and colleagues (2004) concluded that results "support the importance of providing students with specific word-recognition strategies in the context of authentic reading and writing experiences" (p. 305).

Add a Degree of Concreteness

Sounds are abstract. Not only are sounds invisible, they can't be held or made to stay. One way to make sound tasks more concrete is to use physical objects to represent the sounds, such as Elkonin boxes (Griffith and Olson 1992). An Elkonin box is simply a series of boxes drawn on a sheet of paper, one for each phoneme in a given word. As students listen to words and hear discrete sounds, they push markers into the boxes, one for each sound. Later, as children become more familiar with written letters, they can write individual letters or letter combinations that represent individual sounds in the words (see Figures 6.3 and 6.4).

Other ways to make children's learning concrete are also possible. For example, our friend Denise has a "morning stretch" each day. She stretches a large rubber band while inviting children to elongate common words, a process she says helps children learn to segment. Children can also write words or letters in shaving cream or sand, use individual whiteboards, or arrange magnetic letters on cookie sheets. Children find these activities interesting and enjoyable.

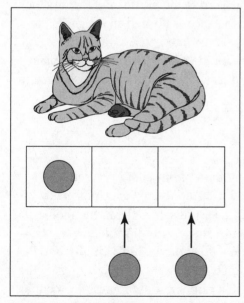

Figure 6.3 Example of Boxes Used for Hearing Sounds in Words

Figure 6.4 Example of Boxes Used for Hearing Sounds and Writing Letters

Sorting Sounds

When students sort or categorize items, they become actively involved in sophisticated analysis of what is to be learned. Indeed, scientists frequently sort or classify to make sense of their area of study. Sorting combines student constructivist learning with teacher-directed instruction (Bear, Invernizzi, Templeton, and Johnston 2012). Word and concept sorting offer opportunities for active student engagement, manipulation, control of the learning task, repeated practice of the learning content, and verbal explanation and reflection of the learning experience in order to deepen what has been learned (Templeton and Bear 2011). Needless to say we are big fans of sorting for students. Sorting can be used to help students develop phonemic awareness through picture sorts.

In a picture sort the teacher provides students with a preselected collection of simple pictures (online clip art is a great source of pictures; *Words Their Way* [Bear et al. 2012] provides another excellent collection). The pictures provide a concrete link to sounds embedded in the words depicted. Then, the teacher asks the students to sort the pictures by a particular category (e.g., words that begin with the *t* sound, words that end with the *s* sound, words that contain the *at* rhyme). As students sort the pictures, they are asked to say the word in the picture and identify the target sound. The teacher provides assistance as needed and engages the students in a discussion on sounds that are represented in the pictures and how the pictures might best be sorted. Students are then asked to explain their sort. As students become more adept at sorting, they can also create and explain their own categories.

In Conclusion

Literacy development involves more than phonics and phonemic awareness. Every day, children need to listen to the best children's literature available, to explore word meanings, to write in their journals, and to work with language-experience stories. Predictable books, big books, poems, and stories should be read chorally, individually, and repeatedly in a supportive environment.

Nevertheless, research tells us that phonemic awareness is essential for phonics and reading success. Children benefit from phonics when they understand and can manipulate speech sounds. Teachers of young children and of older students who struggle in phonics and word recognition should develop curricula that are varied, stimulating, and authentic for teaching and developing students' phonemic awareness.

References

Adams, M. J. (1990). *Beginning to read: Thinking and learning about print.* Cambridge, MA: MIT Press.

Allington, R. L. (1977). If they don't read much, how they ever gonna get good? *Journal of Reading, 21,* 57–61.

Allington, R. L. (1984). Content coverage and contextual reading in reading groups. *Journal of Reading Behavior, 26,* 85–96.

Allington, R. L. (1994). The schools we have. The schools we need. *The Reading Teacher, 48,* 14–29.

Ball, E. and Blachman, B. A. (1991). Does phoneme awareness training in kindergarten make a difference in early word recognition and developmental spelling? *Reading Research Quarterly, 26,* 49–66.

Bear, D. R., Invernizzi, M., Templeton, S., and Johnston, F. (2012). *Words their way: Word study for phonics, vocabulary, and spelling instruction* (5th ed.). Boston: Pearson.

Bradley, L. and Bryant, P. (1983). Categorizing sounds and learning to read: A causal connection. *Nature, 271,* 746–747.

Bradley, L. and Bryant, P. (1985). *Rhyme and reason in reading and spelling.* Ann Arbor: University of Michigan Press.

Catts, H. W. (1991). Facilitating phonological awareness: Role of speech-language pathologists. *Language, Speech, and Hearing Services in Schools, 22,* 196–203.

Clay, M. M. (1985). *The early detection of reading difficulties* (3rd ed.). Portsmouth, NH: Heinemann.

Clarke, L. K. (1988). Invented versus traditional spelling in first graders' writings: Effects on learning to spell and read. *Research in the Teaching of English, 22,* 281–309.

Ericson, L. and Juliebo, M. F. (1998). *The phonological awareness handbook for kindergarten and primary teachers.* Newark, DE: International Reading Association.

Fielding-Barnsley, R. (1997). Explicit instruction in decoding benefits children high in phonemic awareness and alphabet knowledge. *Scientific Studies in Reading, 1,* 85–98.

Griffith, P. and Klesius, J. P. (1990, November). *The effect of phonemic awareness ability and reading instructional approach on first grade children's acquisition of spelling and decoding skills.* Paper presented at the annual meeting of the National Reading Conference, Miami, FL.

Griffith, P. and Olson, M. (1992). Phonemic awareness helps beginning readers break the code. *The Reading Teacher, 45,* 516–523.

Helman, L. (2005). Using literacy assessment results to improve teaching for English-language learners. *The Reading Teacher, 58,* 668–677.

International Reading Association. (1998). Phonemic awareness and the Teaching of Reading: A position statement from the Board of Directors of the International Reading Association. Retrieved from http://www.reading.org/Libraries/Position_Statements_and_Resolutions/ps1025_phonemic.sflb.ashx

Lundberg, I., Frost, J., and Peterson, O. (1988). Effects of an extensive program for stimulating phonological awareness in preschool children. *Reading Research Quarterly, 23,* 263–285.

Maclean, M., Bryant, P., and Bradley, L. (1987). Rhymes, nursery rhymes, and reading in early childhood. *Merrill-Palmer Quarterly, 33,* 255–281.

Meier, D. (2004). *The young child's memory for words.* New York: Teachers College Press.

Morris, D. (1998, December). *Preventing reading failure in the primary grades.* Paper presented at the annual meeting of the National Reading Conference, Austin, TX.

National Reading Panel. (2000). *Teaching children to read: An evidence-based assessment of the scientific research literature on reading and its implications for reading instruction. Reports of the subgroups.* Washington, DC: National Institutes of Health.

Nicholson, T. (2006). How to avoid reading failure: Teaching phonemic awareness. In A. McKeough, L. Phillips, V. Timmons, and J. Lupart (Eds.), *Understanding literacy development* (pp. 31-48). Mahwah, NJ: Lawrence Erlbaum.

Perfetti, C., Beck, I., Bell, I., and Hughes, C. (1987). Phonemic knowledge and learning to read are reciprocal: A longitudinal study of first grade children. *Merrill-Palmer Quarterly, 33,* 283–319.

Smith, M. (2002). *The effects of rhyme-rime connection training on second grade reading performance.* (Unpublished doctoral dissertation). Oklahoma State University, Norman.

Smith, M., Walker, B., and Yellin, D. (2004). From phonological awareness to fluency in each lesson. *The Reading Teacher, 58,* 302–307.

Snow, C. E., Burns, M. S., and Griffin, P. (Eds.). (1998). *Preventing reading difficulties in young children.* Washington, DC: National Academy Press.

Stanovich, K. E. (1986). Matthew effects in reading: Some consequences of individual differences in the acquisition of literacy. *Reading Research Quarterly, 21,* 360–407.

Stanovich, K. E. (1994). Romance and reason. *The Reading Teacher, 49,* 280–291.

Templeton, S. and Bear, D. (2011). Teaching phonemic awareness, spelling, and word recognition. In T. Rasinski (Ed.), *Rebuilding the foundation: Effective reading instruction for the 21st century.* Bloomington, IN: Solution Tree.

Yopp, H. K. (1992). Developing phonemic awareness in young children. *The Reading Teacher, 45,* 696–703.

Yopp, H. K. (1995a). Read-aloud books for developing phonemic awareness: An annotated bibliography. *The Reading Teacher, 48,* 538–542.

Yopp, H. K. (1995b). A test for assessing phonemic awareness in young children. *The Reading Teacher, 49,* 20–29.

7

Onsets, Rimes, and Basic Phonic Patterns

"I use word families because I know they work," says Ellen, a first-grade teacher. Looking into Ellen's classroom about halfway through the school year, you would see print everywhere—students' stories, dictated texts, and lots and lots of word family charts. "We try to work with one or two word families a week. After each is introduced, we write down all the words we know that belong to it." Ellen points to one chart.

> Look at the *-an* chart. At first we brainstormed words like *Dan, man, tan, ran,* and *can.* But later we added longer words that students thought of at home, either with their parents' help, or through their own reading—we added words like *Annie, Anthony, candle, panda,* and *Santa.* What students learn about word families can help them figure out longer words as well as the short one-syllable words. They are intrigued by the word families and use them all the time in their decoding and spelling.

> Phonics is a "way of teaching reading and spelling that stresses symbol-sound relationships" (Harris and Hodges 1995, p. 186). Essentially, this definition suggests teaching children about the consistent relationship between written symbols and sounds. Traditionally this has meant teaching children how individual sounds or blends of consonant sounds are represented by their corresponding letters—for example, that the short *a* sound is represented by the letter *a* as in *bat,* that the long *e* sound is sometimes represented by the letter combination *ee,* that the blended consonant sound is represented by the letters *bl,* or that the *k* sound is sometimes represented by the letter combination *ck.* This approach to phonics has helped many young readers develop a strategy for decoding words.

However, research by Theodore Clymer (1963/1996) casts doubt on the effectiveness of teaching children letter associations or rules for individual sounds. Clymer and his associates gathered phonics generalizations that were taught in various reading programs of the time. Then they found those words, taught in the elementary grades, that contained letters related to the generalizations, and examined the extent to which the letter (or letter combination) actually yielded the appropriate sound, or fit the rule. In other words, the researchers asked, "Would applying this rule help a reader decode this word?" Clymer found that a significant number of the generalizations did not consistently result in the appropriate word. As a result, he questioned the wisdom of actually teaching some of these generalizations. For example, one of the most renowned of all phonics generalizations states that "when two vowels go walking, the first one does the talking and usually says its name"; when a word has two adjacent vowels, the long sound of the first vowel is heard and the sound of the second is not heard. After close examination of words that might fit this rule, Clymer found that over half did not yield the intended sound! (For example, the generalization does not apply to many common words such as *canoe, guest, height, said,* and *steak.*) A large number of other generalizations also were suspect according to Clymer's research. Clymer also found that some rules, although highly reliable, applied to so few words that learning the rule hardly seemed worth the effort.

Does this mean that phonics should be thrown out of the school curriculum? Clearly not. Clymer's (1963/1996) work suggests that phonics generalizations, especially those that are applied after the initial consonant(s) in words or syllables, may be troublesome. Moreover, the notion of going from sound to symbol may also be questionable. Readers begin with the written word and then think about sound representation. Perhaps this is also the appropriate direction for phonics teaching—to begin with written symbols and then move to sounds.

Beginning Letter-Sound (Onsets) Relationships

What written symbols should we teach? Let's start with letters that begin words and syllables, since they are regular, for the most part. To be more precise, the written consonants that precede the vowel in syllables (remember that every syllable has only one vowel sound, unless a diphthong is present) are fairly consistent in the sounds they represent. When a *t* begins a word or syllable and is followed immediately by the vowel, that *t* almost universally produces the *t* sound. The same is true of the consonant blend *bl* and the digraph *sh*. Readers can be confident that those letters represent those sounds.

Thus, one area of great consistency for phonics instruction is the consonants, consonant blends, and consonant digraphs that precede the vowel in words and syllables. These are *onsets,* and their dependability means they can be taught to beginning readers with confidence. Readers can use them. Moreover, initial word onsets tend to be much more useful in recognizing words. As readers our eyes are drawn to the beginnings of words.

For the most part then, traditional phonics instruction for onsets works well. Usually, beginning consonants are taught by associating them with concepts, pictures, or objects that begin with those letters and the sounds normally associated with the letters. For example:

b: bat, ball, barn
d: dog, duck
g: girl, gold
sp: spot, spin

In this approach students learn the sound-symbol relationship by associating the visual form of the letter with the beginning sound of appropriate words. Students may read texts in which most of the words begin with a targeted letter and sound.

Other similar approaches exist. In the Letter People program, for example, students are taught initial sound-symbol correspondence through cartoon-like characters that have bodily features (e.g., Munching Mouth) that correspond with the visual form of the letter, which is displayed on the body of the character. As with most traditional approaches, students engage in a variety of worksheet-like activities to solidify their knowledge of these beginning letter-sound relationships.

A similar yet novel approach to beginning letter-sound phonics, called Action Phonics (Cunningham 1987), teaches the beginning letter-sound associations (and letter combination–sound associations) through physical actions or movements that begin with the targeted sound. For example, the letter *b* might be associated with *bending.*

Teaching beginning letter-sound relationships using Action Phonics requires students to position and move their bodies, which tends to reinforce students' memories of the letters and sounds. Students connect the written letter with the physical position and action they engage in and subsequently with the associated sound. The physical movement acts like a conceptual glue that holds the sound and the symbol together until both the letter(s) and corresponding sound(s) are thoroughly learned.

Each week begins with a review of all the previously learned consonants, actions, and sounds; then one or more new initial consonants are introduced with their accompanying movements and sounds. In one review activity, each child is assigned a consonant and displays its action to the rest of the students in the class, who guess the letter and sound. In another variation, students are gathered in a circle, with one child or the teacher acting as the leader. The leader has all the letters printed on individual cards. The leader shows one letter card to the group, and the entire group displays the accompanying action and says the sound associated with the consonant. The activity moves from one action to another as the leader moves from one letter card to another. This activity is a great way to integrate physical education into phonics and can easily be employed by the physical education teacher to reinforce students' phonics learning.

Teachers who use Action Phonics often find students making the action at their seats when they try to read or spell words on their own. One teacher said, "They are always in motion anyway. They cannot sit quietly and listen. They just naturally move some part of their bodies. Now they all move together purposefully" (Cunningham 1987, p. 249). Action Phonics is a great way to continue teaching phonics and reading, even at those times when students' bodies are ready to get out of their seats and move about. Three key letters and sounds to teach early on—*st* (*stop*), *s* (*sit*), and *q* (*quiet*)—offer a natural ending to the activity.

Moving on to Patterns (Rimes) beyond Initial Letters

After beginning letters are introduced, students need to explore how to construct and decode the remainder of words. Traditionally this has meant introducing short vowel sounds and words containing them, followed by long vowel sounds and the letters that represent them;

however, Clymer's (1963/1996) analysis found generalizations about vowels problematic. Vowels can represent many sounds in English.

Some experts suggest that vowel sounds be taught, not independently, but in the context of the consonants that follow them in syllables (Adams 1990; Gaskins et al. 1996/1997; Goswami 1997, 1998). The combination of a vowel and the consonants that follow it in a syllable is called a rime, phonogram, or word family. *Rimes* are a productive approach to phonics for several reasons. First, rimes consist of several letters, allowing a reader to analyze a word several letters at a time, rather than analyzing letters individually. Rimes make word decoding more efficient because they allow for the use of letter combinations. Second, rimes have a high degree of consistency. When the rime *ack* appears in a word, it nearly always makes *ak*; and when *it* appears at the end of a syllable, it almost invariably makes *it*. Third, rimes are ubiquitous—they are in all words. One common rime such as *at* is present in thousands of English words. In addition, by their very nature, words containing the same rime do in fact rhyme. Thus, it is not difficult to find or compose poems that feature targeted rimes for children, providing superb practice in learning those rimes. Moreover, students can write and celebrate their own rhyming poetry as they begin to understand the connection between the written rimes and their corresponding sounds.

Linguists call rimes and onsets the psychological units of the English language (Moustafa and Maldonado-Colon 1999). Children easily notice them. Children are more able to divide spoken English words into onsets and rimes than into individual phonemes, even before they are able to read (Goswami and Bryant 1990; Trieman 1985). Marilyn Adams (1990) writes this about the use of onsets and rimes as a core element in phonics instruction:

> The onset and rime are relatively easy to remember and to splice back together. Yet another advantage of exploiting phonograms in decoding instruction is that they provide a means of introducing and exercising many primer words with relative efficiency and this, as we have seen, is in marked contrast to the slowness with which words can be developed through individual letter-sound correspondences. Again, this advantage has long been recognized in many instructional programs. (p. 321)

Indeed, research has shown that instruction in rimes (learning sets of words that contain a targeted rime) is effective for beginning and struggling readers (Goswami 2000).

As soon as students have some beginning letter-sound relationships established, teachers can begin concurrently teaching longer letter-sound patterns. This is where rimes come in.

By definition, each syllable contains one rime. There are many rimes worth teaching. Fry (1998) found that 353 different rimes can each generate at least two fairly common one-syllable words. Given that so many rimes exist in English, which ones should be taught first to young students? One approach is to teach those rimes that are most productive in terms of word generation. Fry has identified 38 rimes that make 654 one-syllable words by simply tacking on different onsets to each rime. We combined Fry's rimes with other common rimes identified by Wylie and Durrell (1970), and added a few of our own to develop a list of 75 essential rimes (see Figure 7.1). Students can use these rimes to decode (and spell) over 1,000 one-syllable words simply by adding an initial consonant, blend, or digraph. That's pretty phenomenal. Furthermore, those 75 rimes can be used to decode several thousand longer, multisyllabic words. Teaching approximately two rimes per week, the entire set of rimes can be taught in kindergarten and first grade.

Beyond this initial set, which rimes should be taught at different grade levels? Although instructional materials may provide a rime-teaching sequence, we prefer that teachers themselves establish their own rime curriculum. Here's how it might work:

- Teachers get together in grade-level groups—K through grade 3 or 4.

- Using a set of rimes (see Appendix A), each grade-level group identifies 50 to 100 rimes that are appropriate to teach at its grade level.

- Lists are analyzed and cross-checked across grade levels to ensure that all rimes are taught at one grade level and reinforced at others.

- Each grade level now has its own list of rimes that it is responsible for introducing and is aware of previously taught rimes that need to be revisited.

Now that we have a set of rimes to teach, the question becomes: How do we teach them to our students? In many classrooms, teachers and students brainstorm words that contain targeted rimes. These words and their rimes are listed on a sheet of chart paper and put on display for students to read and use at their convenience.

Figure 7.1 Rasinski-Padak Essential Primary Rimes

ab	cab, crab	eck	deck, check	ir	sir, stir
ace	race, trace	ed	bed, sled	it	pit, knit
ack	back, track	eed	deed, speed	ob	cob, knob
ad	had, clad	eep	peep, sleep	ock	lock, clock
ag	bag, flag	eer	deer, cheer	oil	soil, spoil
ail	pail, trail	ell	bell, smell	oke	joke, smoke
ain	main, stain	en	ten, when	ole	pole, stole
ake	bake, shake	er	her, term	ool	wool, spool
ale	pale, stale	ess	less, dress	op	hop, stop
all	ball, stall	est	nest, crest	or	for, storm
am	jam, slam	ew	dew, flew	ore	core, store
ame	came, blame	ice	nice, slice	ot	hot, spot
an	can, plan	ick	lick, stick	out	pout, shout
ank	bank, blank	id	hid, slid	ow	low, slow
ap	cap, trap	ide	wide, slide	ow	cow, plow
ar	car, star	ig	wig, swig	ub	rub, club
are	care, stare	ight	light, fright	uck	luck, truck
ash	mash, crash	ile	file, smile	ude	rude, crude
ast	past, blast	ill	hill, spill	ug	tug, shrug
at	bat, flat	im	him, trim	um	hum, drum
ate	date, crate	ime	time, chime	ump	pump, stump
aw	jaw, straw	in	win, chin	unk	bunk, chunk
ay	day, stay	ine	fine, spine	y	my, try
eap	leap, cheap	ing	ring, sting		
ear	hear, clear	ink	pink, stink		
eat	meat, cheat	ip	lip, ship		

Source: Based on Fry (1998) and Wylie and Durrell (1970).

Although this is a good start, it does not go far or deep enough in encouraging students to learn rimes. Word recognition requires deep learning of word patterns. This means seeing the patterns in isolation, in words and in texts, and reading plenty of words and text that contain those patterns. What follows is a week-long sequence of activities for teaching two or more rimes per week:

Day 1

1. Introduce one or two rimes—for example, *ack* and *ick*. Print the rimes on a display board and say the sounds they represent several times. Ask students to do the same.

2. Brainstorm and list on chart paper words that contain the *ack* and *ick* rimes. Words should be mostly one-syllable words, though a few multi-syllabic words can be included.

3. Read the words with students several times. Have groups and individual students read the words. Encourage students to read the words on their own throughout the day and into the next. Chant the list of words chorally several times each day. Eventually add the words to the class word wall (see Chapter 9).

4. Challenge students with a Hinky Pinky, written on the board or chart paper, that uses some of the words just brainstormed. A Hinky Pinky is a riddle for which the answer is two or more rhyming words (see Chapter 6).

5. Introduce two or three poems featuring the targeted rime, written by the teacher or another poet, and displayed for all to see on chart paper. Slowly at first, read each poem to students several times, pointing to the words as you read and asking students to join in as they feel comfortable. After a few readings the entire group should be reading the poem chorally. Divide the students into smaller groups and continue to read the poems in parts. Ask a few individual students to read each poem aloud. Ask all students to read the poems throughout the next several days. These authentic reading activities promote reading fluency and sight word acquisition as well as focus children's attention on the targeted rime. The shared experience of reading the poems chorally and repeatedly (Gill 2006) offers children the invitation to join in whenever they feel comfortable and competent—perhaps with the first reading, or after the third reading once a high degree of familiarity with the text has been developed.

   Ellen, the first-grade teacher we introduced to you at the beginning of this chapter, wrote these poems featuring *ack* and *ick*. Some are parodies of common rhymes that are already familiar to many children.

My Duck Jack

Diddle diddle quacking
My duck Jack.
Has a bill that is orange
and wings that are black.
Loves to yack with a
quack quack quack.
Diddle diddle quacking
My duck Jack.

When a Thousand Ducks Quack

When a thousand ducks go quack
And a set of ear plugs I lack
I find my trusty old jacket
Place it over my head.
It softens the racket.
That I truly do dread.

A Duck Named Mack

—I know a duck
His name is Mack
—Makes quite a racket with
his quack quack quack
—He yacks at us all
all manners does he lack
—That's my Mack
the duck who quacks!

Hickory Dickory Click

Hickory dickory click
The chickens are feeling sick
The clock struck nine
Now they're feeling fine
Hickory dickory click.

Hickory Dickory Dare

Dickery dickery dare
The chicken flew up in the air
She looks pretty slick
When she flies so quick
Chickery chickery chair.

Poems can be found in many collections (see Figure 7.2). A second source for poems is the teacher. If you, the teacher, cannot find poems that contain *ack,* surely you can write a couple of four- to six-line poems, as Ellen did, that present students with real texts featuring the targeted rime. Not only does this provide students with a rich source of reading material for practicing their knowledge of rimes, but it shows students that their teacher is also a writer.

Figure 7.2 Poetry Collections and Songbooks for Celebrating Poetry and Lyrics and for Teaching Word Patterns

Bagert, B. (1992). *Let me be the boss: Poems for kids to perform.* Honesdale, PA: Boyds Mills.

Bagert, B. and Rasinski, T. (2010). *Poems for building reading skills.* Huntington Beach, CA: Shell Educational Publishing.

Carle, E. (1992). *Eric Carle's animals animals.* New York: Philomel.

de Paola, T. (1988). *Tomie de Paola's book of poems.* New York: Putnam.

de Regniers, B. S., et al. (1988). *Sing a song of popcorn: Every child's book of poems.* New York: Scholastic.

Harrison, D. L. (2007). *Bugs.* Honesdale, PA: Front Street Press.

Hopkins, L. B. (1993). *Extra innings: Baseball poems.* New York: Harcourt, Brace.

Hopkins, L. B. (1995). *Been to yesterdays: Poems of a life.* Honesdale, PA: Boyds Mills.

Hopkins, L. B. (Ed.). (1995). *Small talk: A book of short poems.* New York: Harcourt, Brace.

Hudson, W. (Ed.). (1993). *Pass it on: African-American poetry for children.* New York: Scholastic.

Hudson, W. and Hudson, C. (Eds.). (1995). *How sweet the sound: African-American songs for children.* New York: Scholastic.

Krull, K. (1992). *Gonna sing my head off: American folk songs for children.* New York: Knopf.

Figure 7.2 (*Continued*)

111

Onsets, Rimes, and Basic Phonic Patterns

Lansky, B. (Ed.). (1991). *Kids pick the funniest poems*. Hopkins, MN: Meadowbrook.

Lansky, B. (1996). *Poetry party*. Hopkins, MN: Meadowbrook.

Larrick, N. (Ed.). (1990). *Mice are nice*. New York: Philomel.

Lobel, A. (1983). *The book of pigericks*. New York: Harper and Row.

Moss, J. (1989). *The butterfly jar*. New York: Bantam.

Moss, J. (1991). *The other side of the door*. New York: Bantam.

Nesbitt, K. (2005). *When the teacher isn't looking*. Hopkins, MN: Meadowbrook.

Nesbitt, K. (2007). *Revenge of the lunch ladies*. Hopkins, MN: Meadowbrook.

Opie, I. and Opie, P. (Eds.). (1992). *I saw Esau: The schoolchild's pocket book*. Cambridge, MA: Candlewick.

Pottle, R. (2007). *I'm allergic to school*. Hopkins, MN: Meadowbrook.

Prelutsky, J. (Ed.). (1983). *The Random House book of poetry for children*. New York: Random House.

Prelutsky, J. (1984). *The new kid on the block*. New York: Random House.

Prelutsky, J. (1990). *Something big has been here*. New York: Greenwillow.

Rasinski, T. and Brothers, K. (2006). *Poems for word study* (K–1, 1–2, 2–3). Huntington Beach, CA: Shell Educational Publishing.

Rasinski, T. and Zimmerman, B. (2001). *Phonics poetry: Teaching word families*. Boston: Allyn and Bacon.

Silverstein, S. (1974). *Where the sidewalk ends*. New York: Harper and Row.

Silverstein, S. (1981). *A light in the attic*. New York: Harper and Row.

Slier, D. (Ed.). (1990). *Make a joyful sound: Poems for children by African-American poets*. New York: Checkerboard Press.

Once the poems have been read, reread, and read again, students find individual words and word parts in the poems. This can mean pointing to, underlining, and circling significant words and word parts on a second copy of each poem (the initial copy is kept clean for future use). At this point you want to draw students' attention to individual words in the poem, particularly those words that contain the targeted rimes. One of our colleagues, Belinda, a first-grade teacher, uses fly swatters as *word whoppers*. She cuts rectangular holes of various sizes out of several fly swatters (see Figure 7.3). She "whops" one of the words from the poem and asks students to identify it. The word whopper isolates the word so that it must be read on its own, without

When a Thousand Ducks Quack

When a thousand ducks go quack
And a set of ear plugs I lack
I find my trusty old jacket.
Placed over my head,
It softens that awful racket.

When the Ducks Return

The ducks are back,
They quack and quack.
What a noisy noise they make.
They return every year
And fill my ears
With quacking that makes me quake!

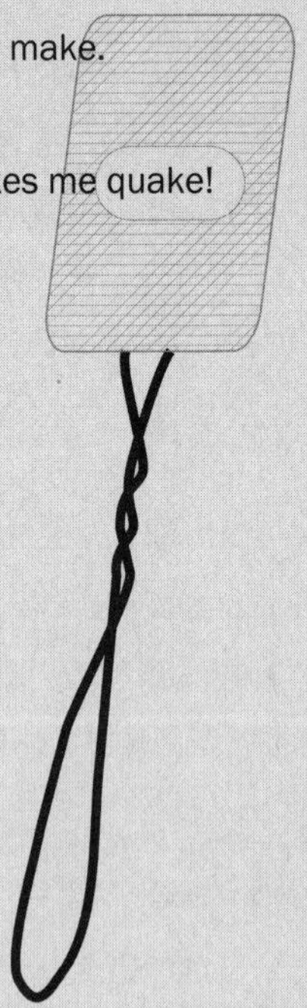

Figure 7.3 Word Whopper

the aid of the general context of the poem. Later, Belinda gives each child a word whopper and asks individuals to whop words and word parts from the poem that she pronounces.

6. The lesson ends with these two assignments:

   a. Students are given a sheet of words containing the rimes brainstormed earlier. They practice reading and spelling the rimes at home. The sheet also contains the poems practiced during the day so that students can practice reading the poems at home with the assistance of a family member.

   b. Students are asked to write their own short rhymes that feature the targeted rime. Students can write their two- to six-line poems on their own or with a family member, a classmate, or a buddy from another grade.

This focus on poetry also allows teachers and students to celebrate a wonderful genre that is often neglected and underused in the language arts curriculum (Benton 1992; Cullinan, Scala, and Schroder 1995; Denman 1988; Lockward 1994; Perfect 1999, 2005; Rogers 1985). Even the simple poems that teachers and children may write say something very important to students—"poetry is valued and celebrated in our classroom. We are poets!"

Day 2

1. Day 2 begins with students copying their poems on chart paper. These are then hung around the room for later use.

2. Next, students read the words and poems from the previous day.

3. Finally, the lesson turns into a poetry festival as students go around the room reading and celebrating each new poem written by a classmate. Stopping at each posted poem, the author first reads the poem to his or her classmates, pointing out key words. Then, the group reads the poem several times, chorally, antiphonally, and finally in pairs and as individuals. Not only does this activity promote practice of key rimes in real contexts, it also gives children another reason to celebrate language and themselves as authors.

   If a classroom aide is available, the poems can quickly be typed, printed, and copied for each student to read several times at home. Eventually, students may make their own individual or classroom poetry anthologies. Imagine children's feelings of accomplishment as they see their own poetry "published" in classroom books.

Day 3

Day 3 is a repeat of Day 1 with other contrasting rimes. If the rimes *ack* and *ick* were targeted in the first part of the week, the rimes for the second half of the week should either include the short *a* sound (*at, ap*) or *ck* ending (*eck, ock*). Before beginning the new lesson, students may want to reread some of the poems and words from Days 1 and 2.

Day 4

The Day 4 lesson is a repeat of the Day 2 lesson with students practicing and making poems using the targeted rime.

Day 5

Day 5 provides students a chance to review the rimes of the week as well as the opportunity to analyze the differences between the rimes when they occur in the same context.

1. The teacher provides students with a short list of words that contain all rimes that were studied during the week. Students can read the words, spell them, sort them into various categories, or any combination of these activities. This activity requires students to discriminate the sounds and spelling of the week's rimes in determining the correct word, spelling, or category.

2. Students read a couple poems or other texts that contain the rimes studied during the week. Again, this provides students with opportunities to examine the rimes within a common context. If it is difficult to locate such poems or other texts, the teacher may write her or his own poem or take a dictated text from students that contains the appropriate rimes.

3. The teacher leads the students in playing one or more word games (see Chapter 14). This provides an additional and enjoyable context for students to study and play with the words and rimes they have studied during the week.

4. Students take copies of the poems and texts home. They practice the texts over the weekend for a possible poetry party performance on Monday.

This sort of lesson routine provides students with the deep analysis and massed practice that allows them to learn the targeted rimes; however, word recognition instruction on these rimes need not be limited to this routine. Children's books provide the impetus for one activity that first- and second-grade teacher Jeannine uses with her students (Rajewski 1994). During a study of ants, Jeannine introduces her students to the book *Antics!* by Cathi Hepworth (1992), an ABC book in which every word contains the rime *ant* and the accompanying illustration features an ant. For example, the *b* word is *brilliant* and the illustration depicts an Einstein-like ant working in a laboratory. After examining the book, students search for other words that have *ant* within them.

Students can emulate Hepworth's book by writing their own alphabet books with other rimes. This is possible because rimes generate an enormous number of words. A rime or phonogram ABC book can become an exciting class project as students are assigned one or two letters and asked to think first of several words that contain the targeted rimes and then of how those words might be illustrated. Students then compile their work into a whole-class ABC book. Students will want to read and reread their phonogram-ABC books for days. Here is the beginning of a rime ABC book using the *ack* phonogram:

a attack
  The army will attack at dawn.

b back, black
  The black ants are back.

c crack, clack
  Clickety clack, the coin fell down the crack.

d diamondback
  A diamondback snake is poisonous.

f firecracker
  Firecrackers scare my dog.

The website www.onelook.com is an excellent tool for finding words that contain a particular phonogram or set of letters. Simply enter the phonogram preceded and followed by an asterisk (for example, *ack*). Then hit enter and an alphabetical list of targeted words containing the phonogram will appear. Figure 7.4 provides additional online resources for teaching word families.

Technology

Figure 7.4 Electronic Sources for Poetry

Word Family Resources

http://www.kidzone.ws/phonics/activity1.htm Provides an introduction to word families and word family instruction. It has several related links.

http://www.readwritethink.org/classroom-resources/student-interactives/word-family-sort-30052.html The International Reading Association and National Council of Teachers of English provide some excellent word family lessons and practice.

http://www.mrsjonesroom.com/teachers/wordfamilies.html Contains several great teacher resources related to phonics and fluency, including word family activities and rhyming poetry.

http://curry.virginia.edu/go/wil/rimes_and_rhymes.htm#This_Week Contains thirty rhymes (one per week) and accompanying lessons that support rime and phonics instruction.

http://www.enchantedlearning.com/rhymes/wordfamilies/ Provides many word family examples along with a wealth of activities that can support teaching word families. It also includes poems and rhymes organized by word families.

Teachers can encourage students to use the targeted words in their talk and writing. Words can be added to each student's word bank (see Chapter 11); students can sort the word bank words by rime or other structural or semantic feature. Students can play games such as Word War, Concentration, or Go Fish with the word bank cards. Teachers can introduce other Hinky Pinkies that feature targeted rimes (e.g., What's another name for John's book bag? Jack's pack). Cloze passages, in which students use the context of a passage along with the rime knowledge to determine unknown words, can be developed and used (see Chapter 12). Words featuring the targeted rimes can become spelling words for the given week. Other word games such as Hangman and Wordo (see Chapter 14) can also be played.

Why Poetry?

Throughout this chapter and, indeed, throughout this book, you will see that we have a strong preference for the use of poetry. We feel that several features of poetry make it an optimal genre for teaching phonemic awareness, phonics, and fluency (Rasinski, Rupley, and Nichols 2008).

Poems for children are often characterized by a defined rhythm and rhyme. The rhythmical language, along with the regularly occurring rhymes, makes them easy to learn to read. Moreover, the brevity of most poems for children means that they can learn to read the entire text in a relatively short period of time (usually in a day). We want children to feel success in learning to read. One way to feel success is to learn to read something well every day. In our reading clinic for struggling readers our goal is for each one of our students to learn to read a text well every day—so that the students (and their parents) can feel that they are achieving success in learning to read.

The rhymes embedded in most poems also makes them real decodable texts for working on phonics. When students read "Rain, rain, go away, come again another day . . ." they are practicing reading the *ay* rime in an authentic text that celebrates language as much as it provides phonics practice for students.

The rhythmical language patterns and rhymes in poems make them fairly easy to emulate. Students (and teachers) can model their own personal poems after the language patterns found in the poems that they have read. Students in our reading clinic regularly write (and perform) poetry that they themselves have written. We collect students' poetry and publish it in a book of poetry that is given to each student at the end of the clinic. The feeling of success and self-efficacy that students have when they see that they have contributed to a book of poetry is hard to duplicate. A few years ago we had students write their own versions of "*Yankee Doodle*":

> Yankee Doodle went to town
> Flying in an airplane.
> There he went to see his friends,
> Jack, Jill, John, and Jane.

> Yankee Doodle went to town
> Riding on a hairless pig.
> He felt sorry for that sow,
> So he bought her a new wig.

> Yankee Doodle went to town
> Hopping on bunny
> All the folks laughed at him
> Because he looked so funny.

In Conclusion

Onsets and rimes are certainly not the only elements of an effective phonics and word recognition program; however, given their efficiency in teaching multiple-letter patterns (rimes and some onsets) as well as their generalizability and consistency, they offer students a wonderful entree into the world of phonics, word recognition, and spelling. We see the systematic and joyful study of onsets and rimes as the foundation to any phonics (and spelling) program. Onsets and rimes can be used in ways that allow students to be creative and constructive in their own learning. They can be used to decode one-syllable words in their entirety, and they are very useful in helping readers at least partially figure out longer, more difficult words.

References

Adams, M. J. (1990). *Beginning to read*. Cambridge, MA: MIT Press.

Benton, M. (1992). Poetry, response and education. In P. Hunt (Ed.), *Literature for children: Contemporary criticism* (pp. 127–134). London: Routledge.

Clymer, T. (1996). The utility of phonic generalizations in the primary grades. *The Reading Teacher, 50*, 182–187. (Reprinted from *The Reading Teacher*, 1963, 16, 252–258.)

Cullinan, B., Scala, M. C., and Schroder, V. C. (1995). *Three voices: An invitation to poetry across the curriculum*. York, ME: Stenhouse.

Cunningham, P. M. (1987). Action phonics. *The Reading Teacher, 41*, 247–249.

Denman, G. A. (1988). *When you've made it your own . . . : Teaching poetry to young people*. Portsmouth, NH: Heinemann.

Fry, E. (1998). The most common phonograms. *The Reading Teacher, 51*, 620–622.

Gaskins, I. W., Ehri, L. C., Creso, C., O'Hara, C., and Donnelly, K. (1996/1997). Procedures for word learning: Making discoveries about words. *The Reading Teacher, 50*, 312–327.

Gill, S. R. (2006). Teaching rimes with shared reading. *The Reading Teacher, 60*, 192–193.

Goswami, U. (1997). Rime-based coding in early reading development in English: Orthographic analogies and rime neighborhoods. In C. Holme and R. M. Joshi (Eds.), *Reading and spelling: Development and disorders* (pp. 69–86). Mahwah, NJ: Erlbaum.

Goswami, U. (1998). The role of analogies in the development of word recognition. In J. L. Metsala and L. C. Ehri (Eds.), *Word recognition in beginning literacy* (pp. 41–63). Mahwah, NJ: Erlbaum.

Goswami, U. (2000). Phonological and lexical processes. In M. L. Kamil, P. B. Mosenthal, R. Barr, and P. D. Pearson (Eds.), *Handbook of reading research* (Vol. 3, pp. 251–267). Mahwah, NJ: Erlbaum.

Goswami, U. and Bryant, P. (1990). *Phonological skills and learning to read.* Hillsdale, NJ: Erlbaum.

Harris, T. and Hodges, R. (Eds.). (1995). *The literacy dictionary.* Newark, DE: International Reading Association.

Lockward, D. (1994). Poets on teaching poetry. *English Journal, 83,* 65–70.

Moustafa, M. and Maldonado-Colon, E. (1999). Whole-to-part phonics instruction: Building on what children know to help them know more. *The Reading Teacher, 52,* 448–458.

Perfect, K. A. (1999). Rhyme and reason: Poetry for the heart and head. *The Reading Teacher, 52,* 728–737.

Perfect, K. A. (2005). *Poetry lessons.* New York: Scholastic.

Rajewski, J. P. (1994). Anticipating antipasto in Antarctica? *The Reading Teacher, 47,* 678–679.

Rasinski, T., Rupley, W., and Nichols, W. (2008). Two essential ingredients: Phonics and fluency getting to know each other. *The Reading Teacher, 62,* 257–260.

Rogers, W. C. (1985). Teaching poetic thought. *The Reading Teacher, 39,* 296–300.

Trieman, R. (1985). Onsets and rimes as units of spoken syllables: Evidence from children. *Journal of Experimental Psychology, 77,* 417–427.

Wylie, R. E. and Durrell, D. D. (1970). Teaching vowels through phonograms. *Elementary English, 47,* 787–791.

Children's Literature Cited

Hepworth, C. (1992). *Antics!* New York: Putnam and Grosset.

8

Teaching Advanced Word Patterns

Justin teaches fourth grade, and he still considers himself a phonics teacher.

> Sure, I teach phonics, but it's not the *b buh, t tuh* phonics that people
> think of when they hear the word *phonics*. I think that phonics means
> helping students see the connection between letters and groups of
> letters and the sounds that they represent. That is just what I do with
> my students, except the groups of letters we work with are the root
> words and prefixes that come from Latin and Greek. I introduce one
> or two roots or prefixes a week and we spend about 10 minutes each
> day exploring the meaning, pronunciation, and real words that contain
> those roots. I ask students to look for the roots we have studied in their
> reading, and I challenge them to use the roots in their school talk. This
> is the first year I've tried this with my students, but I can really see that
> it's turning some kids on to words and how words get their meaning.
> I get a lot more predictions about word meanings when we come across
> unknown words in reading, especially in the different content areas.

Onsets and rimes provide teachers with a powerful tool for helping
students discover how words work. With knowledge of common onsets
and the 75 Essential Primary Rimes (Figure 7.1), students are able to
decode literally thousands of single- and multisyllabic words. However,
as Justin has found, other patterns in words have the added feature of
containing meaning, which can help a reader not only to decode a word
but also provide essential information about its meaning. These types
of patterns (affixes and derivational patterns) are generally taught after
students have studied onsets and rimes.

A *root* is a word part that carries meaning. One type of meaning-bearing word pattern is *affixes,* patterned word parts that are attached to existing words to alter their basic meaning. Prefixes and suffixes are both affixes. The second category of meaningful word patterns or roots is called *derivational patterns*. These are word parts derived from other languages, notably Greek and Latin, that have found their way into many English words, particularly the academic words that students encounter in math and science. Derivational word patterns are important for understanding and decoding unfamiliar words and often appear in new words in English (e.g., *microchip*) as well. Although the study of Latin is often thought of as something taught in the secondary grades, a growing body of research is demonstrating that Latin- and Greek-based roots can be taught successfully in the primary (Biemiller 2005; Mountain 2005; Porter-Collier 2010) and intermediate (Baumann et al. 2002; Carlisle 2000; Kieffer and Lesaux 2007) grades.

Teaching affixes and derivational patterns provides students with several benefits: expanded strategies for decoding unknown words, expanded vocabularies, and strategies for determining the meanings of unknown words. Given this enormous potential, we believe that a good word recognition program should provide direct, systematic, and ongoing instruction in their recognition and use.

Teaching Affixes

Fairly comprehensive lists of prefixes and suffixes are provided in Appendices C and D. Although teaching each affix is unnecessary, the lists provide the raw material for exploring affixes with students.

Teaching affixes can begin in the first grade with suffixes that denote number (*-s* ending) and tense (*-ed* ending). As students begin to develop basic word recognition skills, teachers can introduce other prefixes and suffixes. As a rule of thumb, teaching approximately 50 affixes per year in grades 2 through 8 would cover the entire lists in Appendices C and D. As with rimes, we recommend that teachers in these grades confer with one another to determine which grade levels should take primary responsibility for teaching particular affixes.

Frequently used affixes should be introduced and then revisited throughout the elementary grades. According to Carroll, Davies, and

Richman (1971) the following seven prefix groups represent 66 percent of all words that contain prefixes:

un-

re-

in-, im-, il-, ir- (not)

dis-

en-, em-

non-

in-, im- (in or into)

With suffixes, the frequency analysis yields an even more critical set that should be taught. The following seven suffix groups represent 82 percent of all words containing suffixes:

-s, -es

-ed

-ing

-ly

-er, -or (agent as in presenter or actor)

-ion, -tion, -ation, -ition

-able, -ible

Because no single method has proven more successful than others in teaching affixes, we suggest an eclectic approach focusing on one or two affixes per week. Introduce students to the affix, discuss its meaning, and brainstorm words that contain it. List these on a word wall and encourage students to use the words in their speaking and writing and to be on the lookout for other words to add to the list. Selected words from the brainstormed list can be added to the class's spelling list. Revisit the targeted affixes and words briefly throughout the next several days.

Many of the activities discussed in later chapters can be employed to teach affixes: Making Words and Making and Writing Words (Chapter 10), word banks and word sort activities (Chapter 11), cloze activities using texts that focus on targeted affixes and words (Chapter 12), and word games (Chapter 14). For the most part, affixes are learned through wide reading, in-depth examination, and frequent use. These activities should provide sufficient opportunities for examination and learning.

Teaching Derivational Patterns

Knowledge of derivational patterns, those roots derived from Greek, Latin, and other languages, will help students decode words and discover their meanings. For example, knowing that the root *hem-* or *hemo-* means "blood" helps us with some of the pronunciation and meaning of longer words like *hemodialysis, hemoglobin, hemorrhage, hemostat, hemophilia,* and *hematoma.* An extensive list of Greek and Latin derivatives or roots can be found in Appendix E. (You may also want to check out some of the websites listed in Appendix F for ideas to turn your students on to words and word study.)

Derivational patterns are best taught after students have developed some facility with basic word recognition strategies and affixes. Third or fourth grade is a good time to begin study of derivational patterns, though teachers at any grade level can take advantage of teachable moments to introduce and explore individual patterns.

The same sort of instructional strategies and activities that we suggested for teaching affixes can be used for derivational patterns. Introducing students to one or two roots and their derivations per week should be sufficient to whet students' appetites for learning and exploring derivational patterns. Begin each week by introducing a new root and listing on the class word wall and in the students' word journals the English words that are derived from the root. Then encourage the students to use the words in their speech and writing throughout the week. Additional activities such as word sorts, Making and Writing Words with Letter Patterns, cloze activities, and word games should help solidify students' recognition and understanding of these important word parts.

An alternative or complementary approach to teaching derivational patterns is to begin not with the word part or root itself, but with actual words that are derived from the Latin or Greek root. Our list of essential words and derivations is provided in the appendix at the end of this chapter, and a list of resources for teaching derivations can be found in Figure 8.1. Used as the basis for word of the week, it would take over two years for students to cover all the targeted words. The words on this list contain one or more derivational patterns that can be used to learn the pronunciation and meaning of many other words. The targeted word is really only the starting point for study. Students are exposed to and learn the meaning of other words that contain the derivational root. Word study expands to a wide variety of longer, more difficult, multi-syllabic words.

Figure 8.1   Valuable Resources for Teaching Word Roots

Ehrlich, I. (1988). *Instant vocabulary*. New York: Pocket Books.
 The book highlights 259 derivational patterns, mostly from
 Greek and Latin, used in English. Each pattern is identified with
 its meaning. A list of words and definitions that contain the
 targeted derivational pattern is also provided.

Fry, E. B. and Kress, J. E. (2006). *The reading teacher's book of lists:
Grades K–12* (5th ed.). San Francisco: Jossey-Bass.
 This book of lists is a treasure trove for reading teachers. Among
 other resources, it contains lists of homophones, homographs,
 instant (high-frequency, sight) words, spelling demons, word
 idioms, metaphors, prefixes, suffixes, and Latin and Greek roots.

Lundquist, J. (1989). *English from the roots up: Help for reading,
writing, spelling, and SAT scores*. Bellevue, WA: Literacy Unlimited.
 Individual Greek and Latin roots are presented in lesson-like
 formats. Words derived from each root are presented as well as
 teaching notes for telling the story behind each root.

Rasinski, T., Padak, N., Newton, R., and Newton, E. (2008). *Greek and
Latin roots: Key to building vocabulary*. Huntington Beach, CA: Shell
Educational Publishing.
 An introduction to the study of roots in the elementary, middle,
 and secondary grades. The book provides instructional ideas for
 exploring roots.

Rasinski, T., Padak, N., Newton, R., and Newton, E. (2008). *Building
vocabulary from word roots* (Levels 1–11). Huntington Beach, CA:
Teacher Created Materials.
 This is a comprehensive instructional program for teaching
 vocabulary through word roots from grades 1 through 11.

Model Lessons

In the following sections we offer three instructional strategies
for affixes and derivational patterns that have been successfully
implemented in elementary and middle grade classrooms (Rasinski,
Padak, Newton, and Newton 2008; Rasinski, Padak, Newton, and
Newton 2011).

Divide and Conquer

Divide and Conquer is an instructional approach for helping students
recognize the structure, sound, and meaning of affixes and derivational
patterns. It is an excellent activity for introducing students to particular
roots and then guiding them in studying the essential meaning of the
roots. Here is an example of a Divide and Conquer lesson.

Start with a list of approximately ten words that have the same
prefix (e.g., for the prefix *dis—distract, disinterested, disapprove, disorder,
disrespect, disregard, disown, disloyal, disarm, dishonest*). Read the words
orally with students. Have students choose one or two words from the
list, identify the two basic units of each word, and speculate about what
each means. As students offer explanations, elaborate on their responses
to focus on the critical meaning of the prefix. Help students understand
that the meaning of the full word is obtained through the relationship of
the base word with the prefix.

On a display board or chart, as well as on individual student sheets,
have students list each complete word, divide each into component
parts (prefix and root), and then provide a personal definition for each
word. An example is provided below:

Disinterested	*dis + interested*	to not be interested
Dishonest	*dis + honest*	a person who is not honest, such as a criminal

Word Spokes and Word Charts

Word Spokes is a visual approach for reinforcing a root introduced in
Divide and Conquer. The activity requires a visual display made up
of a center circle with spokes coming from the center, much like the
center and spokes of a wagon wheel. We recommend that you have a
classroom version of the display and that individual students have their
own, say in their personal word journals.

Begin the lesson by reviewing the root that is the topic for the week,
focusing on its essential meaning. Remind students, for example, that
dis- used as a prefix means "not" or "the opposite of." Then, working
alone, in small groups, or as a whole class have students brainstorm
words that contain the *dis-* prefix and list them at the ends of the spokes
on the word spoke chart or paper. In addition to words used in the

Divide and Conquer lesson encourage students to think (or search) for other words, such as *displease* or *disprove*. Once the Word Spokes chart is developed, guide students in a discussion of the meanings of the words and using them in sentences.

We think of the classroom Word Spokes chart as a specialized word wall. Throughout the week make frequent references to the words on the chart and encourage students to add new words they may come across to the Word Spokes chart. Be sure to have students use the words in their own written and oral language.

You can also create simple word charts organized around a particular root. At the top of the chart print the target root. Beneath it, have students brainstorm and list all words that are associated with the target root. For example, on Earth Day you might want to do a word chart about *geo-* (earth or land), with students brainstorming words such as *geothermal*, *geometry*, *geology*, and *geography*. Then throughout the week, you can make specific references to the root and the associated words. Again, encourage your students to do the same in their oral and written language.

Be Creative with Word Study

Behind all this instruction and activity is the idea that students need to learn these important word patterns, but also to develop an intense fascination with words—to become wordsmiths. Unquestionably, one of the greatest wordsmiths of all time was William Shakespeare. Richard Lederer (1998) reported that Shakespeare invented over 8 percent of all the unique words he used in his writings. Words such as *lackluster*, *bedroom*, *frugal*, *dishearten*, *birthplace*, *premeditated*, *submerge*, and *skim milk* have their first known attribution to one of Shakespeare's works. That's pretty remarkable.

If word invention is good enough for Shakespeare, it certainly should be good enough for our students. Help students notice that Shakespeare invented many of his words by combining already known words or roots (e.g., *countless*). Once students gain understanding and control of a fair number of affixes and derivational patterns, they can join the teacher in inventing new words to describe particular phenomena. For example, in one fifth-grade class we recently visited, students who had been studying affixes and derivational patterns came up with the following words and riddles:

What sort of animal might experience *photophobia*?   A mole

In what countries might a person find *paleologs*?   Ancient Egypt,
Greece, Rome

Why might dogs be called *brevorous*?   They eat quickly

What is an *autophile*?   A person who loves himself or herself

What is a *matermand*?   A mother's order

Students enjoy engaging in such creative use of words, especially if it
gives them the opportunity to stump their teacher and classmates.

Another creative use of words is found in poetry writing. Myra
Cohen Livingston (1997) devised a simple poetry game to encourage
her students to think creatively and playfully with words when writing
poetry. Provide students with a set of unrelated words, one to begin
with and then up to six or more. Challenge students to write a poem
that uses all the chosen words. Although some students may find this
challenging initially, with time and practice students can become quite
adept at using words in creative and divergent ways to create a coherent
poem. Livingston published her students' remarkable poetry using this
game technique in *I Am Writing a Poem about . . . A Game of Poetry*.

In Conclusion

Word study need not end after students develop mastery of basic phonic
skills and strategies; rather, we can nurture a fascination with words,
along with a deeper understanding of how words work, by continuing
to explore words throughout students' years in school. Affixes and
derivational word patterns provide wonderful opportunities to continue
our study of words beyond initial phonics.

As Justin, the fourth-grade teacher we introduced in the beginning
of this chapter, discovered for himself, affixes and Greek and Latin
derivations are very useful in helping students decode (pronounce)
and understand particular words. As students move beyond the initial
stages of word recognition, word study should turn toward these
more sophisticated word patterns. Knowledge of word patterns helps
students pronounce and predict the meanings of unknown words
containing the patterns.

The same activities and playful attitude that characterize early
word study should also manifest themselves in learning about these

more sophisticated patterns. If we approach word study with a sense of playfulness and fascination, it is likely that students will be fascinated by words throughout their lives.

Appendix: Essential Words and Derivations for Upper Elementary and Middle Grades

These words (and derivations) are worth teaching at the elementary and middle school levels. Knowledge of the words and their meaningful word parts can be generalized to a large number of words and concepts that students will encounter in various content areas.

The words appear alphabetically. We recommend that the words be presented approximately one per week and that teachers across content areas demonstrate the words to students and discuss the words daily.

	Definition/ Comment	Derivative & Related Words	Derivative & Related Words
1. Acrophobia	Fear of heights.	acro = high *acropolis* *acrobat* *acronym*	phobia = fear *agoraphobia* *hydrophobia*
2. Ambidextrous	Able to use both hands.	ambi = both, all, around *ambiguous* *ambivalence* *ambient*	dexter = skilled *dexterity*
3. Amphitheater	A theater in an oval form with an open center and seats all around and higher.	amphi = both, all, around *amphibian* *amphibious*	thea = to see, to view *theater* *theatrics*
4. Anarchy	Lack of government, law, or supreme power.	an = no *anesthetic* *anonymous* *anomaly* *anorexia*	archos = ruler, chief person *archbishop* *archenemy*

5. Antebellum	Before the war (usually meant to be before the Civil War).	ante = before *antecedent* *anteroom* *antemortem*	belli, bellum = war *bellicose* *belligerent*
6. Antithesis	A contrast or opposition of ideas or words.	anti, anto = against, in opposition to, before *antidote* *antonym* *antiseptic* *antipathy* *antisocial*	thesis = an assertion or statement to be considered *synthesis* *thesis*
7. Appendix	Something added that is often not essential.	pend = to hang *append* *appendicitis* *pendant* *depends* *pending*	
8. Asterisk	A little star.	ast = star *astronaut* *asteroid* *aster* *astrology* *astronomy*	
9. Auditorium	Large room in which to listen.	aud = hear *auditory* *audition*	orium = room, building *sanitorium*
10. Automobile	A car.	auto = self *autobiography*	mobile = to move, moveable *mobile home* *mobilize*
11. Bicameral	A legislature with two houses or chambers.	bi = two *bicycle* *bilingual* *biped*	camera = chamber, house *unicameral* *camera*

(Continued)

129

	Definition/ Comment	Derivative & Related Words	Derivative & Related Words
12. Captain	One who is at the head, who has authority.	cap = head *capital* *capitol* *cap* *decapitate*	
13. Cartography	The practice of drawing maps.	cart, chart = paper *cartoon* *carton* *carte blanche* *Magna Carta*	graph = write, chart *photograph* *phonograph* *telegraph*
14. Centipede	One hundred.	cent = 100 *century* *percent* *centennial* *centigrade* *centipede* *centurion*	ped = foot *pedal* *pedestrian*
15. Centimeter	One one-hundredth of a meter.	cent = 100 *century* *centurion* *percent*	meter = a unit of or device that measures *thermometer* *barometer* *odometer* *kilometer*
16. Chili con carne	A Mexican food made with red peppers (chili) and chopped meat.	con, cum = with *cum laude* *conspire* *constellation* *contact*	carne = meat *carnivore* *carnage* *carnal* *incarnate*
17. Circumspect	Careful, cautious; one who inspects or examines all sides carefully.	circum = around *circumstantial* *circumnavigate* *circus* *circumvent*	spect = look, view *specter* *spectator* *inspect* *spectacles*
18. Cognition	To come to know, to think.	cognos = to know *recognize* *cognizant*	

130

19. Contemporary	Existing or occurring at the same time.	con = with *conscious* *congruence* *confluence*	temp = time *temporary* *tempo* *temporal*
20. Contract	An oral or written agreement.	con = with *contrite* *contribute* *convene* *convent*	tract = pull or draw *abstract* *retract* *traction*
21. Contradict	To deny; to say or assert not to be so.	contra = against *contrary* *contraband* *contrast* *contraception*	dict = to say, speak *dictionary* *dictate* *dictator* *Dictaphone*
22. Contribute	To give; to assign.	con = with *contrite* *contract* *convene*	tribut = to give, to bestow *tribute* *tributary* *attribute* *retribution*
23. Corpus	The body of a person; the collection of laws or writing of one type.	corp = body *corpse* *corporation* *habeas corpus* *corporal punishment*	
24. Countermand	To revoke an order; to change a command to the opposite or reverse direction.	counter = against *counterintelligence* *counterespionage* *encounter*	mand = order, dictate *command* *mandate* *mandatory* *demand*
25. Demented	Insane; out of one's mind.	de = from, out of *demerit* *demoralize* *deport* *derail*	ment = pertaining to the mind *mental*

(Continued)

	Definition/ Comment	Derivative & Related Words	Derivative & Related Words
26. Democrat	A person who believes in rule by the people.	demo = people *demography*	crat = rule; govern *autocrat* *bureaucrat* *theocracy*
27. Demography	Statistics about groups of people.	demo = people *democracy* *democrat*	graph = to write, to chart *graphite* *graphic* *photograph* *phonograph*
28. Doctrine	A particular principle or belief that is taught.	doc, dogma = that which seems true *dogmatic*	
29. Equilateral	Having all sides equal in length.	equi = equal *equinox* *equilibrium* *equidistant*	lateral = side *unilateral* *bilateral* *quadrilateral*
30. Exhume	Remove a body from its burial place.	ex = from *excommunicate* *exhale*	humus = ground *posthumous* *human*
31. Extraterrestrial	Someone from outside the limits of earth.	extra = beyond, in addition to *extrovert* *extravagant* *extraordinary* *extrapolate*	terra = land *terrace* *terrain* *Mediterranean*
32. Fidelity	Faithfulness, observance of duty.	fides = faith *confide* *confidential* *infidel*	

33. Forecast	To make a prediction.	fore = preceding in time, place, or order; at the front of *foremost* *forerunner* *forearm* *foredeck* *forebode*	cast = to throw, calculate, plan *recast* *downcast* *castaway*
34. Fragment	A part broken off.	frag, frac = break *fracture* *fraction* *fractious*	
35. Fratricide	To kill one's brother or sister.	frater = brother *fraternal twins* *fraternity* *fraternize*	cide = murder *suicide* *homicide* *regicide*
36. Hydrophobia	Fear of water.	hydro = water *hydrant* *dehydrate* *hydraulic* *hydroplane* *hydroponics*	phobia = fear *acrophobia* *anthophobia* *agoraphobia*
37. Hypodermic	Under the skin as in a hypodermic needle.	hypo = under, below *hypoglycemia* *hypochondria* *hypocrite* *hypothesis*	derm = skin *dermatologist* *epidermis*
38. Immortal	Cannot die.	im = not *immobilize* *immature*	mort = death *mortuary* *mortal* *mortician*

(Continued)

	Definition/ Comment	Derivative & Related Words	Derivative & Related Words
39. Innate	Characteristics one is born with.	in = within *inland* *inmost* *inmate*	nat = born *nativity* *nature* *native* *prenatal*
40. Intermission	A temporary pause between two periods of action.	inter = between *intermediate* *interfere* *international* *interrupt* *interval*	mission = a purposeful activity *missionary* *dismiss* *remiss*
41. Intramural	Within the limits of a school, organization, or community.	intra = within *intravenous* *intrastate* *intramolecular*	murus = wall *mural*
42. Journey	A travel. Originally the length traveled in one day on foot (20 miles).	jour = day, daily *soup de jour* *bon jour* *journal* *journalist*	
43. Lackluster	Dull; without brightness or vitality.	lack = without *lackadaisical*	luster = brightness, reflected light *illustrious* *illustrate*
44. Macrocosm	The great world; the universe; the entire complex.	macro = large, great, long *macrostructure* *macron* *macrophage*	cosmos = world or universe or entire complex *cosmopolitan* *cosmology* *cosmography*
45. Mandate	A command or order.	mand = to commit, enjoin, command *command* *mandatory* *remand* *countermand*	

46. Maternal	Referring to mother.	mater = mother *alma mater* *matriarch* *matrimony*	
47. Mediterranean	The sea surrounded by (in the middle of) large land masses.	medi = middle *media* *mediocre* *median* *intermediate* *mediate*	terra = land *terrarium* *extraterrestrial* *terra cotta*
48. Megalopolis	A large city or combination of cities—main city and its suburbs.	mega = large *megabyte* *megaphone* *megaton*	polis = city, land area under one government *metropolis* *acropolis* *Indianapolis* *political*
49. Memorial	Something to preserve the memory of someone or something.	memor = mindful *remember* *memory* *memorize* *memoir* *memorandum*	
50. Microscope	A scientific instrument that allows very small items to be seen.	micro = extremely small *microbe* *microfilm* *microwave* *microorganism*	scope = to see a target *telescope* *endoscope* *periscope*
51. Misanthrope	A hater of mankind (people).	mis = incorrect, hate, wrong *miscalculate* *misdirect* *misfile* *mislead*	anthro = pertaining to people *anthropology* *anthropomorphic* *philanthropy* *anthropocentric*

(Continued)

	Definition/ Comment	Derivative & Related Words	Derivative & Related Words
52. Navigate	To steer; to travel, especially by ship.	navis = ship *navy* *navigator* *naval* *navigable*	
53. Novel	Something new.	nov = new *novelty* *novice* *Novocain* *nouveau riche* *nova* *innovate* *renovate*	
54. Omniscient	Having knowledge of everything (all).	omni = all *omnipotence* *omnivorous* *omnibus*	scient (science) = knowledge *conscience* *reminiscent*
55. Orthodontist	A dentist who specializes in straightening and aligning teeth.	ortho = straight *orthodox* *orthopedic*	dont (dent) = pertaining to teeth *dentist* *periodontist*
56. Paralegal	A clerk with some expertise in the law.	para = besides, in addition *paramedic* *paranormal* *parable* *paraphrase*	leg, legis = dealing with the law *legislature* *legal* *legitimate*
57. Parlor	A room for receiving guests; a room for conversation.	parl- (Fr.) = to talk *parliament*	
58. Paternal	Having to do with fathers.	pater = father *patriarch* *patriot* *paternity*	

59. Pathology	The study of the nature of diseases.	pathos = suffering, illness, sorrow *empathy* *sympathy* *pathogen*	logo = discourse, to reason ogy = study of *sociology* *psychology* *logic*
60. Pedestrian	A person in the act of walking (foot travel).	ped (pod, pied) = pertaining to feet *pedestal* *pedal* *podiatrist* *tripod* *piedmont*	
61. Pentagon	Five-sided geometric shape.	pent = five *pentathlon* *pentagram* *Pentecost*	gon = side *polygon* *octagon*
62. Perimeter	The boundary measurement of a figure having two dimensions.	peri = around, surrounding *periscope* *periphery* *perigee*	meter = to measure *barometer* *odometer* *sphygmometer*
63. Periscope	An instrument that allows one to view around objects that are in the direct line of vision as in a submarine.	peri = round, around *perimeter* *pericardium* *periodontal* *periphery*	scope = to see a target *microscope* *telescope* *endoscope*
64. Philanthropy	Love of humanity shown by practical gifts or kindness.	phil, phile = lover or admirer of *Philadelphia* *philharmonic* *bibliophile* *philosopher*	anthropos = having to do with humankind *anthropology* *anthropomorphic* *misanthropy* *anthrophobic*

(Continued)

137

	Definition/ Comment	Derivative & Related Words	Derivative & Related Words
65. Philosopher	A lover of knowledge or wisdom.	philo = love *philanthropy* *philander* *philharmonic* *Philadelphia*	soph = knowledge or wisdom *sophomore*
66. Plateau	A plain (flat place or plate) on the mountains.	plate, plat, pla = wide and flat *platform* *platter* *platypus* *plaza* *place* *misplace*	
67. Polygraph	A machine that charts several features; i.e., a polygraph (truth detector) measures and charts pulse, respiration, and other body functions.	poly = many *polygon* *polygamous* *polymer* *polysyllabic* *Polynesia* *polytheism*	graph = to write or chart *telegraph* *graphite* *seismograph* *graphic* *cartography* *phonograph*
68. Polytheism	Belief in many gods.	poly = many *polygamy* *polymer* *polygraph* *polyglot* *polynomial*	theo (theism) = pertaining to God or gods *theocracy* *monotheism* *theology*
69. Porter	A person who carries another's luggage, especially on a train.	port = to carry *portage* *transport* *export/import* *report*	
70. Pseudonym	A false name.	pseudo = false *pseudoscience*	nym = name *synonym* *antonym*

71. Psychopath	A mentally ill person.	psych = mind *psychology* *psychic* *psychoanalyst* *psychiatry*	path = suffering illness *pathology* *sociopath*
72. Regal	Pertaining to a king (or queen); ruler.	reg = king *regent* *regalia* *regime* *regicide* *regency*	
73. Regicide	The murder/killing of a king or ruler.	reg = king, ruler *regent* *regulation* *regal* *region* *regime*	cide = to kill *suicide* *homicide* *infanticide*
74. Submarine	A boat that is able to travel under the sea.	sub = under *subway* *subterranean* *submerge*	marin = pertaining to the sea *mariner* *marina*
75. Synchronize	At the same time.	syn = same *synonym*	chron = time *anachronism* *chronological* *chronic*
76. Theology	The study of God.	theo = God *theosophy* *theocracy*	ology = the study of *sociology* *psychology*
77. Thermometer	A device for measuring temperature.	therm = heat *thermodynamics* *thermophile* *thermostat* *thermograph* *thermal*	meter = measure *centimeter*

(Continued)

139

	Definition/ Comment	Derivative & Related Words	Derivative & Related Words
78. Transform	To change in form or appearance.	trans = change, across *transcribe* *transfigure* *transfusion* *transfer* *transition*	form = shape, appearance *formal* *uniform* *reform* *deform* *inform* *formula*
79. Unison	To speak with one voice; decide together.	uni = one *uniform* *unicycle*	son = voice, sound *sonic* *supersonic* *sonar* *sonorous* *song* *sonata*
80. Vacuous	Empty; without contents.	vac = empty *evacuate* *vacuum* *vacant* *vacancy* *vacation*	
81. Vagabond	Wandering from place to place; unsettled; worthless.	vag = wander *vagrant* *vagary* *vague* *extravagant*	
82. Variegated	Varied in appearance.	var = to change *varied* *variable* *variance* *variety* *various*	
83. Voracious	Extreme hunger.	vor = eat *carnivore* *herbivore* *omnivore*	

References

Baumann, J., Carr Edwards, E., Font, G., Tereshinski, C., Kame'enui, E., and Olejnik, S. (2002). Teaching morphemic and contextual analysis to fifth-grade students. *Reading Research Quarterly, 37,* 150–176.

Biemiller, A. (2005). Size and sequence in vocabulary development: Implications of choosing words for primary grade vocabulary. In E. H. Hiebert and M. L. Kamil (Eds.), *Teaching and learning vocabulary: Bringing research to practice* (pp. 223–242). Mahwah, NJ: Erlbaum.

Carlisle, J. (2000). Awareness of the structure and meaning of morphologically complex words: Impact on reading. *Reading and Writing: An Interdisciplinary Journal, 12,* 169–190.

Carroll, J. B., Davies, P., and Richman, B. (1971). *The American heritage word frequency book.* Boston: Houghton Mifflin.

Kieffer, M. and Lesaux, N. (2007). Breaking down words to build meaning: Morphology, vocabulary, and reading comprehension in the urban classroom. *The Reading Teacher, 61,* 134–144.

Lederer, R. (1998). A writer of fire-new words. *Writer's Digest, 78*(4), 7.

Livingston, M. C. (Ed.). (1997). *I am writing a poem about . . . a game of poetry.* New York: McElderry Books.

Mountain, L. (2005). ROOTing out meaning: More morphemic analysis for primary pupils. *The Reading Teacher, 58,* 742–749.

Padak, N., Newton, E., Rasinski, T. V., and Newton, E. (2008). Getting to the root of word study: Teaching Latin and Greek word roots in elementary and middle grades. In A. Farstrup and S. J. Samuels (Eds.), *What research has to say about vocabulary instruction* (pp. 6–31). Newark, DE: International Reading Association.

Porter-Collier, I. M. (2010). *Teaching vocabulary through the roots approach in order to increase comprehension and metacognition* (Unpublished master's degree project). Akron, OH: University of Akron.

Rasinski, T. V., Padak, N., Newton, J., and Newton, E. (2011). The Latin-Greek vocabulary connection: Building elementary students' vocabulary through morphological study. *The Reading Teacher, 65,* 131–139.

Rasinski, T. V., Padak, N., Newton, R., and Newton, E. (2008). *Greek and Latin roots: Key to building vocabulary.* Huntington Beach, CA: Shell Educational Publishing.

9

Word Walls

A classroom that fosters word learning looks the part. Words are everywhere—labels, children's writing, chart stories, and other displays. Sometimes children's attention is purposefully drawn to all this print. Other times, the print is a literate backdrop while children engage in other activities. It's been said that interest in words is caught, not taught. We agree, and we think that the physical environment in the classroom can encourage children to catch an interest in words.

Within these word-laden classrooms, several principles drive word recognition instruction (Rasinski, Padak, and Fawcett 2010). Word recognition instruction is an inherent part of, rather than separate from, meaningful reading and other reading activities. Instruction takes on a playful, problem-solving feel, so children think about words actively and develop a thorough understanding of how words work. Children need lots of opportunities to see words and word parts within the context of meaningful activity, a notion that Sandy McCormick (1994) calls multiple contexts/multiple exposures. The teacher's role is to help children see their options for word recognition and to encourage word recognition practice in real reading situations (National Reading Panel 2000).

Word walls can help to achieve these goals. Moreover, word walls send significant messages to students and classroom visitors: "Words and reading are important in this room," "We celebrate words here!" In this chapter, we describe word walls and offer lots of examples of word wall activities.

What Is a Word Wall?

Think of a word wall as a working bulletin board that focuses on words. That's essentially what it is—and more. A word wall can also be thought of as a billboard or advertisement to students about words. To create a word wall, the teacher first places a large sheet of chart paper or butcher paper on the wall. Either alone or in discussion with students, the teacher decides on the focus of the word wall. From that point on, anything goes. Students may add several words to the word wall each day, and the teacher may add words as well. Students may look for and make connections between and among words. The teacher may ask students to read the words on the word wall for practice or may use the words as a source of quick guessing games: "Find a word on the word wall that _____." And of course, the words are easily visible for other student uses, such as checking on spelling.

Although the teacher and children may write directly on the word wall, we advise making word cards that can be manipulated. Words can be printed on large sticky notes or cut-up pieces of newsprint; masking tape or spray-on adhesive can be used to affix the word cards, which should be large enough for easy viewing.

All students should watch and listen when word wall words are added. The teacher should say the word and comment briefly on it. These comments may connect to the word's meaning, its relevance to the focus of the word wall, or even some aspect of word study, such as "What vowel sound do you hear?" or "How many syllables does this word have?" These quick conversations provide just the sort of multiple exposures essential for successful word learning.

Most word walls are temporary; after a few days or weeks, new word walls replace old ones. You might want to keep the old word walls available to children, however; one teacher noted that her students enjoyed adding new words to old word walls as the school year progressed: "These were actually living word walls, and I, and the kids, used them and loved them and loved watching them grow" (Blachowicz and Obrochta 2007, p. 148). Word walls are meant to be used not just viewed.

Sources of Words

Word wall words can come from any area of the curriculum. One caution, though: don't include too many totally unfamiliar words on a word wall. Learning new words in isolation is very challenging for most children. New words or concepts should first be encountered in the context of reading or discussion. After students have gained some familiarity with new words, they will be able to think about them apart from context. This is the time for word wall activity.

English Language
Learners

Beyond this general guideline, teachers will find many uses for word walls. In reading, for example, a word wall might focus on synonyms, particular word families or roots, or vowel or consonant sounds. Word walls are a good choice for vocabulary development activities as well. Bi- or trilingual word walls can provide names for common objects (or other areas of study) in English and other languages spoken by members of the class. Including pictures of these objects will support all children's learning but is especially important for English language learner (ELL) students (Helman and Burns 2008). In writing, word walls may be used to collect powerful verbs, similes, or metaphors. A math word wall might offer synonyms for *addition* or examples of geometric figures (perhaps accompanied by sketches). Figure 9.1 provides several websites that have lots of additional word wall activities and ideas.

Word walls are adaptable. In essence, teachers may use them in any way that supports students' learning, either about words and word parts or about new concepts. This versatility is one of their instructional strengths. Students quickly become accustomed to what word walls are and how they work, so teachers have a useful routine for addressing lots of curricular goals.

Technology

Figure 9.1   Online Resources for Word Walls

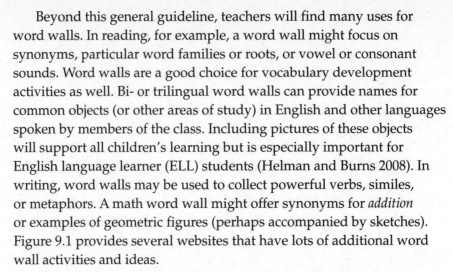

http://www.teachnet.com/lesson/langarts/wordwall062599.html
Information about goals, construction, and possible uses of word walls

http://www.teachingfirst.net/wordwallact.htm
Word wall activities

http://abcteach.com/directory/teaching_extras/word_walls/
Some starter lists of possible word wall words

www.scholastic.com/teachers/article/word-walls-work
An article called "Word Walls That Work"

http://specialed.about.com/od/wordwalls/a/morewordwalls.htm
Lots of quick word wall activities

Using Word Walls

In this section, we offer ways to construct and use word walls. By no means is this an exhaustive list. Our intent is to help you think about possibilities.

Name Walls

Early in the school year, most kindergarten/early primary teachers focus on children's names. The children get to know one another through an immediately meaningful reading activity. Word walls of students' names are a handy instructional tool. Children can read the names each day, with teacher assistance as needed. Names can be sorted into categories such as *boys or girls*, *present or absent*, or *school lunch or brought lunch*. Later in the year, the name wall can be used to introduce alphabetical order or draw children's attention to letters within words. The latter could involve simply counting letters within each person's name, grouping names by numbers of letters, or arranging the entire list from least to most letters (or vice versa). Even quick guessing games, such as "Who has more letters? [Student A or Student B]?" or "How many of us have a B in our names?" provide quick, game-like practice thinking about letters as parts of words. "Who has more letters?" is also a way to teach the mathematical concepts *more* and *less*.

Hall and Cunningham's (1997) "ABC and You" activity is easily adapted to word wall format. First, children's names are listed in alphabetical order; next, each child selects at least one word that begins with the same letter as his or her name. These are added to the alphabetical list:

A . . . Adorable Annie

E . . . Energetic Emily

M . . . Merry Matt

    . . . Mysterious Mike

Children's interest in these name walls sometimes leads to their finding new words to go along with their names. If moveable word cards are used, "Adorable Annie" can easily become "Active, adorable Annie" and so forth. "Hey!" one child said to Mike. "You could add *munching* to yours."

Figure 9.2   Sam's Name Wall

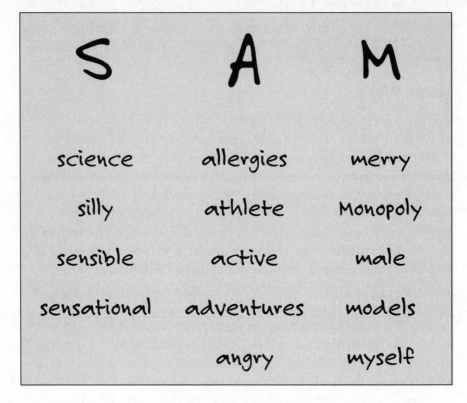

Student of the Week is another feature in many classrooms. Why not create a word wall about the featured student? It might contain words that are special to and descriptive of the student: names of family members, pets, favorite foods, personal characteristics. Or it might be a sort of name poem that includes words other children think are related to the featured child. Figure 9.2 shows an example of this kind of word wall. At the end of the week, the featured student can take the word wall home for further celebration.

Environmental Print Walls

Attention to environmental print is a staple in many early literacy classrooms because of children's interest and familiarity in the words that surround them outside of school. An environmental print word wall may be general—for example, "Words We See." Another option is to select some category of environmental print—for instance, cereal or sneakers—and challenge children to find as many examples as possible. They may even want to bring in logos from empty boxes or look through old newspapers and magazines for homework, to find additions to the wall. Since the logos are often more salient than the print for beginning readers, teachers should also print the words separately, apart from the logos, to provide children with a context-free look at the words.

The resulting wall can be used for practicing words and developing other early literacy notions, such as letter recognition. Depending on the focus of the wall, children's concepts of print can also be addressed. Think of fast-food restaurants, for example, that have one-word names (or two-word names), or a math activity in which children select their favorite fast-food restaurants and create a class bar graph entitled "where we like to eat."

Word Webs

Word webs (Fox 1996) is a small-group instructional activity that focuses students' attention on particular word parts. To engage students in word webbing, the teacher selects a meaningful word part for focus, such as a prefix or Greek or Latin root, and assembles dictionaries, paper, pencils, chart paper, and markers. To begin, the teacher introduces the word part—for example, *port*—and invites students to brainstorm words that contain it. (See Chapter 8 for more on derivations.) These are written on the chalkboard; after a few have been suggested, the teacher asks students to speculate on the meaning of the word part.

Next, small groups assemble. One person in each group circles the word part in the center of a sheet of paper. Now group members search their memories and the dictionary for other words containing the word part. The goal is to find as many words as possible. They list these, talk about word meanings, and ultimately group related words in ways that make sense to them. These word groups are added to the word web as clusters or mini-webs (see Figure 9.3). Finally, groups share their webs with the rest of the class.

After the whole-class discussion, small groups reconvene, make changes in their initial word webs if they desire, and prepare a final copy of their webs using chart paper and markers. These final copies are combined on a *word web wall*, which is a large sheet of chart paper labeled with the word part that children studied. Another alternative, perhaps a bit more challenging, is to ask different groups to create webs

Figure 9.3   A Word Web

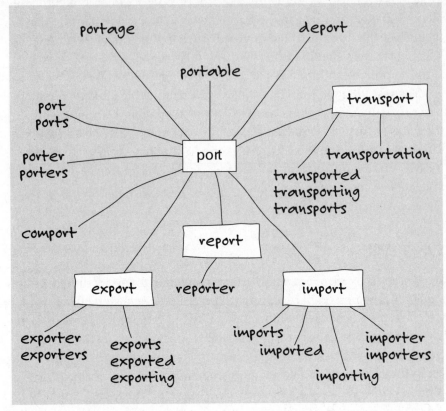

for different word parts, such as prefixes. The resulting word wall, then, would be a compilation of webs about different prefixes.

Word webbing is probably most appropriate for intermediate-level students, but the same idea could be used in primary classrooms to create *word family walls*. Here, students would brainstorm about words that contain a given word family—for example, *ant*—then proceed as described earlier. Reading a book like Cathi Hepworth's (1992) *Antics!* to children beforehand may spark their imaginations.

Content Area Walls

A content area word wall can record words that students believe to be important to some unit of study. As a new unit begins, the teacher can ask students to brainstorm words associated with the topic of the unit: "We're going to study electricity. What words do you think of when I say the word *electricity*?" This brief activity serves two important purposes. First, since it gets students thinking about the topic of the unit, it's a quick and effective prereading activity. A second benefit is the diagnostic value of the resulting list, since teachers can learn about students' prior topical knowledge by examining the quantity and variety of words.

Occasionally throughout the unit, the teacher can invite children to add more words to the content area wall. Word walls can also provide content area cohesion for teachers who use trade books to augment conceptual learning. Here's how Bonnie, an intermediate-grade teacher, explains it:

> Our textbooks are pretty boring and much too difficult for some of my students, so I try to supplement with a few library books. When we started studying electricity last fall, I read *Nikola Tesla: Spark of Genius* [Dommermuth-Costa 1994] to the children, one chapter each day. In addition to learning about this fascinating man's life, the students jotted down words related to electricity as I read, then they talked in small groups to decide which words to add to our electrifying word wall. Sometimes these were interesting and lively discussions—I remember quite a chat about *gigantic streaks of light*, which ended up on the word wall, and *nature's secrets*, which didn't.

Finding important words to add to the wall is a comprehension activity—students must understand the content and select words that are important to the topic under study. The content area wall provides a good record of what children have learned, especially if new additions are written with different colors of markers. A semantic web (like a word web) of all the words is an effective culminating activity.

Sight Word Walls

Sight words are those students recognize instantly and effortlessly. Common, high-frequency words (see Appendix B) are good candidates for learning by sight. Sight words are best learned by lots of contextual reading because students will encounter these high-frequency words often. A sight word wall can reinforce this learning. Five words can be added to the word wall every week and practiced occasionally during spare moments. In one year over 100 words can be added to a sight word wall. Although this may not seem like much, the first 100 words in Fry's Instant Word List (Fry 1980) represent 50 percent of all words elementary students encounter in their reading!

Games can keep children's practice with the words fresh. For example, children can say the first five words in soft voices, the next five in loud voices, and so on. Or one student might read the first word, two the second, three the third—a sort of word symphony! Children also enjoy reading in different voices (e.g., grumpy or happy) or as different characters (e.g., Donald Duck or Superman).

Story Word Walls

Teaching has been described as the process of making visible for learners that which is often invisible to them. When being read to (or reading on their own) students are so involved in the story that they often do not notice the interesting words that the author has used. Yet it is the author's choice of interesting words that makes stories so engaging. When you read to your students (or when they read independently) ask students to take note of any interesting words that the author may have used. Put these words on a story word wall. Talk about the meaning of the words and why the author may have chosen those words over alternatives that may be more common. You may also want to have students add the chosen words to their personal word banks (see Chapter 11). Then, encourage students to use the words in their oral and written language over the next several days. As the teacher, you should take the lead in this and try to use the words yourself. Be sure to point out to students when you do use these words. When they begin to use literary words in their own writing, their writing (and reading comprehension) will certainly improve.

Word Walls for ELL Students

English Language Learners

Word walls are an instructional bonanza for ELL students. Meier (2004) outlines several principles and strategies for promoting second language development. Among them are the following:

- Use of visuals and graphics
- Careful introduction and teaching of key vocabulary
- Informal attention to patterns and regularities in English spelling
- Use of concrete objects and hands-on literacy activities.

Word walls are useful for achieving all these purposes. Words might be illustrated with pictures of the objects they represent. These may even

Figure 9.4 An Illustrated Word Wall

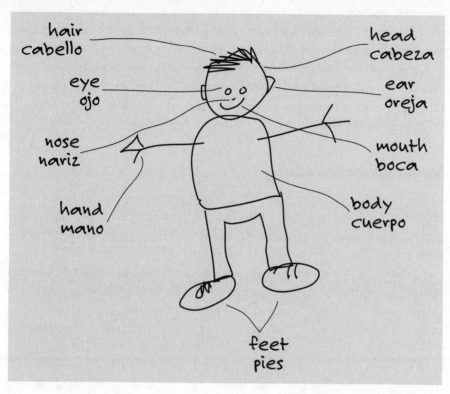

be presented conceptually, as seen in Figure 9.4. Moreover, if children's first languages are included along with the English words, the word wall can be used to draw children's attention to important phonetic contrasts between their first language and English (Helman and Bear 2007), which supports spelling development in English. A bilingual word wall also shows ELLs that their teacher values their first language; other students can learn some about the first language as well.

Writing Word Walls

Drawing children's attention to effective aspects of others' writing can help them see their own options as writers. Word walls are useful here, too (Ziebicki and Grice 1997). For example, the teacher might ask children to collect especially descriptive words, good character descriptions, or powerful sentences from their independent reading. As they find these features, children can write them on strips of newsprint and affix them to a writing word wall. These examples can be used instructionally. Discussions can focus on drawing conclusions based on the examples: What can we learn about effective character descriptions? What makes a powerful sentence?

The notion that students can choose and add words to such walls challenges and empowers them to be on the lookout for good writing—whether words, phrases, or sentences. Students are more likely to be fully engaged in an activity when we give them choice and ownership.

Spelling Word Walls

Certain words—*because*, *of*, and *they*, to name three—seem to cause universal problems for young spellers. At least part of a child's spelling ability depends on visual memory. In fact, we teach children to inspect their writing to see if the words look right. A spelling word wall consisting of a few of these troublesome words may provide additional spelling support for children. Words can be collected from children's unaided writing; good candidates would be common words that many children misspell. The teacher can remind children to check the wall if they are unsure of spelling; some teachers even require word wall words to be spelled properly. In time, when most children have mastered the first group of troublesome words, a new spelling word wall can be created.

A spelling word wall can be a useful instructional prop for lessons that focus on common rules, such as when to double a consonant before adding a suffix. Children and the teacher can collect words, decide about whether the consonant should be doubled before adding the ending, and put both the base word and its inflected forms in one of two columns on the spelling word wall: Double or Do Not Double. In addition to providing visual reinforcement of the rule, the decisions about where to place the words involve problem solving aimed at the spelling rule of interest.

Manipulating words on the spelling word wall can encourage students to use what they have learned in their own writing. In a review of four research studies about developing word knowledge in K–2 classrooms, Williams (2009) concluded that many children don't naturally apply what they have learned about words to their independent writing. She also found that "students were more likely to use the word wall as a resource for their writing when their teacher used it as a teaching tool and also encouraged her students to use it strategically to support their independent writing endeavors" (p. 577).

Quick Word Wall Games

The presence of word walls in the classroom offers lots of incidental word learning and word play opportunities. Jasmine and Schiesl (2009) used these activities in a study with first-graders. They found that word wall games such as the following promoted sight word acquisition:

- Be the Teacher: Children use all words to develop word quizzes or spelling "tests" for peers to solve.

- Guess That Word: Children ask others to guess words they have selected; they offer clues based on the words' formations.

- Let's Be Creative: Partners write a text using as many word wall words as possible.

- Letters in Words: Teacher calls out a letter within a word wall word; students find as many other words as possible that contain the target letter.

In Conclusion

One goal of word recognition instruction is to create a physical environment that invites exploration and play with words. The many possible word wall formats described in this chapter can help to achieve this goal. No matter the variation selected, all these activities meet the criteria we established at the beginning of the chapter for effective instruction about words. Students are free to explore and play with words; thinking and sharing are featured. Developing a word wall is a meaningful way for children to work with words, and using the word wall becomes a joint venture that interests all children. As such, word walls are an easy and effective addition to the classroom.

References

Blachowicz, C. and Obrochta, C. (2007). Tweaking practice: Modifying read-alouds to enhance content vocabulary learning in grade 1. In D. Rowe, R. Jimenez, D. Compton, D. Dickinson, Y. Kim, K. Leander, and V. Risko (Eds.), *56th yearbook of the National Reading Conference* (pp. 140–150). Oak Creek, WI: National Reading Conference.

Fox, B. (1996). *Strategies for word identification*. Englewood Cliffs, NJ: Merrill.

Fry, E. (1980). The new instant word list. *The Reading Teacher, 34*, 284–289.

Hall, D., and Cunningham, P. (1997). *Month-by-month reading and writing for kindergarten*. Greensboro, NC: Carson-Dellosa.

Helman, L. and Bear, D. (2007). Does an established model of orthographic development hold true for English learners? In D. Rowe, R. Jimenez, D. Compton, D. Dickinson, Y. Kim, K. Leander, and V. Risko (Eds.), *56th yearbook of the National Reading Conference* (pp. 266–280). Oak Creek, WI: National Reading Conference.

Helman, L. and Burns, M. (2008). What does oral language have to do with it? Helping young English language learners acquire a sight word vocabulary. *The Reading Teacher, 62*, 14–19.

Jasmine, J. and Schiesl, P. (2009). The effects of word wall activities on the reading fluency of first grade students. *Reading Horizons, 49*, 301–314.

McCormick, S. (1994). A nonreader becomes a reader: A case study of literacy acquisition by a severely disabled reader. *Reading Research Quarterly, 29*, 156–176.

Meier, D. (2004). *The young child's memory for words*. New York: Teachers College Press.

National Reading Panel. (2000). *Report of the National Reading Panel: Teaching children to read. Report of the subgroups*. Washington, DC: National Institutes of Health.

Rasinski, T., Padak, N., and Fawcett, G. (2010). *Teaching children who find reading difficult* (4th ed.). Boston: Allyn and Bacon.

Williams, C. (2009). Word study in the K–2 classroom. *The Reading Teacher, 62*, 570–578.

Ziebicki, S. and Grice, K. (1997). Building walls and opening doors. *Primary English, 16*, 7–9.

Children's Literature Cited

Dommermuth-Costa, C. (1994). *Nikola Tesla: Spark of genius*. Minneapolis, MN: Lerner.

Hepworth, C. (1992). *Antics!* New York: Putnam.

10

Building Words

Beth has just finished "Making Words" with her first-grade students. As she and some students were picking up the letter cards, other students were still buzzing about the challenge word that required them to use all their letters for that day. Clearly, these kids were engaged in the process of manipulating letter cards to make and spell words.

We use the term *constructivism* to describe how children learn by actively engaging in and manipulating their environment. Students learn science by engaging in scientific experiments in the school laboratory. Social studies comes alive when the teacher turns her classroom into a mini United Nations or City Council and engages in the issues of these bodies. Carpenters learn carpentry not by sitting in a lecture hall day in and day out but by working with a master carpenter. Together they build things and engage in instructional conversations that allow the learner to move toward mastery.

Students can learn words by building words under the teacher's guidance. In a study of word building, McCandliss and his colleagues (2003) found that elementary grade students experiencing difficulty in reading made significant gains in word recognition, phonemic awareness, and reading comprehension through an intervention called word building. In this intervention students were guided by their teacher in building a chain (series) of words by changing, adding, or subtracting one letter and sound at a time from various positions in words in the chain.

Making Words (Cunningham and Cunningham 1992) is a word-building activity. As one part of a more comprehensive reading curriculum for elementary students, Making Words has become a very popular and effective approach for teaching students about words (Cunningham, Hall, and Defee 1998; Snow, Burns, and Griffin 1998; Stahl, Duffy-Hester, and

Research-Based Strategies

Stahl 1998) claim that Making Words appears "to be effective as part of an overall approach to teaching reading" (p. 347).

As originally described by Pat and Jim Cunningham, in Making Words, individual students manipulate a limited set of letter squares or cards (one letter per card) in order to form words under the teacher's guidance. It is much like the age-old activity in which the teacher provides a word and challenges students to make other words using its letters. The major differences between Making Words and that traditional activity are that the letters in Making Words are not initially provided in the context of any one word—they are simply listed for the children; the teacher predetermines words to be made from the letters and guides students in making the words. Also, the Making Words activity moves on to making new words that are not fully represented by the original set of letters, and students sort the words they make into various categorical schemes.

Here's an example of a Making Words lesson that Beth does with her students toward the end of grade 1. She plans the lesson in advance and arranges for each student to have letter cards for the vowels *e* and *i* and the consonants *c, d, h, l, n,* and *r.* The vowels are usually written in a different color from the consonants in order to differentiate them. Beth also has a larger set of the same letters in a pocket chart at the front of the room in which she (or an assigned student) will make the words she asks students to make.

After distributing the cards, Beth begins by saying individual words, first short words and then longer ones. By this time of the year students know that their job is to make the words as Beth calls them out. Beth has determined the words earlier and now she dictates them— *Ed, in, red, hid, lid, rid, chin, ice, rice, nice, hide, ride, chide, child.* The final word is one that uses all the letters (the word that Beth started with in planning her lesson). Students are challenged to figure it out without any clues except that the word uses all the letters. Of course, the word is *children,* and most of Beth's students are able to figure it out in a minute or two. As suggested by Cunningham and Cunningham (1992), Beth picks her challenge word from a story students will be reading, a topic under study in a content area, or an upcoming holiday. Next, Beth directs her students' attention to her pocket chart and demonstrates how new words can be formed from some of the patterns just written. For example, she shows students how the words *slid* and *slide* can be made from the *id* and *ide* patterns. Students also change *chin* to *chip,* *chirp,* *chick,* and *chicken.* On the following day Beth has students write these words on word cards, practice them with a partner, and sort them in various ways—by word family, by beginning sound, or by presence or absence of a consonant blend or digraph.

Beth becomes quite animated when she talks about Making Words.

> I think it's a fabulous activity! My kids never seem to get tired of it. In fact, they often ask me when we are going to do it again. I've even taught some of my parents how to do it at home with their children. . . . I've seen my students make progress in learning to decode and spell words through this activity that I hadn't seen before.

Making and Writing Words

Although Making Words is very effective in its original form, Tim has developed a variant called Making and Writing Words (MWW) (Rasinski 1999a). Rather than use letter cards or squares, which can be cumbersome (Beth hasn't mentioned this, but we have noticed that it takes her a few minutes to distribute and collect the letter cards with every lesson), Making and Writing Words uses a form sheet on which students write the words as they are made. Because the form sheet is generic and can be used for any MWW lesson, it alleviates problems associated with creating letter squares, sorting them before and after lessons, and keeping track of letter squares during the lesson. In short, the sheet makes the activity logistically less complex. Since MWW requires some facility in writing, students in the first half of first grade or below may be better suited for the Making Words using the letter squares.

As in Making Words, MWW begins with the specification of letters (vowels and consonants) to be used in the lesson. These are listed at the top of the MWW sheet in the appropriate box (see Figure 10.1). Beneath this listing of letters are empty boxes in which students will write words under the teacher's guidance and direction. The teacher reminds students that for any one box, they may use only those letters that are listed at the top of the page, and only one use per letter is allowed for any word unless more than one of the same letter is listed at the top.

The first part of the activity begins with the teacher pronouncing words or providing clues for words to be written in each of the boxes. The teacher should have a transparent blank form or access to a computer and projector so that he or she may do the activity with the students. Figure 10.2 shows a typical scenario of how Making and Writing Words might be used.

Figure 10.1 Making and Writing Words

Vowels		Consonants	

1	6	11
2	7	12
3	8	13
4	9	14
5	10	15

Transfer

T-1	T-2	T-3

Figure 10.2 Making and Writing Words

159

Building Words

Vowels	Consonants
a, a, e, i	c, m, r

1 car	6 race	11 ✗
2 care	7 cram	12 ✗
3 ram	8 cream	13 ✗
4 arm	9 crime	14 ✗
5 rim	10 America	15 ✗

Transfer

T-1	T-2	T-3
crust	carpet	hammer

Each student has a blank Making and Writing Words sheet. The teacher instructs the students to write the following letters in the appropriate boxes:

Vowels a, a, e, i ; Consonants c, m, r

For Part 1, the teacher either pronounces words or gives clues to the words and asks students to write them in the appropriate boxes, beginning with short words and moving on to longer words.

"OK, in box number 1 write a three-letter word that is another name for an automobile."

(Students write the word *car* in box 1.)

"Good, now write *car* again in box 2 and add one letter to make the word *care*."

(Students write the word *care* in box 2.)

"Now in box 3, write the word *ram*. Does anyone know what *ram* means?"

(Students write *ram* in box 3.)

"In box 4 use the same letters as in *ram* to make a word that is a part of your body; your hand is attached to it."

(Students write *arm* in box 4.)

"In box 5 please write the word *rim*."

(Students write the word *rim* in box 5.)

The teacher may lead the students in a discussion of other words that have the *am* and *im* phonograms or rimes. These could be listed on the board.

The teacher continues through other words such as *race, cram, cream,* and *crime*. The MWW activity sheet has room for 15 words, but a teacher can stop anywhere. The last word in any MWW activity is a secret word that uses all the letters. Without further clues, students are challenged to determine and spell the final word. In this case the secret word, *America*, goes in box 10. The final word could relate to something that is under study in another part of the curriculum, an introduction to a story about to be read, or a word related to a current event or time of year.

As in Making Words, after all the words have been written, the teacher guides the students to transfer words they used in Part 1 to new words that follow some of the patterns or principles found in the words just written (Part 2). In making transfer words, any letter of the alphabet can be used—students are not limited to the letters used in Part 1 of the lesson.

In the boxes marked T-1, T-2, and T-3, the teacher directs students to write words related to those in boxes 1 through 10. In this example the teacher asks students to look over the words they have just written and write the words *crust* in T-1, *carpet* in T-2, and *hammer* in T-3. Students give it a go and then talk about the information they used in Part 1 to figure out the transfer words.

Part 3 of Making and Writing Words involves students sorting the words. Students cut out each word written on the MWW sheet into individual word cards, which can be kept in an envelope as students work with them over the next several days. In the word sorts, the teacher provides students with categories and the students sort their word cards into the appropriate piles. Here are some of the sorts the teacher may pose with the 13 words from the MWW activity:

- Sort 1: Words that belong to the *am* family, and those that don't.
- Sort 2: Words that have one syllable, two syllables, and three or more syllables.
- Sort 3: Words that contain consonant blends, and those that don't.
- Sort 4: Words that contain long vowels sounds, and those that don't.

Not all the sorts have to be letter-sound related. Teachers can also have students sort words into semantic or meaningful categories, such as:

- Sort 5: Words that are things, and words that aren't things.
- Sort 6: Words that describe things you shouldn't do inside a home.

Eventually, students can assume more responsibility, including leading the word sorts. Many students will demonstrate a lot of creativity in leading this part of MWW. Additionally, older students can write the word sort categories and words, rather than cutting the words into word bank cards and sorting them manually.

Once words have been made, transferred, and sorted, the words made in the MWW lesson can be added to the classroom word wall and to students' personal journals for further use. The words can also be used for word games and, perhaps, can be added to a spelling list for further study.

Planning for MWW

As in Making Words, planning for MWW begins with the final or challenge word. Once the challenge word is determined, teachers simply brainstorm words that can be written from the letters, going from short words to longer words, and developing clues. Online resources (see box) are useful for planning MWW. From a list of anagrams for the challenge word, it's easy to make note of appropriate words.

Technology

Online Resources for MWW

Wordsmith.org (includes links to anagrams in non-English)
www.wordsmith.org/anagram/

Specialist Online Dictionary
www.specialist-online-dictionary.com/word-unscrambler.html

Anagram Links and Resources
www.anagrammy.com/resources/generators.html#finder

The challenge word and sequence of words used in Making and Writing Words should be guided by students' abilities. Beginning readers may benefit most from five- and six-letter challenge words containing one vowel. Students in late grade 1 through 3 may find words with six to eight letters and two vowels appropriate. Older students in grades 4 through 6 will be appropriately challenged by secret words longer than eight letters and containing three or more vowels. Beth has found that challenge words in the seven- to eight-letter range work very well with her first-graders in April.

Making and Writing Words Using Letter Patterns

Readers use letter patterns to help them decode unknown words (Adams 1990; National Reading Panel 2000). The basic patterns readers use are the parts of syllables known as onsets (initial consonant in a syllable) and rimes (the vowel and succeeding consonants in a syllable). Other common patterns are also useful: prefixes, suffixes, and derivations primarily from Greek and Latin.

Making Words and its variation, Making and Writing Words, are powerful activities in and of themselves. Students use individual letters to think about and make words that conform to their teachers' pronunciation and other cues. This instruction may be made even more powerful, especially for older students, if instead of using individual letters, students engage in the activity using onsets, rimes, and other patterns. Such an activity helps students develop a greater sensitivity to patterns in unknown words they will encounter in their contextual reading. Thus, Making and Writing Words Using Letter Patterns (MWW-LP) (Rasinski 1999b) is a somewhat more complex activity to promote word knowledge among older students.

As in MWW, a form simplifies the MWW-LP process (see Figure 10.3). To prepare, the teacher identifies the onsets, rimes, and other patterns to be used. One of the best and easiest ways to plan such an activity is to begin with a long word that contains several onsets and rimes. These are then listed in the appropriate boxes. From here the teacher adds other onsets, rimes, and patterns, creating a wide range of words with one, two, and three or more syllables. In Appendix A are a number of letter patterns and words that can be used for a MWW-LP lesson.

Once the patterns and the words to be used are planned in appropriate order and students have copies of the form, the fun can begin. In the example presented in Figure 10.4, the onsets *b, c, l, r, t*, the rimes *ace, ake, et, ice, ink, ise, y*, and the prefix *pre* are used. To come up with this set of letters and patterns, we began with a multi-syllabic word, in this case *bracelet*. Using these onsets and rimes, we brainstormed several single and multi-syllable words. Next, we determined other onsets, rimes, and patterns to use with the original set in order to make more words.

Figure 10.3 Making and Writing Words—Letter Patterns

Onsets	Rimes	Other Patterns

1	6	11
2	7	12
3	8	13
4	9	14
5	10	15

Transfer

T-1	T-2	T-3
T-4	T-5	T-6

Figure 10.4 Making and Writing Words—Letter Patterns

165

Building Words

Onsets	Rimes	Other Patterns
b, c, l, r, t	ace, ake, et, ice, ink, ise, y	pre

1 prerace	6 baker	11 brace
2 trace	7 bakery	12 ice rink
3 Tracey	8 blink	13 trinket
4 rice	9 brink	14 try
5 rise	10 brake	15 bracelet

Transfer

T-1 icy	T-2 crinkle	T-3 practice
T-4 letter	T-5 laced	T-6 spiced cake

Now, given this set of patterns we would guide students in making the words listed below. The words are listed with some semantic clues, although in many cases the teacher may want the students to make the words after simply hearing them.

1. prerace

2. trace

3. Tracey   a girl's name that uses the word in box 2

4. rice   a grain food that is used often in Asian and Mexican dishes

5. rise

6. baker

7. bakery   a place where a baker works

8. blink   when your eyes shut and open quickly

9. brink   on the edge

10. brake

11. brace

12. ice rink   a place to go skating in the winter (two words)

13. trinket

14. try

15. bracelet

In the transfer section of the MWW-LP form, the teacher challenges students to make and write new words. The new words contain some of the word parts and patterns used in the initial section of the activity, but not all. Students use existing knowledge to make and write the words in this transfer section. Here are some words that the teacher may have asked students to write in the transfer section.

T-1. icy

T-2. crinkle

T-3. practice

T4. letter

T5. laced

T6. spiced cake

As with MWW, the third and final part of MWW-LP has the students cutting apart the words and using them for practice, word games, and word sorts. Word sorts for words in Figure 10.4, for example, could include the following:

- By word family: words containing the *ace* rime, words containing *ice*, words containing *ake*, and all other words

- By number of syllables: one syllable, two syllables, and three or more syllables

- Words that have more than one meaning, and those that don't

- Words that describe things (nouns), words that describe actions (verbs), and all other words

- Words that have positive connotations for you, words that have negative connotations for you, and words that have neither negative nor positive connotations.

The word sorts and word card games and activities (see Chapter 14) can take place over a day or two. Words can also be added to a word wall. Students can be encouraged to use the words in their oral speech and writing to further enhance their knowledge of the structure and the meaning of the words.

MWW-LP is a good activity for older students who must deal with considerably longer and more complex words than in the previous grades. MWW-LP allows students to examine in detail the structure of more sophisticated words, thus giving them some strategies for decoding them.

Word Ladders

Word ladders (Rasinski and Zutell, 2010) is another word-building activity, similar in nature to the intervention used in the McCandliss study described earlier in this chapter. In doing a word ladder, the teacher guides students in writing a series or ladder of words by manipulating one or more letters and sounds in order to make each subsequent word.

In the process of building the words in the ladder, the teacher engages students in an instructional conversation in which she draws students' attention to the meaning of the words, their pronunciation, and spelling features within each word (e.g., blends, digraphs, etc.). Below is a word ladder that begins with *word* and ends with *read*:

Word	Change one letter to make the activity a person does when he or she has a job.
Work	Change one letter to make something that can be used as a stopper for a bottle.
Cork	Change one letter to make the center of an apple.
Core	Change one letter to make a word that means to protect or look out for another person, animal, or thing.
Care	Subtract one letter to make another word for an automobile.
Car	Change one letter to make a word that means a long way off or a long distance.
Far	Add one letter to make a word that means the price paid to ride on a bus or train.
Fare	Change one letter to make a word that means to act with boldness or courage.
Dare	Rearrange the letters to make what you do with *words* (the first word in the ladder)
Read	

Although it is not necessary for the first and last words in a ladder to connect in some meaningful way, doing so makes the word ladder a game-like activity (Rasinski 2005a, 2005b, 2008). After having done word ladders regularly with their teacher, students can create their own word ladders to share with their classmates. As with the other activities presented in this chapter, once the words have been made, they can be sorted in various ways, added to the classroom word wall and to students' personal word journals, and used for other word game activities throughout the week.

In Conclusion

Manipulating a limited set of letters, with the guidance and support of the teacher, in the process of building words challenges students to explore the nature of the sound-symbol relationship in a way that allows all students to be successful. We have found that most students thoroughly enjoy these game-like activities. Done as a regular part of the word study portion of the reading curriculum, students develop their understanding of how words work and overall facility in spelling and writing.

References

Adams, M. J. (1990). *Beginning to read*. Cambridge, MA: MIT Press.

Cunningham, P. M. and Cunningham, J. W. (1992). Making words: Enhancing the invented spelling-decoding connection. *The Reading Teacher, 46*, 106–115.

Cunningham, P. M., Hall, D. P., and Defee, M. (1998). Nonability-grouped, multilevel instruction: Eight years later. *The Reading Teacher, 51*, 652–664.

McCandliss, B., Beck, I., Sandak, R., and Perfetti, C. (2003). Focusing attention on decoding for children with poor reading skills: Design and preliminary tests of the word building intervention. *Scientific Studies in Reading, 7*, 75–104.

National Reading Panel. (2000). *Report of the National Reading Panel: Teaching children to read. Report of the subgroups*. Washington, DC: National Institutes of Health.

Rasinski, T. V. (1999a). Making and writing words. *Reading Online*. Retrieved from www.readingonline.org/articles/words/rasinski.html

Rasinski, T. V. (1999b). Making and writing words using letter patterns. *Reading Online*. Retrieved from http://readingonline.org/articles/art_index.asp?HREF=/articles/rasinski/index.html

Rasinski, T. (2005a). *Daily word ladders: Grades 2–3*. New York: Scholastic.

Rasinski, T. (2005b). *Daily word ladders: Grades 4–6*. New York: Scholastic.

Rasinski, T. (2008). *Daily word ladders: Grades 1–2*. New York: Scholastic.

Rasinski, T. and Zutell, J. (2010). *Essential strategies for word study*. New York: Scholastic.

Snow, C. E., Burns, M. S., and Griffin, P. (Eds.). (1998). *Preventing reading difficulties in young children*. Washington, DC: National Academy Press.

Stahl, S. A., Duffy-Hester, A. M., and Stahl, K. A. M. (1998). Theory and research into practice: Everything you wanted to know about phonics (but were afraid to ask). *Reading Research Quarterly, 33*, 338–355.

11

Word Banks and Word Sorts

We visited an elementary school in our area not long ago. When entering Sam's first-grade classroom, we were immediately struck by the variety of activity—children were reading, working with words, writing—literacy activity was everywhere. Little Jeremy soon approached us. "Hey!" he said, beaming. "I learned 17 words last week! Wanna see?" Of course we did, so Jeremy took us to his desk and proudly extracted several words from his word bank. "Here they are. These came from the poem we have been reading. Did I tell you I can read the poem? And these are from the science story we dictated to Mr. Johnson. Want me to read the words to you?" Jeremy was proud of his accomplishments and enthusiastic about the words he had learned. He was well on his way to becoming a reader.

Upstairs, in Chris's fifth-grade class, we saw small groups of students clustered around words written on slips of paper. Kids were talking and moving words around on their tables. Chris explained, "We just finished a social studies unit about the American Revolution. Students are sorting important vocabulary words into one of three categories: battles, government, or both. I've been eavesdropping. The discussions are fascinating, especially for words like *liberty* and *independence*. They're really thinking!"

Beginning readers like Jeremy need meaningful, familiar text to read and reread. They also need to work with words, particularly to develop and maintain their sight vocabularies and to discover features of the graphophonic cueing system. Older students, like those in Chris's class, need opportunities to think about and use academic vocabulary. Word banks and word sorts, the focus of this chapter, are very useful for these purposes (Stauffer 1980).

What Is a Word Bank?

A word bank is a collection of words that a child knows (or is in the process of learning). Beginning readers primarily use word banks to reinforce word learning. Beyond the beginning stages of reading, word banks are used as a reference for spelling and writing and as a source of words for instruction and practice in phonics or other related reading skills. Hall (1981) outlines several major functions for word banks:

- To serve as a record of individual students' reading vocabularies
- To serve as a reference for writing and spelling
- To serve as examples and context for group language study or skills instruction
- To provide reinforcement through repeated exposure to words

Word bank words can come from anywhere. In fact, the child's own name, family members' names, and words related to outside-of-school interests often appear in children's word banks. Inside the classroom, dictations, predictable pattern books, poems, and songs are supportive texts for beginning reading instruction. As children read and reread these texts, they learn the words within them. Older students also keep word banks, in which they deposit interesting or important words they encounter from the literature they read and the content areas they study.

Because word banks consist almost exclusively of words the child already knows, it's easier for them to focus on the similarities and differences among words that are so necessary for word learning (Bear, Invernizzi, Templeton, and Johnston 2012). Children may also select some words to add to their word banks because of personal interest. Although they may not know these words at sight, they can usually decode them. In our summer reading program, we have found that the added incentive of learning "my words" enables successful learning. Working with too many unfamiliar words in isolation is frustrating, however. Asking children to underline the words that they know as they read individual copies of their texts is an easy way to find word bank words. This is a positive approach to word learning because the emphasis is on what students know and what they want to learn (Stauffer 1980).

Word bank cards should be rather small, about 1" × 2", and sturdy, since children use them often. Index cards or oaktag work well. Envelopes work well initially for storage, but larger containers, such as plastic recipe boxes, are soon needed. Some teachers punch holes at one end of word bank cards, and children use large metal shower rings to keep the cards together.

Students' word banks grow slowly and steadily. At first, cards can be stored in random order, but soon children need a system for organizing their words so that they can locate needed words quickly. Storing words in alphabetical order provides a natural reason for learning and practicing alphabetizing skills and sound-symbol relationships. Suppose, for example, that a child has envelopes labeled with letters of the alphabet and that the envelopes are stored in alphabetical order. To locate a word, a child needs to think about the word's beginning sound, decide what letter of the alphabet to look for, and find the corresponding envelope in alphabetical order. So even the process of finding a word offers many word-learning opportunities!

When word banks become cumbersome because of the number of cards children have accumulated, the teacher may want to suggest that children add only a specific number of words from each text they read or add only new, special, or more difficult words. The sheer volume of accumulated words is an important indicator of learning for some students, though, so we urge caution in providing too many restrictions on the size of a child's word bank.

When most children in the class have more than 200 words in their word banks, it may be time to discontinue their active use. Students' ease in reading words in teacher-made sorts is another sign for termination. If students can read teacher-selected words easily, they may not need word banks anymore (Bear et al. 2012). Many children keep word cards with them even after the entire class eliminates work with word banks, however. Some keep cards of their individual spelling demons for easy reference. Word banks for English language learner (ELL) students might contain both first language and English versions of new words, perhaps accompanied by simple sketches. Older students also find word banks useful for learning foreign language vocabulary or for subject area study.

**English Language
Learners**

Using Word Banks

Having a large sight vocabulary doesn't guarantee reading success, but it certainly helps. The more words a reader knows by sight, the fewer times he or she must stop reading to figure out unknown words.

Reading interesting, easy, familiar material affords children many opportunities to encounter words repeatedly in meaningful contexts, thus increasing the possibility that they will become sight words.

Instruction also helps children acquire sight words. Stauffer (1980) describes the overall instructional approach as cue reduction. Initially, children encounter words in the context of a familiar text. Children listen to and look at the words as the teacher reads them. A gradual cue reduction occurs when children read with the teacher, and more cues are reduced when children read chorally without the teacher or take turns reading parts of the text by themselves. Next, children read the whole texts independently, underlining words they know. Finally, the child reads the underlined words apart from their context, and known words are added to the word bank. Such a meaningful and context-rich instructional approach, based on the idea of gradual cue reduction, helps facilitate the acquisition of sight vocabulary.

Beyond the general principle of cue reduction, a great deal can be done with word bank words. Next, using Hall's (1981) broad categories, we suggest many uses for word banks.

Recording Individual Reading Vocabulary

Jeremy, whom we introduced at the beginning of this chapter, was very proud of his 17 new words. Children often benefit from concrete proof that they are learning. In many classrooms, children keep simple charts in their reading folders that record the date, perhaps every two weeks or so, and the number of words in their word banks.

Teachers can keep track of students' individual reading vocabularies as well. Since word banks contain words that students *know* (or want to know), not simply those the children have seen or the teacher has introduced, their contents provide a safe estimate of word learning. Quick calculations of quantity, quality, and rate of learning can provide indications of a child's ease and progress in learning to read as well as the overall size of the child's sight vocabulary.

Class activities with word bank words offer natural opportunities to differentiate instruction. Students who are learning English can add pictures or other visuals to their word bank cards, which will facilitate their word learning (Helman and Burns 2008). Moreover, concepts can be taught with words of different difficulty levels, which is useful in Response To Intervention environments. Imagine the variety of words

English Language
Learners

that might be selected in response to teacher questions like these: "Find words that could take the *–ed* ending" or "Find words that could be used to describe someone."

Because no two word banks are alike, teachers sometimes worry that children are not learning high-frequency words. This concern is almost always unfounded. Since a high-frequency word is, by definition, used frequently in written text, the odds are great that children will encounter it often and eventually learn it. Nevertheless, to set their minds at ease, teachers may wish to keep high-frequency word lists in students' reading folders. Periodically, students can mark the words on the list that they know by sight, perhaps by using a different symbol each time (a check mark in October, a plus sign in December, and so on) to show growth.

Word-learning information can be shared with parents. Children can complete simple charts (or better yet, computer-made certificates) to take home each month. These feature the number of new words learned that month and the total number of words in the word bank. In some classrooms, children use the computer to create triple-spaced lists of their word bank words. Mary, a first-grade teacher, notes that "this is an easy way to introduce elements of word processing. Besides that, children take their lists home, cut the words apart, and play word games with their families." What a positive way for parents to learn about their children's reading progress! And the children get the added benefit of having everyone at home congratulate them for their learning.

Technology

Serving as a Reference for Writing and Spelling

Since children know the words in their word banks, it's fair for teachers to expect the words to be spelled accurately in final drafts of children's writing. For this expectation to be realized, it must be clear to children.

Word banks can also be used to focus on issues related to language in writing. For example, teachers might ask students to find possible synonyms for commonly used words (e.g., *good* or *said*) from their word banks. In some classrooms, we have seen charts of alternatives to common words posted on walls for easy reference. These charts, usually titled "Instead of _____, try . . . ," contain lists of synonyms from students' word banks. Matt's second-graders have a chart of words to use instead of *nice*, including *kind, friendly, good, pretty, beautiful,* and *favorite*. Matt says that the list grows steadily during the year and that he frequently sees students looking at the list while writing.

Serving as Examples for Group Language Study and Skills Instruction

In general, it's easier to learn something new using what we already know. Several years ago, for example, our young friend Lee was trying to tell one of us about her new interest—lacrosse, which she described as "kind of like field hockey but you can't body check and there's a net on the stick." By relating the unknown game to one we already knew, Lee was able to explain her new interest. This same principle applies to one of the most powerful uses for word banks—that is, using words children know to teach them about language or to teach skills and strategies that will help them grow as readers. The examples we provide here illustrate how this instruction can work.

Judy knew her Title I students needed to learn about hard and soft *c*. As she listened to children read, she noted situations where lack of this knowledge was hampering children's decoding ability, so she planned a lesson to introduce these sounds. She prepared by finding pictures of common objects that had the two *c* sounds—celery, cereal, circle, circus; cat, car, comb, comics, cup, cucumber. She showed the pictures to children and asked them to say the words. Then she showed the pictures again, this time asking children to listen carefully to the beginning sounds of the words. Children quickly discovered that the words began with either the *s* sound or the *k* sound. Together Judy and the children sorted the words into *s* sound or *k* sound categories. Judy used magnets to attach the words to the chalkboard, where she also labeled each picture.

At this point, Judy asked that children find all the words in their word banks that began with *c* and to make three groups of words—*s sound*, *k sound*, and *other* (to accommodate words like *chop* and *church*). After individuals had completed this task, they shared with the larger group. Judy made two large charts containing everyone's *s sound* and *k sound* words. When the list was complete, she asked children to look for spelling similarities among the *s sound* words and *k sound* words. Children were quick to hypothesize about the vowels after the *c*. Judy concluded the lesson by asking children what they had learned and how that new information might help them if they encountered unknown words that began with *c*. By developing new knowledge (the two sounds of *c*) based on words children already knew, Judy focused their attention where she wanted it—on the beginning sounds.

Judy's instruction is an example of a *closed word sort*, an activity in which students sort word bank cards into predetermined categories. Here are some examples of categories that teachers can use in different word sorts:

■ Words that contain/don't contain some word family

■ Words with/without some phonic element

■ Words with/without affixes

■ Words that are/are not naming words, describing words, action words, and so on

■ Words that do/don't express feelings or some other feature

Within just a few minutes, students can complete several different types of sorts with the same set of words. With every sort, students get practice on each word in their word banks, each time from a different structural, syntactic, or semantic perspective. And, with each sort, students develop deeper knowledge and insights into important word and intraword characteristics.

Maintaining a sight vocabulary requires practice with the words. Two instructional activities, *open word sorts* and *odd word out*, which is a type of closed word sort, are effective practice techniques. Word sorts are small-group activities that invite students to categorize or classify words. Students either use their word bank words or other sight words for word sort activities. If other words are used, the teacher makes small word cards for students to manipulate.

An *open word sort* is a divergent thinking activity. Students may group words however they wish—there's no right answer. Instead, the focus is on the process that students use to arrive at groupings and the reasons for their choices. Students may work individually in an open word sort, but pairs or triads are often more successful because of the talking that occurs as students consider possible groupings. The teacher simply tells students to put word bank words (or other sight words) into categories that make sense and reminds them to be ready to explain their groupings to others. After a few minutes of discussion and grouping, children either explain their categories, or the teacher asks students to share their word groupings with others in the class, who are invited to guess the categories.

As mentioned earlier, the teacher provides categories in a *closed word sort*. Other than this, the activity is completed just like an open word sort. Although closed word sorts tend to yield more convergent responses, the goal is not only to produce "correct" responses. Again, students' thinking and reasoning processes are of primary importance.

Kay and her kindergarten students worked with blocks and then dictated a language experience story, "The Crazy Monster," about what their block monster looked like:

The Crazy Monster

The crazy monster has lots of eyes. The crazy monster has two hats. The crazy monster has twelve eyes. The crazy monster has six pairs of eyes. He has two necks and two heads. The crazy monster is scary. The monster is funny. The monster has two eyes on each head.

After reading the text to the children and reading it with them, Kay gave children individual copies of the text to read with partners and on their own. Two days later, to prepare for word study, Kay selected several words from the text and printed each on a 3" × 5" index card:

eyes, heads, funny, necks, twelve, monster, crazy, scary, six, two

She and the children used these word cards for an open word sort and for playing odd word out.

For the open word sort, Kay put the word cards on the carpet so all the children could see and manipulate them. She then invited pairs of students to find words that could go together. Here's what the children decided:

- *twelve*, *two*, and *six* "because they're number words"
- *crazy* and *monster* "because the monster's crazy"
- *scary* and *funny* "because they both end in *y*"
- *heads*, *necks*, and *eyes* "because they're parts of the body" (Another child added, "Yeah, but it could also be that they all end with *s*.")
- *scary* and *six* "because they're *s* words"

In the diversity of children's responses, we see that they thought about word meanings, word parts, and sounds to arrive at their answers.

In the "odd word out" activity, the teacher provides at least two related words along with one unrelated word, and children guess which word doesn't belong, again providing reasons for their decisions. Kay placed these two groups of words on the chalkboard using magnets: *twelve*, *two*, *six*, and *monster*, and *eyes*, *funny*, *heads*, and *necks*. Children easily found the odd words. Students can also play odd word out with partners using their own word bank words.

Former first-grade teacher Francine Johnston (1998) explored three ways to support young children's development of sight vocabulary. Children in three first-grade classrooms read three easy books each week. On a rotating basis, they also participated in three types of follow-up activities: repeated readings, in which they simply read and reread the stories at least 10 times each; sentence strips, in which they read text-only versions of the books and reassembled the stories from sentence strips; and word banks, in which children read text-only versions of the books, developed word banks, and participated in many of the word study activities we describe in this chapter. Although children learned words with all three methods, Francine found that children of all ability levels learned the least number of words with repeated readings and the greatest number of words with the word bank activities. The word bank activities gave "students in each achievement level a slight edge over the students in the next higher level who simply read and reread the text" (p. 671).

All three of these examples—Judy, Kay, and Francine—demonstrate an important principle of word study with word banks: working from the whole to the parts. In each case, the teacher began with something that was meaningful for students—pictures, a dictated text, or simple storybooks. Children were familiar and comfortable with these *wholes* before the teacher focused their attention on *parts*—sounds, words, or both. This balance among wholes and parts can be tricky to achieve but is well worth attaining. Too much exclusive attention to whole texts can lead children to memorize or to rely too heavily on picture cues (National Reading Panel 2000). Too much exclusive attention to words or word parts can be overly abstract and confusing for children. In whole-to-part instruction, children "begin with the full support of the text, but they also work with sentences, words, letters, and sounds in a way that demands close attention to print" (Johnston 1998, p. 668). This balance enables children to maximize their word learning.

Providing Reinforcement through Repeated Exposures to Words

Word banks are excellent sources for independent practice activities and word games. Since some of these activities involve children sharing word bank cards with others, the teacher may want to ask children to write their initials on the backs of their own cards. This will facilitate cleanup after the activities.

Although classified as primarily word study or concept development, many of these activities and games engage children in categorizing and sorting known words. This not only anchors the words in children's sight vocabularies, it also helps them discover the parts of the words, useful in solving the mystery of unknown words. Indeed, categorizing, sorting, and finding similarities and differences is a very powerful learning activity (Marzano, Pickering, and Pollock 2001). Several authors have described many other word bank activities (Bear et al. 2012; Fresch and Wheaton 1997; Garton, Schoenfelder, and Skriba 1979; Hall 1981).

Word Study

- Children can sort word bank cards according to consonant or vowel sounds. The teacher can provide a key word ("Find words with the vowel sound you hear in *box*"), a chart can be used to organize children's sorting ("long *a*, short *a*, other"), or the sorts can be left open for student exploration.

- Children can sort by word families (e.g., *-it* or *-ate*).

- Students can sort words by function (e.g., naming words, action words, describing words).

- Children can sort words according to the numbers of syllables they contain.

- Learners can find words that contain (or could contain) prefixes or suffixes.

- Students can fold pieces of paper into three columns and select word bank words that begin with different consonants (or contain different vowel sounds) for each column. Then they look through old magazines or junk mail like catalogs to find pictures of objects that match the selected sounds. These are pasted into the appropriate column.

- The teacher can ask children to find all the words in their word banks that could have -*ing* (or other endings) added. These can simply be shared, or children can sort the words according to a spelling rule, such as words that need a doubled consonant (e.g., *hop—hopping, bat—batting*), and words that do not (e.g., *read—reading, rain—raining*).

- Children can play Go Fish or Match (see Chapter 14) with beginning sounds, ending sounds, rhyming words, or vowel sounds. Singular and plural forms, synonyms, contracted and uncontracted forms, and other categories can also be used. ELL students can match pictures and English words or English words and words from their first languages.

- Students can practice their words with a partner occasionally as a quick warm-up.

- A student can select two word bank words to read to a partner and then ask one or more of the following questions: Do they begin the same? Do they end the same? Do they have the same vowel sound? Do they rhyme?

- The teacher can suggest a word. Children find additional words from their word banks based on inflectional or derivational forms (e.g., *rain—rains, raining, rainy, rained, raincoat*).

- Learners can play Change Over, which is like Crazy Eights. Words played must match the beginning consonant sound or medial vowel sound from the previous word. A wild card allows the player to change to a new consonant or vowel sound. The winner is the first person to use all his or her cards.

- Children can play Word War (see Chapter 14).

- Berne and Blachowicz (2009) tell of second-graders who made this game to use with their word bank words. They made a stack of "types" word cards—e.g., words that start with *B*, words with three syllables, action words, and so on. One at a time, children select a "type" card and roll dice (or just one if you want the game to go faster). They then pull word bank cards that match the criteria (type and number). If a child doesn't have enough of a particular type, play goes to the left. The player who uses all his/her cards first wins.

- One partner names a word bank word. The other partner finds a word bank word that comes before (or after) in alphabetical order.

Concept Development

- Children can sort word bank words into semantic categories, such as people words or color words. They can also look for some of these words in old magazines or in junk mail and create collages.

- Children can find words that have more than one meaning. They can also look for synonyms, antonyms, or homonyms.

- Students can make and share sentences using their word bank words.

- Children can use word bank words to make short sentences as long as possible.

- Learners can make compound words using words from their word banks. Children may want to make up and then illustrate their own compound words as well.

- Partners can use both their word banks to write a story.

- The teacher can prepare modified cloze exercises: The dog is _____ the table; I saw a _____ balloon; Tim has a _____. Children find as many words from their word banks as possible to complete the sentences.

- Children can make riddles using their word bank words:

  I am small.

  I am brown.

  I eat carrots.

  I am a _____.

- Students can create picture dictionaries using their word banks as a source.

- Children can find word bank words related to concepts being discussed in science or social studies. Or they can complete *concept sorts*, such as a *seasons sort* in which children find and categorize word bank words that belong with spring, summer, and so on.

- Class members can play Word Bingo. Each child lays out 9, 16, or 25 words, face up, in rows like a Bingo card. The caller says, "Turn over a word that . . ." and gives a characteristic common to some of the words. For example, a word that begins or ends like [another word], a word that has an ending, a word that tells something to do, a word that names an animal, a word that has two syllables, your shortest word, your favorite word, and so on. The winner is the first child to turn over an entire row, column, or diagonal.

Word Banks for Stories and Content Study

An alternative (or complement) to a master, ongoing word bank is a temporary one based on a story or content area study. These temporary word banks can be developed based on texts that students read or on teacher read-alouds.

Before reading a story to students (or asking them to read it), the teacher asks students to write down or remember interesting words they encounter during the reading. After the reading, a group list is written on the board or chart paper; the teacher can add a word or two (12 to 24 words is a good number). Students then write the words on word bank grids, which are simply plain sheets of paper with one vertical line and three horizontal lines, resulting in eight rectangles (one word is written in each rectangle). They cut the grids into individual word cards, look over the words, and then put them in envelopes for storage.

Over the next several days, students can do open and closed word sorts, play word games, practice the words, and use them in their talk and writing. Before long, they learn the words, and they also practice examining the words for important word features. When most students have learned the words, a new story word bank can be developed.

Blachowicz and Obrochta (2007) studied a process they called "tweaking"—making small modifications to read-alouds in grade 1 content area instruction to focus more on content words. Teachers looked for words within each read-aloud text that could be used for "vocabulary visits." Before reading, teachers asked students to list all the words they knew about the topic under study. These words were put on a poster along with the teacher-selected vocabulary. Then the teacher showed a picture that was related to the topic and asked students to identify more related words, which were added with sticky notes. While the teacher read aloud, students used "thumbs up" when they heard a target word. After reading, students made word bank cards and did semantic word sorts with them. These small modifications enhanced students' word learning.

These examples illustrate the versatile nature of word banks, as well as the whole-to-part model that supports student learning so well. Students begin with a whole text, choose and study individual words from it, and finally, through word sorts and other activities, examine the intraword features of the words. As a bonus, students learn the important notion that good writing contains interesting words.

In Conclusion

Children learn about words and written language as they successfully encounter words, stories, and other types of texts. They learn individual words in the same manner that they learn to read, through repeated exposure in familiar, dependable contexts. Word banks show evidence of this word learning while providing fertile ground for additional learning. Word sorting activities reinforce the recognition of the words themselves. Equally important, they offer children the opportunity to generalize about sound-related characteristics of words.

References

Bear, D. R., Invernizzi, M., Templeton, S., and Johnston, F. (2012). *Words their way* (5th ed.). Englewood Cliffs, NJ: Prentice-Hall.

Berne, J. and Blachowicz, C. (2009). What reading teachers say about vocabulary instruction: Voices from the classroom. *The Reading Teacher, 62,* 314–323.

Blachowicz, C. and Obrochta, C. (2007). Tweaking practice: Modifying read-alouds to enhance content vocabulary learning in grade 1. In D. Rowe, R. Jimenez, D. Compton, D. Dickinson, Y. Kim, K. Leander, and V. Risko (Eds.), *56th yearbook of the National Reading Conference* (pp. 140–150). Oak Creek, WI: National Reading Conference.

Fresch, M. J. and Wheaton. A. (1997). Sort-search-discover: Spelling in the child-centered classroom. *The Reading Teacher, 51,* 20–31.

Garton, S., Shoenfelder, P., and Skriba, P. (1979). Activities for young word bankers. *The Reading Teacher, 32,* 453–457.

Hall, M. A. (1981). *Teaching reading as a language experience* (3rd ed.). Columbus, OH: Merrill.

Helman, L. and Burns, M. (2008). What does oral language have to do with it? Helping young English language learners acquire a sight word vocabulary. *The Reading Teacher, 62,* 14–19.

Johnston, F. (1998). The reader, the text, and the task: Word learning in first grade. *The Reading Teacher, 51,* 666–675.

Marzano, R., Pickering, D., and Pollock, J. (2001). *Classroom instruction that works: Research-based strategies for increasing student achievement.* Alexandria, VA: Association for Supervision and Curriculum Development.

National Reading Panel. (2000). *Report of the National Reading Panel: Teaching children to read. Report of the subgroups.* Washington, DC: National Institutes of Health.

Stauffer, R. G. (1980). *The language-experience approach to the teaching of reading* (2nd ed.). New York: Harper and Row.

12

Contextual Word Recognition

We asked young Gabe if he ever encountered difficult words in his reading. He replied, "Oh, sure. Some of them are real tricky." "What do you do with those tricky words?" we asked. Gabe answered, "I say blank," and then told us how he had learned to say "blank" at the difficult spot, read to the end of the sentence, and try again. "It usually works," he commented, "but you have to look at the word, too. The sounds have to match."

Maria, Gabe's teacher, was pleased that he was able to explain his word recognition strategies. "Most of the children know something about phonics by the time they get to me in second grade. Many know about context, too, but few understand the power of using them simultaneously. I've been working on helping the children see how all these decoding options work together," she said. Maria has the right idea. Although both phonics and context are helpful alone, they work far more effectively together. In this chapter we explore issues related to context—what it is, why it's important, and how teachers can encourage its use.

What Is Context?

When talking with children, we describe context as the neighborhood where a word lives. Put more formally, contextual analysis is a word identification strategy; a reader attempts to determine the meaning and/or pronunciation of an unknown word by the way it is used in the text (National Reading Panel 2000). To do this, the reader uses one or more cues. Illustrations, graphic aids, or typographical cues can provide clues to meaning. When a reader sees quotation marks, for example, the reader can guess that someone is saying something, a guess that is usually but not always correct.

Pragmatic context refers to the general structure of the text as well as the situation in which the reader is reading. With regard to the former, consider the opening phrase "Once upon a time." What would you expect to find in a text that begins with those words? Your experience with fairy tales provides a rich resource for decoding and understanding such a text.

Sometimes the context in which the reading is done affects understanding. Here's an example:

> Both f_____ and m_____ have problems with ch_____that are not easy to s_____.

How did you fill in the blanks? We use this example in our teaching, and students almost invariably decide that the sentence refers to *fathers*, *mothers*, and *children*. Makes sense, doesn't it? But if the sentence were used in an agriculture class, students might decide that it referred to *farmers*, *merchants*, and *chickens*. We even develop and use expectations related to reading that are based on the reading situation.

But the most powerful context clues are the linguistic ones provided by the positional nature of English (syntax) and by the knowledge the reader has of the meanings of other words and ideas (semantics). Below we consider these important clues in a bit more detail.

Syntax refers to the way words go together to form sentences. Even very young speakers of a language understand its syntax and how to form sentences. The linguist Noam Chomsky (1957) offers this example:

> Colorless green ideas sleep furiously.

Could this be a sentence of English? Although it doesn't make sense—something can't be both colorless and green; ideas have no color and don't sleep—it is syntactically allowable in terms of word order and expresses a complete, if bizarre, thought. Even though few of us would be able to articulate the grammar rules that make this an allowable sentence, as speakers of the language we know that it could be.

This point has important instructional implications: children do not need to be able to articulate syntactic (grammar) rules in order to use their knowledge of language to guide their reading. Teachers can help children understand syntactic context by offering examples such as:

Sally watched as the wind blew her _____ balloon away.

Children will offer adjectives to fill in the blank. The teacher can underscore the necessity that what we read must sound like sentences in English.

Although a strong contextual aid for native English speakers, syntax can pose challenges for English language learners (ELLs), particularly if English word order differs from the syntax of their first languages. Knowing the major syntactic differences between English and children's first languages can assist teachers in helping children move past confusion and use what they know about the syntax of one language as an aid to learning the syntax of another. The websites in the text box provide resources to learn about the major points of difference (and possible interference) between English and other languages.

Web-Based Resources for Learning about Syntax and Vocabulary

http://esl.com

http://spanish.about.com
http://en.wikipedia.org (enter the language you are interested in plus the word "syntax" in the search box)

Technology

Semantics refers to word meanings. In essence, the reader asks, "What would make sense here?" and, using information from the text along with prior knowledge and experience, makes a guess. Put another way, words represent concepts, which reflect experience. Most linguists argue that individual words have little or no real meaning apart from their use. For example, most of us would say we know what *window* means. But consider these uses:

The eyes are a *window* to the soul.

What is our *window* of opportunity?

You make a better door than *window*.

These windows are semantically related to the panes of glass we ordinarily think about, but they're not exactly the same. Meaning resides not so much in individual words but in the way they're used.

Semantic context is a powerful way to identify a word. Here's a little test: What's this word? _____ Were you able to get it? No? OK, try this: w_____ Got it? Still not enough? Here's a third clue: You make a better door than a w_____. There. We bet you have it now. The power of semantic context is one reason why children need to practice decoding by reading meaningful text.

Why Is Context Important?

Context helps us make predictions about the text. In a summary of research related to context use, Johnson and Baumann (1984) explain how this works: "It has been theorized . . . that a reader uses this tacit knowledge of language by reducing the number of possible alternative candidates for an unfamiliar word and thereby enhances his/her chances of making an accurate identification" (p. 599). Stanovich (1991) calls this the *notion of expectancy*—when readers use context to develop notions about what they expect to see, the subsequent reading is more fluent and successful. This is probably why most of us read connected text more fluently than lists of words. But good readers are probably not consciously aware of using context. In fact, poor readers appear to rely heavily, perhaps too much, on context (Stanovich 1991). Some researchers see context as a compensation strategy, as a way to figure out an unknown word when no other tools are available for use.

This raises another important issue for teachers to consider: how to help children see that word recognition is essentially a problem-solving activity that works best when they rely on all cueing systems for information. The problem is the unknown word; the solution involves finding a word that makes contextual sense and bears graphophonic resemblance to the unknown word. Another way to think about word recognition is in terms of prediction and confirmation. A reader predicts what a word is likely to be using syntactic and semantic contextual information, and confirms the prediction using graphophonic information and subsequent contextual information. In other words, proficient readers orchestrate context and phonics as an overall word recognition strategy and as a prompt for self-correction, should it be necessary.

Information about the graphophonic cueing system is valuable for word recognition, particularly when readers attend to the beginning portions of words, which generally contain the best and most useful information (Johnson and Baumann 1984). However, phonics works best when the reader knows what a word is likely to be in the first place. "If you know that the word you're looking at is probably *horse*, *cow*, or *donkey*, phonics will enable you to tell the difference. But here you do not have to run through all 11 alternatives for the first two letters of *horse*—you just have to know that a word beginning with *ho* could not be *cow* or *donkey*" (Smith 1985, p. 54). So all cues—graphophonic and contextual—help readers reduce alternatives, which makes determining the unknown word more efficient and effective.

Although our emphasis in this chapter is primarily on using context to recognize words, most reading authorities agree that context can be a powerful tool for word learning (National Reading Panel 2000). Most also agree that context is not enough. Consider the following:

Research-Based
Strategies

> My sister Ginger has blonde hair and a light complexion. She is very slim. Her best friend Sam, however, is corpulent.

Suppose you didn't know the meaning of *corpulent*. From context (specifically the word *however*), you can determine that *corpulent* is something that Ginger is not. Does Sam have some other color of hair? Does he have a dark complexion? Is he chubby? The passage contains some clues but not enough to solve the problem with assurance. Using context clues and reading in context are, however, important aspects of vocabulary learning.

Nagy's (1988) model of vocabulary instruction shows how important they are. To learn new concepts, we must first link them to what we already know. Helping children learn concepts related to different forms of government—for example, dictatorship—may begin with a discussion of what they already know about their own form of government. The next stage in Nagy's model is repetition, in which readers need many meaningful encounters with the new concept in context. This leads to automatic access, so that the reader doesn't have to stop and think, "Now what is this again?" when encountering the new word. The final stage, meaningful use, also involves many encounters with the new concept, but this time children use the concept in their own writing and speaking rather than reading someone else's use. As can be seen, both the second and third stages of the model involve contextual reading and using the concept in writing and oral communication.

These are important points to remember when planning how to help children use context as they read. First, when using context to decode, children need to confirm their contextual guesses at unknown words, perhaps using beginning letters and sounds. They should learn to ask, "Does it make sense? Does it look right?" as a means of checking contextual guesses. Second, contextual reading can facilitate word learning or vocabulary acquisition; indeed, it's one of the very best ways to do so, but children will need instruction as well. In fact, most children, especially struggling readers, need instruction in what context is, how using context can help them, and especially how to double-check their contextual guesses (Johnson and Baumann 1984; Stanovich 1991).

Talking about Context

Read-aloud sessions offer a "powerful context for word learning" (Kindle 2009, p. 202) and a great opportunity to model using context. Selecting engaging books that contain some challenging vocabulary will offer teachers modeling opportunities. Before sharing, teachers should identify a word or two for focus. Then, in the process of the read-aloud, teachers can take a moment to explain how they think about context when encountering an unusual word. This sort of in-process explanation can help children see how to use context as they read.

Discussion can also help children learn how and why to use context. Teachers can encourage children to talk about how context helped them figure out unknown words (or didn't) by using a strategy called Reader-Selected Miscues (Goodman, Watson, and Burke 1996). In this procedure, students keep track of tricky words during independent reading time by making a light pencil mark in the margin or jotting down the word and page number on a separate piece of paper. After reading, the teacher asks children to return to their tricky words to see if they can now figure them out. Then a discussion ensues, in which children talk about how they solved word-related problems in their reading. Questions like these can guide the discussion: "How did you

figure out the tricky word?" "How did you know _____ was right?"
Teachers' comments during these discussions can also help students to
see the benefits of using the strategies their classmates describe.

Teachers can also use reader-selected miscues collected from a
group to find productive topics for mini-lessons. To use the strategy
in this way, children will need small 3" × 5" slips of paper. When they
encounter a tricky word, they insert a slip of paper at that spot in their
books and continue reading. After reading, they return to each slip of
paper, write the sentence in which the word appears, and underline the
word in question. Some teachers ask that children also note the title of
the book. When the papers are complete, the teacher collects them for
later categorization and analysis. Looking at the types of words that
give children difficulty can provide direction for small-group or
whole-class lessons.

In many classrooms, teachers and students occasionally discuss
ways children have identified unknown words. This discussion
might simply begin with the teacher asking, "Who has figured out a
hard word?" "How did you do it?" "How did you know you were
correct?" Discussions like these help children see that all readers
encounter problems from time to time, which is an important aspect
of an accurate concept of reading. Additionally, children's attention
is focused on the problem-solving nature of word identification, and
they may get new ideas from their peers. Together they may make
charts of their successful word identification strategies to post in the
classroom.

Cloze and Maze Activities

Many instructional activities supporting the use of context rely on
some sort of fill-in-the-blank format. This makes sense because to fill
in the blanks, children must use context. Reading professionals call
these *cloze exercises*, after a term coined by Wilson Taylor (1953). Cloze
takes advantage of the natural human tendency to find closure—if we
see almost all of a photograph, for example, our tendency is to fill in
the missing detail so that we perceive a complete photo. This happens
almost automatically; we are often not even conscious of our thinking.
To complete a cloze activity successfully, the reader does the same thing,
and in the process, thinks along with the author.

Figure 12.1   Cloze for Testing and Teaching

Feature	Assessment	Instruction
Length	150+ words	At least a sentence; length can vary
Materials	Usually instructional level or higher	Usually independent level; easy for child
Deletions	First sentence intact; then delete every fifth word for a total of at least 25 deletions	Varies; teacher decides
Evaluation	Exact or close to exact replacements only	Synonyms acceptable
Follow-up	Usually none, although teacher may analyze responses for syntax or semantics	Teacher and student discuss replacements and how/why they were made

Source: Adapted from Tierney, Readence, and Dishner (1995).

As described in Chapter 3, cloze can be used to test whether a child can read a particular text successfully. When used as a testing technique, the rules for developing and scoring cloze exercises are fairly well set. Teachers have much more latitude in developing cloze activities for instructional purposes. Figure 12.1, which we have adapted from Tierney, Readence, and Dishner (1995), shows the major differences between these two uses of cloze. Although some children find cloze tests frustrating, most students enjoy solving the puzzles represented by instructional cloze activities.

Before children can benefit from instructional activities based on cloze procedures, they need to understand the concept of closure. Oral cloze activities can help in this regard (Leu and Kinzer 1999). For example, the teacher might recite a line from a familiar poem, song, or pattern book, leaving a word out and asking children to replace it. Because the language is familiar, children will easily fill in the blanks.

Doing so will help them see that language users naturally fill in the blanks while listening or reading.

Another way to help children understand the principle of closure is to invite children to complete a sentence:

I wish I could eat some _____.

As children offer possibilities, the teacher can write and affix word cards to complete the sentence. This activity also provides opportunities for indirect learning about print conventions, such as left-to-right progression, learning that letters make up words, and developing a concept for word in print.

Oral cloze is also helpful for showing children how to use context and phonics together. For example, the teacher might change the sentence to:

I wish I could eat some c_____.

Children can then offer possibilities that fit the context and begin appropriately. Often this activity presents opportunities for teachers to distinguish possible completions (e.g., *cabbage* or *celery* in the example above) from likely ones (e.g., *cake* or *cookies*), which shows children how easy it can be to double-check their guesses as they read.

To make a cloze activity, the teacher first selects a passage, usually from something children have read. Keep the first sentence intact in order to allow students to develop a contextual background for the text. Words chosen for deletion should be those that can be determined from context and require a variety of strategies to figure out. Instructional modifications include providing initial letters or onsets for the deleted words or cueing the replacement word's length by the length of the space. Here are some examples from Ludwig Bemelmans's (1939) book, *Madeline*:

Cloze

They left the _____ at_____ past nine in two straight _____ in rain or _____.

Initial Letter/Onset Modification

They sm_____ at the g_____ and fr_____ at the bad and
sometimes th_____ were very s_____.

Word Length

She was ___ afraid __ mice—she loved _____, snow, and ice.

Once students complete the task, engage them in an instructional
conversation about the strategies and knowledge they used to
determine the deleted words.

Interactive cloze (Ruddell and Ruddell 1995) is a discussion activity
that can help children see how context works to aid decoding. To
prepare for this activity, the teacher develops a cloze passage with a
few deletions that are chosen to spark conversation. Either individually
or with a partner, students complete the passage. Then they join with
others in small groups to share and discuss their replacement words.
Children are sometimes surprised when others select the same words
or when someone shares a completely different, yet sensible, word.
A whole-class conversation can conclude the session.

Indeed, we think that no cloze or maze activity is complete until
students and the teacher discuss it. Through discussion, students
can share the strategies they use to determine the deleted words. For
example, in the preceding cloze, the final blank can be completed
by reading beyond the deletion, developing a sense for the items
enumerated (_____, *snow*, and *ice*) and using that knowledge to
choose a word that fits the sequence. This is a nice demonstration of the
strategy of reading on when one meets a difficult or unknown word.

Maze (or multiple-choice cloze) activities can also help children
learn to use context. In one version of maze, the teacher provides words
to be replaced; the student's job is to decide which goes where, as in this
example from Ezra Jack Keats's *The Snowy Day* (1962, p. 7):

One _____ morning Peter woke_____ and _____ out the
_____. Snow had fallen _____ the night. [during, window,
looked, up, winter]

Maze activities can also be developed to draw children's attention
to how syntactic and graphophonic information combines with

semantic information. To achieve this goal, the options should be graphophonically similar, at least in the beginning portions of words, but syntactically different. Again, from *The Snowy Day* (p. 28):

> (Beater, Before, Befuddled) he got into bed, he looked (if, is, in) his pocket. His (snowman, sandbox, snowball) wasn't there.

"I put maze activities on the computer," says Lou, a second-grade teacher. "It's pretty easy, actually. I create a master file and then copy it for everyone. The children enjoy cutting and pasting their choices, and they reread the sentences to make sure they make sense. The children save their work on the computer so that later I can look at what they've done." Cloze and maze activities can also be constructed by retyping a passage with underscores for deleted words. An alternative and significantly less time-consuming approach is to photocopy the original text and use a dark marker to line out the words to be deleted. Deletions should be numbered, and students can use a numbered answer sheet to record their word choices.

Technology

These activities are powerful ways to help students strengthen their abilities to use context. The teacher's task in all these activities is to help children become accustomed to looking at and thinking about the surrounding context to guess unknown words. Once children understand the principle of cloze, teachers will find it an adaptable instructional strategy.

Helping Readers See Their Options

What do children think they're supposed to do when they encounter an unknown word? We routinely ask this question of children who attend our summer reading program, all struggling readers, and their responses are surprisingly similar. Primary-age children think they're supposed to "sound it out." Older students believe that they must "look it up." Although both of these can be effective ways to solve the problem of an unknown word, we strive to help students see that they have other options, which may sometimes be more successful than their old standbys. We have found that incidental but purposeful in-process teaching is a powerful way to help children expand their word recognition repertoires.

Perhaps the best time for this incidental teaching comes when a child encounters a difficult word when reading aloud to the teacher. This can be a golden opportunity to help the reader see his or her options. For using context, three types of teacher support are possible, depending on what the reader seems to need.

Some readers need encouragement to predict an unknown word. These are the readers who stop when they encounter difficulty, often waiting patiently for someone else to solve the problem (a surprisingly effective strategy in some classrooms!) To help the reader see that making a guess is appropriate, the teacher can:

■ Say nothing for two or three seconds. This silence sends two important messages to the reader: "This is your problem to solve." "I believe you can do it." Many teachers find that this strategy alone makes a remarkable difference in their students' willingness and ability to decode unknown words.

■ Ask, "Why did you stop?" to ensure that a word difficulty is the reason and to learn which word is providing trouble.

■ Ask, "What would make sense there?" This prompt reminds the reader to make a guess based on contextual clues.

■ Say, "Read to the end of the sentence. Now try again. Think of a word that makes sense and looks like [point to difficult word]." A similar prompt is "Look at the word, get your mouth ready for the first sound, and think of a word that would also make sense." Both of these prompts show the reader a way to use context and graphophonic cues together. They also remind students that clues can often be found after the unknown word and not just before it.

Other readers need to learn how to confirm their contextual guesses as well. These are the readers who make inappropriate guesses but read on, apparently not thinking at all about the sense (or lack of sense) of what they have just said. To help these readers, teachers can:

■ Say, "Was that OK? How do you know?" This reminds the child about confirmation, checking that a word is "OK."

■ Say, "How did you decide what that word was?" or "How do you know that word is _____?" These questions, too, point back at meaning, but they also give the teacher a glimpse into the child's strategies, at least the ones he or she can articulate.

■ Say, "Does that make sense?" This directs the child's thinking to the author's message and to using context as a confirmation tool.

Children sometimes know they've made mistakes but don't know that they should correct them. These readers typically pause and sometimes look puzzled but read on. To encourage self-correction, the teacher can:

■ Say nothing for two or three seconds to ensure that the reader needs additional support and to signal that the reader is responsible for solving the problem.

■ Ask the child to read the sentence again. This enables the teacher to see if the mistake was a careless error or if the reader may have corrected it mentally without saying the correction aloud.

■ Ask the child to tell you the sentence in his or her own words and then ask if the sentence makes sense. An alternative is to say, "You said _____. Does that make sense?" Teachers should wait to use both of these strategies until the child has finished reading so that the incidental instruction doesn't interfere with the flow of the child's reading. The teacher can simply make note of the problem sentence and return to it later.

Like many of the other teacher comments we have described, these comments guard against the careless error while focusing the reader's attention on contextual meaning. By basing their comments on what children seem to need, teachers can help children develop a well-rounded word recognition strategy that takes advantage of all available linguistic cues.

In Conclusion

Contextual analysis is a very important strategy for recognizing unknown words. Determining a word by scrutinizing its surrounding context is efficient and, most often, effective, especially when double-checked against graphophonic information.

Although filling in the blanks is, to some extent, a natural cognitive activity, some students need help thinking about context clues as a tool for reading. Through activities such as Reader-Selected Miscues, cloze, and maze, teachers can show children the power of contextual information. Talking about context-based decision making is particularly critical. And independent reading—lots of it—offers students excellent practical opportunities to apply this knowledge about context. Together, these activities can help children see what decoding tools they have and how they can work together.

References

Chomsky, N. (1957). *Syntactic structures.* The Hague: Mouton.

Goodman, Y., Watson, D., and Burke, C. (1996). *Reading strategies: Focus on comprehension* (2nd ed.). Katonah, NY: Richard C. Owen.

Johnson, D. and Baumann, J. (1984). Word identification. In P. D. Pearson, R. Barr, M. Kamil, and P. Mosenthal (Eds.), *Handbook of reading research* (pp. 583–608). New York: Longman.

Kindle, K. (2009). Vocabulary development during read-alouds: Primary practices. *The Reading Teacher, 63,* 202–211.

Leu, D. and C. Kinzer. (1999). *Effective literacy instruction* (4th ed.). Upper Saddle River, NJ: Prentice Hall.

Nagy, W. (1988). *Teaching vocabulary to improve reading comprehension.* Newark, DE: International Reading Association.

National Reading Panel. (2000). *Report of the National Reading Panel: Teaching children to read. Report of the subgroups.* Washington, DC: National Institutes of Health.

Ruddell, R. and Ruddell, M. (1995). *Teaching children to read and write.* Boston: Allyn and Bacon.

Smith, F. (1985). *Reading without nonsense* (2nd ed.). New York: Teachers College Press.

Stanovich, K. (1991). Word recognition: Changing perspectives. In R. Barr, M. Kamil, P. Mosenthal, and P. D. Pearson (Eds.), *Handbook of reading research,* vol. 2 (pp. 418–452). New York: Longman.

Taylor, W. (1953). *The cloze procedure: How it predicts comprehension and intelligence of military personnel.* Urbana, IL: University of Illinois, Human Resources Research Institute, Division of Communication.

Tierney, R., Readence, J., and Dishner, E. (1995). *Reading strategies and practices* (4th ed.). Boston: Allyn and Bacon.

Children's Literature Cited

Bemelmans, L. (1939). *Madeline.* New York: Viking.

Keats, E. J. (1962). *The snowy day.* New York: Viking.

13

Student-Created Texts and Word Learning

To prepare for a math lesson about categorization, Gloria, a first-grade teacher, brought two small cardboard boxes of buttons to school. After the students were seated around her, but before she opened the boxes, she shook them and then asked the children, "What's in the boxes?" The children became curious, of course, and began making guesses: shells, rocks, buttons, keys, marbles. While children guessed, Gloria continued shaking the boxes. She said, "Listen again. What do you hear? What do you think?" By the time the boxes were emptied on the table, the children were interested in the lesson to come.

Next, Gloria said, "Look these over. Just use your eyes. What can you discover about these buttons?" The children examined them, and after a while, Gloria said, "What did you notice about the buttons?" A lively discussion ensued, with some children pointing to interesting buttons and others remarking about the variety of buttons. Finally, Annie said, "They're different," and Kevin agreed: "They're different colors."

This gave Gloria the opening she was looking for. She asked the group, "What did you notice about the different colors?" Molly said, "Some are dark and some are light." So Gloria asked the children to sort the buttons into two piles, dark and light. The children talked informally with one another as they completed this task.

When they were finished making their piles, Gloria pointed to one pile and asked, "What would you call this group?" She also asked if the children agreed that all buttons in the dark category belonged there, which led to an interesting debate about a dark pink button. When the children were satisfied with their dark category, Gloria repeated her questions, this time with the light category. Then she asked the children, "Now, what did we do?" Jenny replied, "These are dark and these are light." Jose added, "We sorted them into two groups—dark and light."

Next, Gloria put all the buttons back into one big pile and asked the children what else they noticed about them. Eventually, the children sorted the buttons three more times, according to size, luster, and texture. Finally, Gloria invited a summary: "What have we been doing? What did you find out? Let's talk about it. Who can make an observation?"

At this point, the children were ready to talk about what they had done and discovered. They offered their ideas, and Gloria recorded them on chart paper exactly as they were said. She also spoke each word as she wrote it and reread each sentence after it was written, asking the child who offered it, "Is this what you want to say?" Each child contributed to the dictation. When it was finished, Gloria encouraged the children to read the text silently as she read it aloud (again pointing to words as she read them):

Buttons

We made piles for the buttons. Some buttons are big, and some are small. Some buttons are medium-sized. The buttons were rough or smooth or lumpy. Some are shiny, and some are not. Some are different and some are the same. We called the piles categories.

By Annie, Kevin, Molly, Jenny, and José

What Is LEA?

Gloria and her students participated in language-experience approach (LEA) activities, such as this button lesson, nearly every day and in all content areas. In the language-experience approach, students' experiences are represented first by their oral language and later re-represented, or converted to written language, by the teacher or another scribe. This written text, which is based on students' own experiences and understanding, becomes reading material. LEA activities feature attention to the interrelationships among oral language, written language, and readers' thoughts and experiences. In this chapter we describe LEA and offer practical suggestions for obtaining and using dictations for early reading instruction. (This discussion relates to Chapter 11, which focuses on word banks and their uses.) We also address copy change activities, another good source of early reading material, in this chapter. Both LEA and copy change transform children's oral language into written texts that can be read and used as a springboard into word study.

Language-experience approach is not a new idea. In the years following the Civil War, Colonel Francis Parker advocated experience-based learning, as did John Dewey in the early 1900s (Rippa 1984). LEA activities are also described in Edmund Burke Huey's *The Psychology and Pedagogy of Reading* (1908/1968). In her book *Teacher* (1963), Sylvia Ashton-Warner provides a detailed description of LEA as used with Maori children in New Zealand. At about the same time, U.S. scholars such as Russell G. Stauffer, Roach Van Allen, and Jeanette Veatch advocated LEA and conducted research in LEA classrooms.

Over all these years, scholars have amassed a lot of evidence to show us the benefits of LEA-related instruction. For example, the U.S. Office of Education's massive First Grade Studies research project, conducted in the late 1960s, provided "evidence that language experience approaches do result in good achievement" (Hall 1985, p. 7). Another research review, conducted almost two decades later, showed

> very convincingly that language experience programmes work. . . . And not only that it works in the attainment of good achievement scores but that it does far more than that. It promotes learning that is pleasurable and that is congruent with how language competence flourishes. (Hall 1985, p. 10)

The LEA philosophy is based on several related theories: how people learn, how people read, and how others can help. At the intersection of these theories are notions about what makes learning easy. Hall (1985) notes that LEA is "rooted in the elements of success, relevance, involvement, attitude, interest, and motivation" (p. 6). Relationships among thinking, problem solving, and reading are another aspect of the foundation of LEA. Stauffer (1969) describes reading as "a phenomenon of mental activity akin to thinking" (p. 4). To comprehend, he says, readers restructure meaning from experience; they think and reason while they read. In other words, "reading is never treated as something apart from language and thought" (Allen 1976, p. 10), or, as Stauffer says, "meaning is the important thing—not saying words. Reading is a thinking process and not a parroting process" (p. 186).

To create a classroom environment that reflects these beliefs, Veatch (1986) advises teachers to "utilize some aspect of the internal world of the pupil. There must be some kind of personal choice, some kind of individual input into the task of learning" (p. 32). This sort of environment features student freedom and choice, to be sure, but also student responsibility. Let's take a closer look at how we can create such a dynamic learning environment.

LEA: The Basics

Students of all ages find success with LEA activities. In general, LEA works well if a learner's oral language (i.e., vocabulary and sentence structure) is more complex than the written language the learner can read successfully. Both beginning readers and struggling readers fall into this category. In fact, a search of the professional literature (Padak and Rasinski 1996) shows that LEA-related activities can be used effectively with beginning readers, to be sure, but also with middle school, high school, college, and adult readers, including those with special needs. Many teachers who work with English language learner (ELL) students rely heavily on LEA. Barone's (1996) year-long case study of bilingual (Spanish and English) first-graders showed LEA in both languages to be an important routine to foster children's learning of English. More recently, Helman and Burns (2008), who found a relationship between ELL children's oral proficiency in English and their ability to learn sight words in English, advised use of LEA to provide a bridge between oral and written language. Thus, teachers who know the basic assumptions and procedures underlying LEA have a flexible set of instructional procedures that can be implemented in many classrooms with a wide variety of learners.

To obtain dictated texts with groups of students, teachers follow six steps:

**English Language
Learners**

1. Provide a stimulus: some event or interesting happening (in or out of the classroom), a field trip, a story read aloud or viewed, a classroom visitor, and other activities. Content area connections are also fruitful sources for dictated texts. In science, students may observe weather patterns or plant growth, for example, and in social studies they may dictate texts about famous people, current events,

holidays, or elections. Family events, stories, and experiences can also be the basis for individual LEA activities. Several additional examples are described in the next section.

2. Initiate discussion. Encourage students to talk about their thoughts, opinions, or feelings. Facilitate the discussion by acknowledging learners' contributions, inviting summarization, and encouraging further exploration.

3. When discussion seems complete, begin to take dictation. Encourage children to recapture the discussion so that you can write it for them. The length of dictated texts varies, but for beginners, short texts (perhaps six to eight sentences) work well. Write on chart paper, the chalkboard, an overhead transparency, or the computer if you have access to an LCD panel. Use print that is large enough for the whole group to read. Space words clearly. Say the words as you write them. Use standard spelling and adhere to capitalization and punctuation rules. Don't edit the text in any other way, though. Record students' language exactly as expressed.

4. After the dictation is complete, reread it aloud. Encourage learners to read it silently as well. Ask children if they want to make changes, and make those requested. Finally, ask learners to provide a title for their text (i.e., the main idea).

5. Read and reread the dictation several times as a group, which also builds fluency.

6. Draw students' attention to interesting words within the text they developed. Use these words as the basis for word study.

7. Make individual copies of the text for further use. Study individual sentences, lines, phrases, words, and word parts within the text. (See the next section, Obtaining Dictations.)

The same procedures work for taking individual dictations. The text can be written on regular paper or the computer. With individuals, it's often helpful for the child to sit at your side (to the left if you are right-handed), so that he or she can watch as you print the words on the page.

Obtaining Dictations

Although children are often interested in speculating about outside-the-classroom events, most teachers also plan classroom experiences that will lead naturally to dictation. These experiences need not be spectacular; in fact, the typical classroom routine offers

Technology

many opportunities for LEA. What happens during the experience and how the teacher facilitates children's learning, however, are very important.

Think about Gloria's role during the buttons lesson described at the beginning of the chapter. The lesson was successful, we believe, because of what she did and did not do. She encouraged the children to express their thoughts and to share their ideas with one another, but she did not tell children what to think or say. For example, she asked children, "What did you notice?" and let children generate categories, rather than telling them which categories to use. She facilitated language and learning without controlling it. She also encouraged summarizing at appropriate points in the lesson by asking questions such as, "What have we been doing?"

In other words, Gloria's primary function was to keep conversation flowing. She chose her words carefully because she knew their importance. As Joan Tough (1979) notes, "If we are to use talk as a means of supporting and extending children's learning then we must select what we say with the same awareness and deliberateness as we would when we select and use other resources" (p. 80).

At the dictation stage, Gloria encouraged children to summarize their learning. She recorded children's comments verbatim rather than making editorial changes or even suggestions. This, too, was done purposefully. Gloria wanted children to maintain interest in the dictated text so that they would want to reread it, and she knew that children would be more interested in language that was their own. She also knew that maintaining the children's exact language would facilitate their learning about connections between oral and written language and about the conventions of print. As LEA evolves in the classroom, it may be possible to address issues of revising and editing the text that children present orally to demonstrate that written text is often revised and is rarely a direct transcription of talk. But especially at first, teachers should write down exactly what students say.

Dictation can occur in whole group, small group, or individual situations. The overall LEA procedures remain the same. Good LEA activities feature lots of language, sharing, exploration, and problem solving. Here, for example, is part of a book dictated by several children who were just beginning a library unit in their special reading class. They had discussed how valuable the library was for finding answers to questions, and Gary, their teacher, asked them what they would like to learn:

"I would like to learn about dinosaurs. I know almost everything, but how big is T. Rex? I know how big some dinosaurs are."

By Akio

"I would like to learn how the world spins around. I want to learn if it spins on anything or not."

By Alison

The children didn't just ask questions. With help from Gary and the school librarian, they found answers. These, too, were dictated. Eventually, Gary and the students put the questions and answers into a class book about the library project.

Sometimes LEA activities can promote the use of specific vocabulary. Kay, a kindergarten teacher we introduced in Chapter 11, wanted children to learn color words, number words, and names for parts of the body. So she arranged an activity where children worked together to make a creature out of large, colorful, interlocking blocks. Her hope was that the activity would encourage children to dictate some color words, number words, and words for body parts. Here's the children's text:

The Crazy Monster

We made a crazy monster. It had twelve eyes. It had two necks for its two heads. It had a hat on each head. It had eyes on each head. We thought the monster was funny. But the crazy monster is also a little scary.

Kay's plan worked pretty well. The children dictated number words and names for parts of the body. They didn't use color words, though, and Kay didn't force the issue. She knew that the text must reflect the children's ideas, not hers. She also knew she could plan another LEA to invite focus on color words.

Content area study offers LEA opportunities. Dorr (2006) suggests that dictations can serve as transitions between children's prior knowledge and the texts they will encounter, which helps to broaden and deepen their content knowledge base. Another natural use of LEA is to summarize an entire unit of study. The text shown next, also from Kay's kindergarten classroom, was created at the end of several weeks' study about birds. Children had heard and read stories, poems, and nonfiction texts about birds; listened to recordings of bird sounds; and visited the bird exhibit at the local zoo. The dictation offered them an opportunity to summarize and synthesize what they had learned, and the resulting text became a permanent record for their continued use.

Birds

Birds have feathers. A lot of birds can fly. Some birds walk. Some birds swim. Birds are different colors. Birds can be big or small. Some birds have crests. All birds have bills. All birds lay eggs. Birds eat different things.

Literature, too, can serve as a stimulus for dictation. After hearing a favorite book, children can dictate their reactions or recount their favorite episodes. They can also create their own versions of a story or poem, a procedure called copy change (introduced in Chapter 5 and also described later in this chapter). Many of the words from the original text show up in students' dictated or copy change texts. Wayne's students enjoy dictating stories to accompany wordless picture books. The classroom library contains copies of the children's texts in large ziplock bags along with copies of the wordless books. "Children love these!" he says. "It's not unusual to see a student spend lots of time—sometimes almost an hour—poring over different versions of a wordless book, comparing them to each other and the pictures. It's amazing."

LEA activities can also "glue" several aspects of a lesson together. For example, Sue, a Title I reading teacher, read the book *Shadow* (Brown 1986). Then she and her second-grade students, all of whom were beginning readers, talked about shadows, what makes them, and where they are found. Next, each child stood in the light beam of the overhead projector, and Sue traced the child's shadow using white chalk on a piece of black construction paper that had been taped to the chalkboard. Children cut their silhouettes out and glued them on large pieces of construction paper.

The next day, Sue read some of the sentences from June Behrens's (1968) book *Who Am I?* She selected only sentences beginning with *I* because she wanted to encourage her beginning readers to dictate sentences beginning with *I*. Then she and the students discussed things that were different about each person, such as eye color, length of hair, color of skin, and gender. Children dictated riddles about themselves that ended with "Who am I?" They copied their riddles onto the construction paper next to their silhouettes. Each child then made an answer key by putting his or her name on an index card and placing it inside a library pocket card that was pasted onto the construction paper.

Sue found the entire LEA very rewarding. "The children were surprised to see how much their silhouettes resembled them," she commented. "They were fascinated by the shadows. Before we even wrote the riddles, they were trying to guess whose was whose. And then when the riddles were written, they LOVED reading them and guessing. I think each child preferred his or her own riddle, though. I noticed that they read their own riddles again and again."

Language-experience approach is an obvious and successful instructional activity for ELL students. The conversations that precede dictations and the talk surrounding preparing the dictated texts are just the types of social interactions that support new language learning (Perez 2004). ELL students may use words or even entire sentences from their native languages as they dictate (Meier 2004). Maria's dictation about the class parakeet (el perico) offers an example of this kind of code mixing:

> Our perico is blue. El perico sings and chirps. Food of the bird he eats. El perico sleeps when we put a cloth on his cage. We will try to teach el perico to talk.

> by Maria

Autumn, Maria's teacher, uses these dictations to support Maria's English learning. "I'll add the English word using a different color marker to Maria's texts. That way when she practices the texts, she has the support of her familiar Spanish." Autumn has taught Mrs. Gomez, a parent volunteer who speaks Spanish, how to serve as a scribe so that she can take Maria's dictations in Spanish. Then she and Maria translate them into English. All children in the class have access to Spanish and English versions of the same text. Autumn has noticed positive benefits: "My English-speaking students are fascinated to compare the two texts. They really puzzle over words, and I've noticed them picking up some Spanish. And Maria seems to love this. I think the whole procedure shows her that we really do value her language."

English Language
Learners

LEA and Individual Students

Dictations with individuals have the added benefit of bringing the child's unique interests into the classroom. Most children have interests that may not be addressed during instruction in school. Providing texts for students to read that reflect their interests can be a powerful motivator for reading growth.

For example, Nancy's son Matt is a sports fanatic. When he was a little boy, he used to spend hours poring over the sports pages in the newspapers and magazines about professional sports. He was particularly drawn to charts, such as the ones shown in Figure 13.1, which came from a magazine about professional football that reviewed the 1986 season and made predictions about the 1987 season.

Matt used these three charts, which summarized the 1986 seasons for the Buffalo Bills, the Cleveland Browns, and the Chicago Bears, to dictate the following text to his mom.

What I Like about Football

What I like about football is to watch it on TV because it has a lot of tackling and sacking and stuff like that. Now we go on to the statistics.

OK, I'll tell about the Bills, the Browns, and the Bears. In the Bills' first game they lost to the New York Jets to kick off the football season. The final score was New York 28 and poor Buffalo had 24. In the second game of the season they lost again, a surprising loss for the Bills. Except this time they lost it 33–36. But luck is going to change for the Bills. It finally turns around, 17–10 for the Bills. Bills in front; Cardinals in back.

In the Browns' first game of the 1986 season, they lost to the Bears, 31–41. But luck may change for the Browns, and it does, 23–20. They pick up a win against the patriotic Patriots. Then luck turns around again. This time the Chiefs beat the Browns, believe it or not, 33–13.

I want to tell about the Bears because they're my favorite team. The first game of the season they won against the Browns, but we already know that, 31–41. Then they beat the Steelers, and then they beat the Giants. Then they picked up another win off Kansas City, 44–7.

Why do I like the Bears so much? Because they've had great talent over the years. Another reason is the Bears are just a winning team.

Like they won the Super Bowl, 46–10. And the Pats are good, but not too good for the Bears. It was one of the great challenges of my life to see my team win the Super Bowl!

By Matt, age 6

We might add that Matthew is today a college graduate and successful business executive who uses his own words and language in his work. He also continues to be a football fanatic!

Figure 13.1 Matt's Football Charts

Buffalo Bills 1986 Results		
Sept. 7	NEW YORK JETS	24-28
Sept. 14	at Cincinnati	33-36
Sept. 21	ST. LOUIS	17-10
Sept. 26	KANSAS CITY	17-20
Oct. 5	at New York Jets	13-14
Oct.12	at Miami	14-27
Oct.19	INDIANAPOLIS	24-13
Oct. 26	NEW ENGLAND	3-23
Nov. 2	at Tampa Bay	28-34
Nov. 6	PITTSBURGH	16-12
Nov. 16	MIAMI	24-34
Nov. 23	at New England	19-22
Nov. 30	at Kansas City	17-14
Dec. 7	CLEVELAND	17-21
Dec. 14	at Indianapolis	15-24
Dec. 21	at Houston	7-16

Cleveland Browns 1986 Results		
Sept. 7	at Chicago	31-41
Sept. 14	at Houston	23-20
Sept. 18	CINCINNATI (Thurs.)	13-30
Sept. 26	DETROIT	24-21
Oct. 5	at Pittsburgh	27-24
Oct.12	KANSAS CITY	20-7
Oct.19	GREEN BAY	14-17
Oct. 26	at Minnesota	23-30
Nov. 2	at Indianapolis	24-9
Nov. 10	MIAMI (Mon.)	26-16
Nov. 16	at Los Angeles Raiders	14-27
Nov. 23	PITTSBURGH	37-31
Nov. 30	HOUSTON	13-10
Dec. 7	at Buffalo	21-17
Dec. 11	at Cincinnati	34-3
Dec. 21	SAN DIEGO	47-17

Chicago Bears 1986 Results		
Sept. 7	CLEVELAND	41-31
Sept. 14	PHILADELPHIA	13-10
Sept. 22	at Green Bay (Mon.)	25-12
Sept. 28	at Cincinnati	44-7
Oct. 5	MINNESOTA	23-0
Oct.12	at Houston	20-7
Oct.19	at Minnesota	7-23
Oct. 26	DETROIT	13-7
Nov. 3	L.A. RAMS (Mon.)	17-20
Nov. 9	at Tampa Bay	23-3
Nov. 16	at Atlanta	13-10
Nov. 23	GREEN BAY	12-10
Nov. 30	PITTSBURGH	13-10
Dec. 7	TAMPA BAY	48-14
Dec. 15	at Detroit (Mon.)	16-13
Dec. 21	at Dallas	24-10

Dictated texts are valuable and effective as reading materials for beginning readers. LEA activities enhance written language awareness and demonstrate the connection between spoken and written language. As children watch their words being recorded, they learn that print is meaningful; they also learn about the conventions of printed language. And they learn that writing is valuable for preserving information, ideas, and feelings. Teachers who rely on LEA also note its flexibility. Any curricular area can provide the stimulus for dictation, and subsequent reading can foster content area learning as well as reading growth.

Later, as children mature in their writing ability, students can write texts based on their own experiences. This is LEA at its zenith and, we contend, the type of experience-based writing that many professional writers do for a living!

Using LEA Texts for Extended Reading and Word Exploration

Dictations can be used like any other reading material. For example, children can read and reread current and previous dictations, either silently or with a partner. Many teachers make dictation notebooks, individual three-ring binders, so that students have easy access to the texts they have helped to prepare.

Sometimes teachers prepare their own versions of students' texts to provide extra practice with texts and words. These teacher-developed texts contain the same content and most of the same words but differ in form from the students' original text. Here, for example, is Gloria's version of *Buttons*:

> We put the buttons into piles called categories. One pile was smooth buttons, and one pile was rough buttons. Some buttons were lumpy. Some were shiny. We made categories for the buttons.

Gloria's version contains the same ideas and the same words as the children's version, but the words have been reorganized into different sentences.

The teacher can also develop questions to accompany dictated texts, such as "How many categories did we have?" or "One pile was smooth buttons. What was the other pile?" Cloze exercises (see Chapter 12) can also be developed from dictated texts (e.g., "We put _____ into piles called _____").

Children can illustrate their dictated texts. They can also make books by cutting longer dictations apart. Each sentence can be pasted on a different page and illustrated. Some teachers make story puzzles by cutting dictated texts into sentences and asking children to reassemble the sentences in ways that make sense to them. All these activities involve reading and rereading the texts and, as such, are valuable for building sight vocabulary and developing fluency in reading. Many word- and sound-related activities, which we discuss extensively in other chapters, are also possible. For example, children can find words containing word families in their dictations.

Dictated texts can be used for teacher-directed instruction as well. Beginning readers need to learn about the conventions of print, the ways written language is similar to and yet different from oral language. Oral language is a steady stream of speech, but in writing, words are separated from one another on the page. And then there's directionality: in English, letters in a word and words on a line are arranged from left to right, and lines on a page are generally arranged from top to bottom. Readers take all these aspects of written language for granted, but beginners must develop these understandings for themselves.

Much of this learning happens informally. When children watch something being read, they gain knowledge about the conventions of print. This is one reason why it's so helpful for teachers to say words while writing them during dictation. Some teachers even provide running commentaries about the conventions of print while they record children's words. They say things like, "OK, that's the end of the sentence, so I'll put a period here. This new sentence will need a capital letter." Over time, such informal and incidental learning pays dividends in terms of children's understandings.

More formal instruction can also be planned. In the Crazy Monster lesson described earlier, Kay's follow-up activities focused on print conventions. She conducted the lesson the day after the children had built the monster. The children were seated around a large copy of their dictated text.

- Kay asked about the title: "How many words are in the title?" "Where's the first word in the title?" "Where's the last word?" "Who can circle all the words in the title?"

- She asked about the first and last words in the story. The children found them and circled them.

- She asked children to find sentences: "Where does the first sentence begin?" "Where does it end?" "How can we tell when a sentence begins?" "How can we tell when a sentence ends?" "How many sentences are in our story?" "How many lines?"

- She used her word whopper (see Chapter 7) to isolate words in the text that students were asked to read.

- She asked children to match lines from the story with strips of paper that contained the lines. In each case, Kay and the children discussed how many sentences the lines contained and whether or not the lines made sense by themselves.

- She asked children to match words from the story with word cards that contained the words.

- She played word sort games (see Chapter 11). Kay and the children also played word-changing games, which involved changing letters to make new words (e.g., *hats* became *rats* and *bats*; *scary* became *Mary*; *funny* became *fun*). Kay invited all children to participate in these activities; the kindergartners who were beginning to read had the most success with these word-level games. Kay didn't worry about frustrating the others, however, because they found success with other activities more focused on print conventions. In this way she was able to differentiate instruction to accommodate all children's needs and abilities.

In this lesson, Kay's students worked with parts of written language—lines, sentences, and words. Nevertheless, they were also working with familiar and meaningful text, which provided support and allowed them to discover the relationship between the parts and the whole. Over time, activities like these can help beginning readers learn about the conventions of print.

Many of these same activities can serve diagnostic functions. Consider the preceding questions, for example. Which could Kay use if she were interested in determining students' conceptual knowledge of sentences? Words? Teachers can also gain insight into children's literacy development while they practice reading individual copies of their dictated texts. For example, teachers can see who has mastered directionality, who has mastered the concept of word, who is able to read fluently, and who can use word recognition strategies to help them recognize words. Comprehension can be checked by asking children to read old dictations and retell them in their own words. Retellings can be evaluated according to breadth and sequence. Many additional diagnostic suggestions are provided by Ann Agnew (1982); we have used variations of her ideas for more than a decade and have found them helpful for exploring children's growth in literacy.

Copy Change

As we saw with Sue's shadow lessons, children's literature or poetry can be an effective springboard for dictation or writing. After the teacher reads several fairy tales to the class, for example, discussion and subsequent dictation can focus on common elements. Children can use these dictated notes to create their own tales, perhaps by changing the characters or updating the plots. In this manner, "Little Red Riding Hood" might become "Dirty Old Baseball Hat" or Goldilocks might visit the home of three roller-bladers.

As we noted in Chapter 5, predictable literature is a good choice for copy change. *The Important Book* (Brown 1949/1999), for example, has a readily recognizable pattern that children can easily use to create their own versions. This book is particularly useful during the first days of school. After having read or listened to Brown's descriptions of important things, students can write or dictate descriptions of themselves using the same format ("The important thing about Karen is . . ."). Individual student contributions, as well as one the teacher writes, can be collected to form a class "Introductions" book. Copies of the book can also be made for each student to take home to read with family members, perhaps inspiring development of a "Family Important Book."

Poetry is another good choice for copy change activities. Judith Viorst's (1981) poem "If I Were in Charge of the World" is a favorite among teachers and students we know. Its four stanzas follow a pattern, with the first line of each stanza repeating the contrived scenario of the poem's title. Marala read this poem several times over several days to her third-grade students. Then she asked the children what they noticed about how Judith Viorst created the poem: "What did she say again and again? How did she set up the verses?" As students offered ideas, Marala wrote them on the chalkboard:

- Every one starts the same.
- The kid wants to change bad things or to get good things.
- There are usually four things in the verse.

After the students had dictated their thoughts about Viorst's patterns, Marala invited them to create their own versions. Here are two:

If I was in charge of the universe
I could do anything I wanted to do.
I could play computer games all day long.
I could run really fast and even fly.

By Patrick

If I was in charge of the school
Everyone would have computers.
Nobody would have worksheets.
We would have lots of recesses.
We could play outside or swim in a pool.

By Amanda D.

Students can also recast a favorite story in the form of a script to be performed for others. This, too, is a copy change because the original story serves as a framework for the new version. Here, for example, is the beginning of a script based on *Ira Sleeps Over* (Waber 1972) that Bonnie's second-graders developed and later performed:

Ira: I'm going to sleep over at Reggie's house.

Sister: Are you taking your teddy bear?

Ira: Take my teddy bear? No, I'm not taking my teddy bear!

Sister: But you've never slept without your teddy bear. Won't you feel funny?

Ira: I'll feel fine!

Narrator: Now Ira started thinking. Maybe he did need his teddy bear.

To support children's script development, Bonnie first read the book to them a couple of times. Then the children decided who the characters would be and what they would say. Bonnie took dictation during this discussion.

An instructional routine developed by Smith, Walker, and Yellin (2004) combines reading children's literature, developing phonological awareness, dictation, and copy change. The routine reflects the whole-to-part-to-whole framework we advocate throughout this book. It begins with shared reading of a predictable book (see Chapter 5), after which the teacher and students focus first on rhyming words from the book and then on the rimes they represent. Rimes are listed, children dictate a frame from the book to be used as copy change, and then they create and read their own books. Research with this routine, which elegantly connects word study, dictation, fluency practice, and writing instruction, shows that it yields significant growth on a standardized reading test.

Like LEAs, students' copy change texts and their scripts can be used to help beginning readers develop concepts about printed language; build a sight vocabulary; and learn about the features of words, sentences, and sounds. Copy change activities encourage careful reading, listening, and thinking so that children can discover and subsequently use the author's pattern. They also provide a structural framework or scaffold that makes writing easier for students. And, like other LEA activities, they yield lots of interesting material to read and perform.

In Conclusion

Language experience is an elegant and well-articulated approach to literacy instruction that is grounded in decades of research and professional practice. Whether dictated texts originate in a classroom experience or are based on a piece of literature, the familiarity afforded by children's own language provides a strong scaffold to support beginning reading success and word learning.

Children enter school as competent and creative language users who already know how to learn. Children will approach reading with the same enthusiasm and problem-solving ability they used in learning to talk if instruction focuses on thinking, communication, interaction, and their own experiences. Experience-based instruction offers all this and more; LEA experiences demonstrate a genuine caring for learners and respect for their experiences, interests, and motivations. This caring and respect helps to create self-confident learners who know how to work with one another in cooperative and responsible ways. To us, LEA is more than a reading method. It's a way to help children learn about life inside and outside the classroom. More important, it's a vehicle for helping children develop as informed, confident, and caring human beings.

References

Agnew, A. T. (1982). Using children's dictations to assess code consciousness. *The Reading Teacher, 35*, 450–454.

Allen, R. V. (1976). *Language experiences in communication*. Boston: Houghton Mifflin.

Ashton-Warner, S. (1963). *Teacher*. New York: Scholastic.

Barone, D. (1996). Whose language? Learning from bilingual learners in a developmental first-grade classroom. In D. Leu, C. Kinzer, and K. Hinchman (Eds.), *Literacies for the 21st century: Research and practice* (pp. 170–182). Chicago: National Reading Conference.

Dorr, R. (2006). Something old is new again: Revisiting language experience. *The Reading Teacher, 60*, 138–146.

Hall, M. (1985). Focus on language experience learning and teaching. *Reading, 19*, 5–12.

Helman, L. and Burns, M. (2008). What does oral language have to do with it? Helping young English language learners acquire a sight word vocabulary. *The Reading Teacher, 62*, 14–19.

Huey, E. B. (1908/1968). *The psychology and pedagogy of reading*. Cambridge, MA: MIT Press.

Meier, D. (2004). *The young child's memory for words*. New York: Teachers College Press.

Padak, N. and Rasinski, T. (1996). LEA in ERIC. *Language Experience Forum, 26*, 2, 4–5.

Perez, B. (2004). Language, literacy, and biliteracy. In B. Perez (Ed.), *Sociocultural contexts of language and literacy* (2nd ed., pp. 25–56). Mahwah, NJ: Erlbaum.

Rippa, S. A. (1984). *Education in a free society* (5th ed.). New York: Longman.

Smith, M., Walker, B., and Yellin, D. (2004). From phonological awareness to fluency in each lesson. *The Reading Teacher, 58*, 302–307.

Stauffer, R. G. (1969). *Directing reading maturity as a cognitive process*. New York: Harper and Row.

Tough, J. (1979). *Talk for teaching and learning*. Portsmouth, NH: Heinemann.

Veatch, J. (1986). Teaching without texts. *Journal of Clinical Reading, 2*, 32–35.

Children's Literature Cited

Behrens, J. (1968). *Who am I?* Chicago: Children's Press.

Brown, M. (1986). *Shadow*. New York: Aladdin.

Brown, M. W. (1949/1999). *The important book*. New York: HarperCollins.

Viorst, J. (1981). *If I were in charge of the world and other worries*. New York: Atheneum.

Waber, B. (1972). *Ira sleeps over*. Boston: Houghton Mifflin.

14

Word Games

Excitement is in the air. It's Friday afternoon and Angie's second-grade students spend the last 30 minutes of the school week playing word games. Angie has introduced students to a number of word games throughout the year, and this afternoon Wordo and Team Scattergories are on the agenda. Her students love to play these games.

> Many children who show up in my classroom early in the morning or have to wait for their bus after school find word games a good way to spend those few extra minutes. In fact, so many parents have asked about our games that I did two Make-It-Take-It workshops for parents this year. In October we made a reading game and in January we did a math game. My parents find that this is an easy way to help their children and have some fun at the same time.

As proficient adult readers, you automatically recognize nearly all the words you encounter in everyday reading. How did you achieve this proficiency? Most likely through repeated exposures—the more you saw certain words, the stronger your mental image became for them, to the point where they became sight words.

The goal of any word recognition program is for readers to recognize nearly all words automatically or by sight. Sight vocabulary develops through repeated exposure to words. Gates (1931) determined that learners of average intelligence require approximately 35 exposures to a word before it can be easily recognized; less able learners need about 55 exposures.

Most of the many exposures to words that lead to sight vocabulary growth come from wide reading. That is why the most frequent words (e.g., the Dolch list or the Fry Instant Word List) are good candidates for sight learning—the reader sees frequent words repeatedly, easily adding them as sight words. Lots of contextual reading, including independent reading in school and pleasure reading at home, helps to build sight vocabulary. Again, then, we return to the notion that the foundation of any good word recognition reading program is lots of reading for real purposes.

We (Tim and Nancy) love to play games in our family gatherings. We were stunned a while back when we inventoried all the games our families have played—Scrabble, Boggle, Balderdash, Wheel of Fortune, Password, Buzzword, Taboo, Quiddler, Bananagrams, Scrabble Slam!, crossword puzzles, and others. What stunned us what not that we liked to play games, but that so many of the games we played were word games in one sense or another. If we as adults love to play games with our family members, why wouldn't students in school?

Students' exposure to (and thoughtful consideration of) words can also be enhanced through word games in the classroom and at home. In this chapter we suggest some successful word games that provide additional practice for students in learning to recognize and understand written words. Word games can also be devised to reinforce phonics patterns, generalizations, word meanings, or other significant word recognition skills and strategies.

Many word games can be developed or adapted for classroom use. The ones described in this chapter are only a beginning. Some games are designed for children to play independently and so may be useful in classroom centers, and others may involve you or a more capable other, such as a parent volunteer or older student. We encourage you to develop your own word games for your students. The key is to ensure that all students participate all the time. If only one or two students in a group of 25 are attending to the game at any one time, then only those one or two gain from the experience.

Wordo

One of our favorite word games is Wordo, a takeoff of Bingo. A 5 × 5 game card grid is used, very similar to the one in Bingo; however, instead of each box being filled with a number, in Wordo, each box contains a word.

To play, select at least 24 or 25 words and provide a Wordo card for each player (see Figure 14.1). The words can be spelling words or words

Figure 14.1 Wordo Card

from specific word recognition lessons, a word bank, or various content areas. List the words on the chalkboard and ask students to copy them randomly on their game cards, one word per box. The center box can be marked Free. Random word placement is important; if everyone uses the same order, all players win at the same time! The teacher also writes the words on a set of 3 × 5 cards, shuffles them, and spreads them out, written side down, on a table.

The game begins when the teacher (or a student) draws a word card from those spread out and calls out the selected word. Students search for this word, and if it appears on their card, they cover it with a marker (dried lima beans make good, inexpensive markers). The game continues in this way until a student achieves Wordo by getting a line of markers in a row, column, or diagonal. A small prize is often given to the winner, game cards are cleared, and a new game begins.

Rather than simply call out selected words, the moderator may want to give other clues such as the definition, a sentence in which the selected word is deleted, or structural clues, such as "The word I selected has two syllables, begins with a consonant blend, and contains a diphthong."

To use these more subtle clues students must examine the words on their cards in a little more depth.

Younger students may be a bit overwhelmed by games cards that contain 24 empty boxes. For students just beginning to learn about words and Wordo, you can use games cards that are made up of a 3 × 3 or 4 × 4 matrix.

The Wordo concept can also be used to teach initial letters and letter sounds. In this version of Wordo, usually done with a 3 × 3 game card for younger children (see Figure 14.2), students write initial consonant letters or blends on their cards in random fashion—one letter or blend for each box . Then, the teacher calls out words that contain one of the sounds or shows a picture that begins with one of the sounds. Students find the appropriate beginning letter or blend and cover it with a marker. The same idea can also be employed with ending letters and sounds, affixes, and vowels and their corresponding sounds.

Students love to play Wordo. It is certainly an enjoyable way to review words you want students to learn and to provide the necessary practice for adding the words to their sight vocabularies.

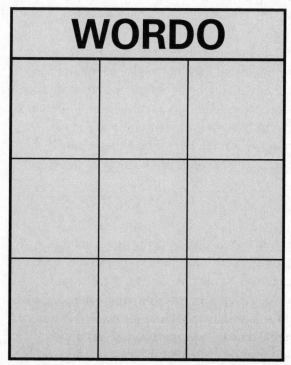

Figure 14.2 3 X 3
Wordo Card

Word War

Word War, a version of the card game War, is best played by a group of two to four students. A deck of word cards is needed. This can be accomplished by giving each group of students a deck of 3 × 5 cards, asking students to divide them up, and having them write a word on each card. Students can use word wall words (see Chapter 9), words related to some area of study, or interesting words. Once created, the Word War cards can be used for many weeks, and new words can be added to the deck as needed.

Students can also use words from their word banks (see Chapter 11 for more on word banks). Of course, if you choose this option, students will need to mark their own cards in some way (perhaps their initials) so that they can retrieve their cards at the end of the game.

Once the deck is established, all the word cards are put together, shuffled, and distributed to each player, face down. An agreed-on time limit is set, usually 5 or 10 minutes, and the game begins. Each player plays one card face up from his or her deck. The player must be able to pronounce the word in order to continue the play. Once each player presents a card and pronounces it, the player with the longest word wins the round and all the cards that were played. These words go to the bottom of the player's pile.

New rounds are the same. If, however, the longest word is shared by two or more players, then a war ensues. Each of the players involved in the tie plays another card face down and then one face up and pronounces it. The player with the longer of the second face-up cards wins all the cards played in that round. Another tie brings on another war, and so forth.

Play continues in this manner until the timer bell goes off. At this point, players count their cards. The player with the most cards wins.

Pick Up Sticks

Played with two to four students, Pick Up Sticks requires a set of popsicle sticks with words to be practiced written on one end of each stick. One stick has the word ZAP! written at the end. All sticks are placed word-end down, into a can, cup, or some other opaque container.

Play begins with one student pulling a stick up from the container. If the player can pronounce the word, he or she gets to keep the stick. If the word cannot be pronounced quickly it must be returned to the container. In turn, each player pulls one stick at a time. Play continues until the ZAP! stick is pulled. At this point, the player with the most sticks is the winner. Students love the suspense that develops as the number of remaining sticks becomes smaller and smaller.

Match (Concentration)

Match is another word card game and is best played in pairs. Two word cards are made for each word used in the game. Usually, between 10 and 15 words (20 to 30 cards) are sufficient. Students can make word cards from a clean deck of 3×5 cards, or they can be drawn from students' personal word banks. If drawn from word banks, the cards need to be marked for easy return to the owner, and players must ensure that each card has a match.

The card deck is shuffled and laid out in a grid, face down. Students take turns turning over and pronouncing two cards at a time. If the two word cards match, the student wins the pair and selects another two cards. If the cards do not match, the cards are turned back over and the next player takes a turn. Play continues until all cards have been matched. Players count the cards they have accumulated, and the player with the most cards is the winner.

Variations of the game can be created by changing the criteria for matching cards. The matched pairs could be rhyming words; words with the same beginning letter, letter combination, or sound; words with the same ending; words with the same number of syllables; or words that are synonyms or antonyms. Match can also be played with pictures and words, which is a useful adaptation for English language learner (ELL) students.

Go Fish

Another matching game is a variation of the classic card game Go Fish. Go Fish also requires a deck of word cards that match in some way (e.g., same words, rhyming words, words that begin with the same letters or sounds, words with the same meaning). Ideally played with four or five players, students are each dealt five cards and the remaining cards are spread out in the middle of the table as the card pond. The object of the game is to find matches to the words in your hand.

A turn begins when a player examines his or her cards and asks a second player for a card that matches a criterion (e.g., "Do you have a word the rhymes with *cat*?"). If the second player has such a card, it's given to the first player, who matches it and lays the pair down face up. The first player then makes another request for a card. If the second player doesn't have the requested card, the first player must "go fish" and draw a card from the pond. If the card matches one in the player's hand, he or she lays it down, face up, and takes another turn. If a match cannot be made, the next player's turn begins. Play continues until one player matches all the cards in her or his hand.

Scoring is variable; usually players get one point for each card matched but must subtract a point for each card that remains in their hands at the end of a round. The game continues until one player's cards are all on the table or until a certain point limit is reached, usually 50 to 100.

Make Words with Cubes

Make Words with Cubes requires a set of blank cubes or dice that can be purchased at many teacher supply stores. Individual letters or letter combinations are written on each side of the cube. If cubes cannot be found, you can take a set of dice, white out the dots, and write in individual letters and letter combinations. Alphabet blocks can also be used. (Another variation is simply to list 6 to10 letters or letter combinations on the chalkboard.)

The game can be played in groups of three to five or with a larger group in which teams of two to three students work together. If cubes are available, they are shaken and spilled out on the table. A timer is set for 5 to 10 minutes and students are challenged to make as many words as they can from the given list of letters. Bear, Invernizzi, Templeton, and Johnston (2011) suggest that students record the words they make by length (see Figure 14.3). Once time has expired, students check their words and assign points (one point per letter). Other recording and scoring sheets are possible. For example, students could sort their words by number of syllables, number of consonant blends and digraphs per word, or short and long vowel sounds, with more points given to words with more syllables, more blends and digraphs, or long vowel sounds.

Figure 14.3   Cube Word Record Sheet

2 letters	3 letters	4 letters	5 letters	6 letters	7 letters	8 letters	9 letters	10 letters

Word Maker Cups

One age-old practice is to have students blend beginning consonants and blends with rimes or word families to determine the words that can be made, such as *pr + ay = pray*. Often this involves creating "sliders" in which a strip containing the beginning consonants, consonant blends, and consonant digraphs is slipped through slits in a larger piece of construction paper that contains the rimes. Moving the beginning consonant slider through the rime sheet, the student determines all the words that can be made.

This is a good activity for students learning how to blend onsets and rimes, but making sliders is time-consuming. Furthermore, sliders tend to fall apart easily when used a lot by young hands.

An alternative is to use large Styrofoam coffee cups. When two cups are stacked, their lips fit together nicely; they can also be rotated. The lips of one set of cups, then, can contain beginning consonants and blends (8 to 10 per cup should do). And the lips of the other set of cups show rimes or word families (two to four rimes per cup work best).

Figure 14.4 Word Maker Cups

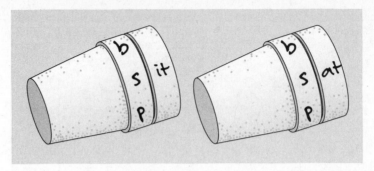

Then, have students simply take one of the beginning consonant and blend cups and one of the rime cups, fit them together, and rotate them so that all the combinations of consonants, blends, and rimes can be analyzed (see Figure 14.4). Students should jot down the words they make. Although this is not necessarily a game, it is enjoyable practice in using rimes to decode and spell words. Since word cups are inexpensive (usually 100 for a dollar or less) and easy to make (even students can make them), this is an attractive option for busy teachers (isn't that all teachers, all the time?).

Scattergories

Scattergories can be played with large groups of students; we find it best, however, if students work in teams of two or three. Scattergories is a generative game that is a great way to get students thinking about word patterns. The only requirement is a Scattergories sheet for each student or team (see Figure 14.5).

Along the top row, the teacher (and students) brainstorm about five word patterns—rimes, derivational patterns, and so on. Down the left-hand column, the teacher provides a random set of consonants and consonant blends. Then, for the next 5 to 10 minutes students think of words that begin with each consonant or blend and that contain one of the targeted patterns (see Figure 14.6 for an example).

At the end of the given time period, students score their sheets. If students are allowed to put only one word into each box, they can be given a point for every letter used in each acceptable word. This

Figure 14.5 Scattegories Form

227

Word Games

Scattergories
Word Families

Initial Letters

encourages students to think of longer words containing the targeted patterns. In another scoring scheme, students list all the words they can think of that fit each box. One point is given for each acceptable word. In this case, students are rewarded for thinking of many words that fit the given specifications.

Figure 14.6 Scattergories

Scattergories				
Word Families → **Initial Letters**	ack	ick	at	it
t	track	ticker	tattle	tacit
p	packet			pitiful
m			Matthew	
d				ditto

The game has many variations. For example, the left-hand column could contain prefixes or semantic categories that require students to orchestrate their knowledge of word patterns with the meanings of words that contain such patterns. For example, word patterns such as *il(l)*, *en*, *ack*, *ip*, and *on* could be used on the top row. The left-hand column could contain semantic categories such as *people's names*, animals, *cities and states*, and *plants*. For *people's names*, Bill, Dennis, or *Jack* could be used. For *animals*, killer whale, hen, and *hippo* would work. *Philadelphia*, *Hackensack*, and *Boston* would fit the *cities and states* category, and *dill* and *tulip* would be in the *plants* category. The many variations of Scattergories that can add depth and interest make it a very useful game for the later primary to middle school grades.

Sentencing

Word recognition also involves the ability to use context to determine unknown words in texts. One of the best games we have found for supporting this ability is called Sentencing (Hall 1995), a game similar in nature to Wheel of Fortune and Hangman, except that it uses sentences instead of individual words. Sentencing challenges students to use syntactic and semantic cues to reconstruct a sentence the teacher creates or extracts from an appropriate level text. The game involves teams of three to eight students and can be played with students in grade 3 and up. Student teams try to determine unknown words in a sentence.

After teams are set, the teacher finds a meaningful sentence of 7 to 15 words that makes strong use of syntax. The sentence should not include proper nouns or contractions. For example:

If you are hungry, look inside the refrigerator.

The sun has been shining all week long, and I love it.

Each team gets two "free letter" cards to use during the game.

The game begins with the teacher listing the sentence on the chalkboard with only one key word revealed (see Figure 14.7). This word should help students use background knowledge in making predictions about the sentence. Also, the teacher should point out to students any clues such as punctuation.

Figure 14.7

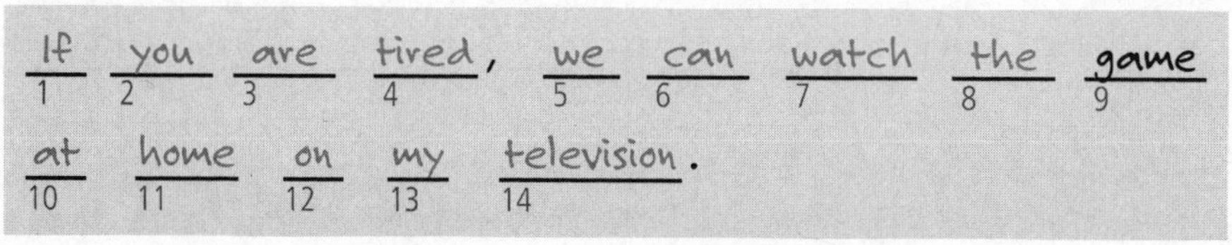

Each turn begins with the revelation of one unknown word of the team's choice. Upon revelation of the word, the team can either guess another word in the sentence, for which they will receive 2 points if correct, or they can use their "free letter" card in order to get the first (or another) letter of any unrevealed word. After seeing this letter, they must guess any unknown word in the sentence. Guessing a word that has one or more letters revealed earns 1 point.

Correct guesses allow the team to continue. An incorrect guess ends that team's turn. Play is over when the entire sentence is guessed, at which time the score is tallied for each team.

In the example shown in Figure 14.8, Team One asked for word five to be revealed. It then used its "free letter" card for the first letter of the first word of the sentence. They correctly guessed *If* after the *I* was given and earned 1 point. They then guessed *the* for word eight and received 2 more points. Their next guess, *we* for word two, was incorrect, so the turn went to Team Two.

Team Two began by asking for word fourteen to be revealed. The word was *television*. Then they used a "letter card" for the first letter in word four. This was a *t* and Team Two then guessed word two to be *you* and word three to be *are*. These guesses were worth 2 points. Team Two then guessed *tardy* for word four, which was incorrect (see Figure 14.9).

Figure 14.8

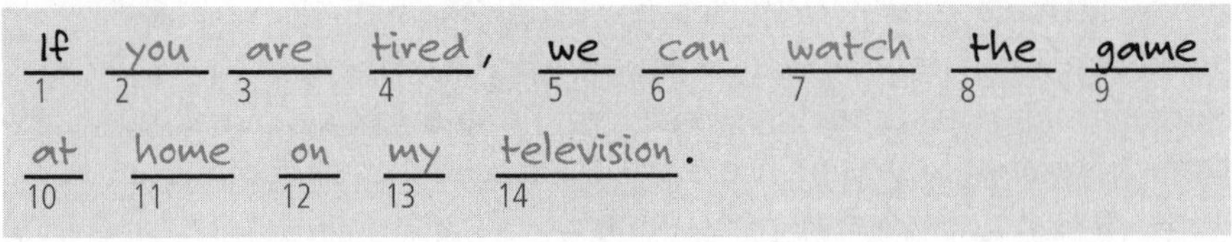

Figure 14.9

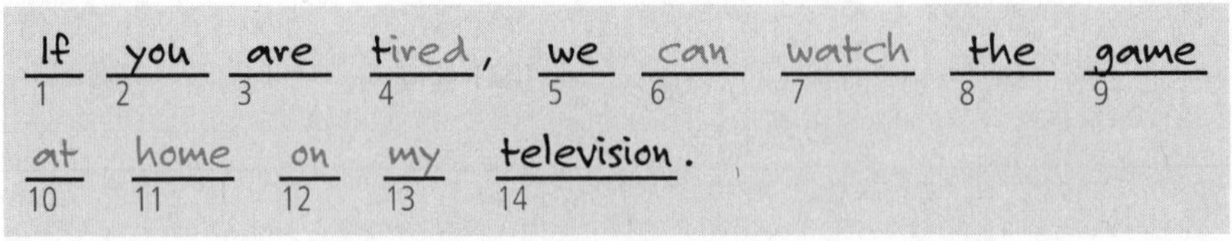

Figure 14.10

If	you	are	tired,	we	can	watch	the	game
1	2	3	4	5	6	7	8	9

at	home	on	my	television .
10	11	12	13	14

Figure 14.11

If	you	are	tired,	we	can	watch	the	game
1	2	3	4	5	6	7	8	9

at	home	on	my	television .
10	11	12	13	14

Team One then used its last "letter card" for the second letter of word four—an *i*. Team members correctly guessed the word to be *tired* for 1 point. From this point, Team One correctly guessed word seven to be *watch*, but missed word six by guessing *will* (see Figure 14.10).

Team Two asked for word ten, which was *at*, and used its "letter card" for the first letter of word eleven—an *h*. At this point, Team Two guessed word eleven to be *home* (1 point) and then correctly guessed the remainder of the sentence: word six *can* (2 points), word twelve *on* (2 points), and word thirteen *my* (2 points) (see Figure 14.11). Points were tallied: Team Two—12 points and Team One—6 points.

Although the game may seem somewhat complex, it is simple to play, and once students become familiar with the format, games tend to take no more than five minutes. Once the game is over, the teacher engages students in a quick debriefing, asking what strategies they used and what helped them figure out the sentence. Students will inform one another, within teams and later between teams, of significant and useful syntactic and semantic clues.

Word Sketches

Word Sketches (Padak and Rasinski 2009) is based on Pictionary. To play it, choose words from a text your students are currently reading or have read. Be sure to choose words that lend themselves to images. Write each word on a slip of paper, and put the slips in a cup or container. Students form teams of four to five players per team and play the game the same way they would Pictionary. One student on each team selects a word and makes a sketch that reflects its meaning without saying the word itself. Other members of the team try to guess the word. Determine the time required to guess the word correctly (limit the time to about a minute per word). Once a word is guessed, the other team has its turn. The game ends when all members of both teams have had a chance to be the "sketcher." The team that takes fewest total seconds to determine their words is the winner.

Word Theater

Word Theater (Padak and Rasinski 2009) is a classroom version of Charades. Set the game up in the same way that you set up Word Sketches—you'll need a set of words on paper slips in a cup and two teams of students. Then play the game as you would Charades. Instead of drawing sketches of the words, students act out their chosen word while other members of the team attempt to guess it. Each member of both teams has a chance to choose and act out a word. The team that requires the least time to guess their words wins the game.

Word-Part Rummy

This is a card game in which the cards contain word parts (prefixes, suffixes, roots) that can go together to form words (Padak and Rasinski 2009). Prepare about 10 cards per player, shuffle, deal five to each player, and place the remaining cards face down in a stack. Players look for cards that create words (prefix-root, root-suffix, prefix-root-suffix, root-root) and place them face up on the table. Then they take turns drawing cards from the pile. If the drawn card does not make a match, the player discards a card, which the next player may take. Play continues until someone has matched all of his or her cards. The player with the most cards used is the winner.

Other Games

We have only scratched the surface of the possible word games teachers and students can develop and enjoy. Note also that word games can easily be adapted for home use as well (Padak and Rasinski 2009).

What could you do with cookie sheets and magnetic alphabet letters, for example? Online resources, such as those listed in the box, may also work well. Many of the word activities described in previous chapters (e.g. Making Words, Making and Writing Words, Word Ladders) also have game-like qualities.

Online Resources for Word Games

Preschool Home Activities for Parents and Children (See Rhymes and Alphabet)   www.preschoolrainbow.org

Word Central.com   www.wordcentral.com/

Puzzlemaker.com   http://puzzlemaker.school.discovery.com/index.html

Text Twist   http://games.yahoo.com/game/text-twist-applet.html

Billy Bear 4 Kids   www.billybear4kids.com/jigsaw-puzzles/main-page.html

Reading Is Fundamental   http://www.rif.org/kids/readingplanet/gamestation.htm

PBS's "Between the Lions"   http://pbskids.org/lions/games/

Miscellaneous word game sites
http://www.funbrain.com/words.html

http://www.eastoftheweb.com/games/

http://www.wordgames.com/

http://wordplays.com

http://games.yahoo.com/word-games

Games derived from the words on the word wall (see Chapter 9) are also possible. Second-grade teacher John has students do word sprints using the word wall words. Throughout the school year John adds five sight words each week to the sight word wall. The words come from the second group of 100 words from the Fry Instant Word List (Appendix B). Students pair up about once a week and each pair is given a stopwatch. While one student keeps time and checks for errors, the other student tries to read the wall as accurately and quickly as possible. The student records his or her scores, and the roles are reversed.

Scores for accuracy and time are recorded on a "personal best" sheet that each student keeps. "It's really only a tiny part of my word study and reading program, 10 minutes a week or so, and I want to make sure the students compete against themselves not others," John says, "but the improvement that the students make . . . is simply amazing. Based on their original readings of the wall, students set a goal for themselves for accuracy and speed, and if they can meet or beat their individual goals they win a certificate. The level of intensity as students practice the words on their own is impressive."

In Conclusion

Word learning and automatic word recognition require repeated exposures to words. Word games are a superb way to add those exposures, which build students' sight vocabularies. Children love to play games, and the nature of words themselves—their meaning, their grammatical categories, their orthographic makeup—make them excellent material for classroom and home reading games. Although games are only a minor part of any reading or word recognition program, they can play a significant role in adding variety, life, and practice to students' word learning.

References

Bear, D., Invernizzi, M., Templeton, S., and Johnston, F. (2011). *Words their way: Word study for phonics, vocabulary, and spelling instruction* (5th ed.). Englewood Cliffs, NJ: Prentice-Hall.

Gates, A. (1931). *Interest and ability in reading*. New York: Macmillan.

Hall, A. K. (1995). Sentencing: The psycholinguistic guessing game. *The Reading Teacher, 49,* 76–77.

Padak, N. and Rasinski, T. (2009). The games children play. *The Reading Teacher, 62,* 362–365.

15

Spelling and Word Learning

Jason, age 7, was writing a story (Harste, Woodward, and Burke 1984). One of his characters "tried again," which Jason wrote as *chridagen*. Later, while rereading his story, *chridagen* stopped him. He solved the reading problem by thinking about the meaning of the story, but the spelling bothered him. He knew it wasn't right, so, like his character, Jason tried again. His second spelling was exactly the same as his first!

Think about Jason's efforts, and you will see why we have included a chapter about spelling in a book about word learning. Say the *t* and *ch* sounds to see how your tongue is in the same place for both. Note that Jason has used the letter *i* for the long *i* sound. And *agen* is a pretty good phonetic representation of *again*. Most important is that rethinking the words, which he knew were wrong because they didn't look right, led Jason to the same spelling. Jason's story shows us that children's invented, approximated, or temporary spellings are neither random nor careless errors; they are reasoned, rule governed, and represent children's best thinking about the relationships between sounds in oral language and words in writing.

Writing instruction can play an important role in children's word learning. Writers learn about writing, reading, and words. Young writers learn how printed language works—how to make letters and words do what they want them to do. And as we can see from the story of Jason, children think carefully about how to spell the words they want to write. Thus, a strong focus on unaided writing can help children learn how to work with words.

Our focus in this chapter is not on all aspects of spelling instruction. (For more comprehensive discussions, see Bear et al. 2012; Ganske 2000; or Henderson 1990.) We examine spelling from the perspective that learning to spell augments word recognition development. Actually, many of the activities described in this book, such as Making and Writing Words (Chapter 10), support spelling development as well as word recognition.

Scholars have focused on spelling development for decades. Although the stages of children's development as spellers are well understood, there's still much that we don't know about how to support children's growth in spelling. Fortunately, teachers can use the following widely accepted guiding principles to integrate spelling instruction into their reading and writing programs (Bear et al. 2012; Fresch and Wheaton 1997; Heald-Taylor 1998; Templeton and Morris 1999):

- Learning to spell is a complex, developmental process. Spelling proficiency is related to maturation and experience in writing. Knowledge about spelling begins globally and develops gradually as children become able to develop, differentiate, and integrate insights about how letters and sounds are related.

- Spelling instruction should be a functional component of a complete writing program.

- Of several guiding principles related to instruction (Heald-Taylor 1998), two are particularly important for our purposes in this chapter. Teachers should accept children's inventions or approximations, especially initially, and use them diagnostically. In a research review related to this point, Invernizzi and Hayes (2004) concluded that whole-group instruction that is not based on students' needs is ineffective, particularly for struggling spellers. By determining what children know about letter-sound relationships, teachers can ensure appropriate emphases for instruction.

In this chapter, we address spelling issues that are directly related to children's word learning: what children learn about written language through invented spelling, how teachers can discover what children know about the way that written language works, ways to support word learning through spelling, and how and why to inform parents about this aspect of the reading-writing program.

Learning about Written Language through Spelling Approximations

Young literacy learners begin to think about written language as a system and hypothesize about how it works. They learn that lines of print in English run from left to right and top to bottom on a page, for example. Children also develop concepts about units of written language. They learn that print carries meaning and that we use certain rules or conventions of print to represent meaning. Developing a concept of word as a unit of written language is particularly important, and this is no small task. First, the child must think about language as a system, to separate the form of language from its function. Then the child must segment a steady stream of oral speech. Think about this for a moment. Recall the last time you heard someone speaking a language that was foreign to you. Could you segment the oral speech into words? Probably not, because you lack a concept for word in that language. This demonstrates the enormity of children's conceptual learning about written language. They must learn to separate, think about, and become aware of individual words within spoken language. And then, of course, children must use their knowledge of oral speech to discover that words are also units of written language. As children write (not copy), they must think about written language and about how letters and letter combinations represent sounds in language.

Children learn about written language gradually and informally. The overall learning process is the same as for any other language learning: hypothesis generation and testing. For example, simply telling children that words have spaces around them may not do much good. Children must invent their own concepts and then test them through reading and writing. This same principle applies to sound-symbol relationships in writing. Children who invent spellings get valuable practice with the sound-to-letter system. Moreover, young writers learn that the beginning-to-ending sequences of sounds in words relate, although not exactly, to the left-to-right sequences of letters in words. And this practice pays off in word learning:

> The value of encouraging and allowing young children to invent their spelling has been strongly supported by well-conducted studies. . . . When children attempt to represent their speech with letters, they are applying phonics in a truly authentic context. (Templeton and Morris 1999, p. 108)

Research-Based Strategies

Discovering What Children Know about Sounds through Spelling

Scholars have been exploring the characteristics of young children's spelling since the early 1970s, when Charles Read's (1971) landmark work showed us that young children's spelling errors are predictable and change in predictable ways over time. This research has helped us understand how spelling develops: from random, incomprehensible strings of letters (and sometimes other symbols) to spellings that show some understanding of sound-symbol relationships to conventional spelling.

Children's spelling ability begins to develop well before they enter school. In this "extended period of emergent literacy . . . children learn much about the forms and functions of print. This understanding lays the groundwork for moving into the exploration of the *alphabetic* layer of spelling" (Templeton and Morris 1999, p. 105). Exploring this alphabetic layer of spelling involves thinking about the relationship between sounds and individual letters of the alphabet. Eventually, children's focus shifts to patterns in language, such as groups of letters (e.g., *-tion*) or conceptually related words (e.g., *act*, *act*ion, re*act*or). Thus, children show us their knowledge of words and sounds through their approximations or inventions.

A great deal of this learning occurs during children's preschool through primary years. Here we explain some key features of spelling development for children at these ages, using examples from Ben's writing. Ben was a kindergartner, and his ability was average among the children in his urban classroom. Each day Kay, his teacher, encouraged students to visit the writing center, which was stocked with a variety of writing paper and instruments. The children had access to printed letters of the alphabet, which they could use or not as they wished. Ben had no other writing or spelling instruction.

Figure 15.1 is an example of the prephonemic or precommunicative stage of spelling development. At this stage, children know how letters are formed but not how they work. They have not yet discovered that letters represent speech sounds in words. Some children write random strings of letters, numbers, other symbols, or scribbles. Gentry and Gillet (1993) compare this stage to babbling as children learn to talk. In

BEN

Figure 15.1   Ben—October

late October, Ben chose to draw about Halloween. He has memorized
the spelling of his name.

By March (see Figure 15.2), Ben has progressed to the early
phonemic or semiphonetic stage of spelling development. At this stage,
children begin to use letters to represent sounds, but only very sparsely.
They sometimes begin words with one or two letters/phonemes
and end them with a random string of letters. Or they may represent
an entire word with one letter/phoneme. Teachers will see more
consistency in consonant sounds than vowel sounds. In fact, some early
phonemic spellers don't even use vowels yet. Lack of a stable concept of
word is another characteristic of early phonemic spelling.

Note that Ben is beginning to write, a sign of growth from October.
Note, too, that he knows how to spell *to* and that he can hear and
represent middle consonants (e.g., *Legos, store*) as well as beginning and
ending consonants. Examine Ben's sound-symbol understanding for a
moment. What consonant sounds does he know?

Figure 15.2   Ben—March

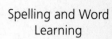

Figure 15.3   Ben—April

i like The zoo. I saw A
Porcepin. I saw all the
annumels.

By April, Ben has progressed to the letter-name or phonetic stage of spelling development (see Figure 15.3). Letter-name spellers have discovered *word* as a concept, and we can see this in Ben's writing. They spell consonant phonemes with some regularity but may omit (or have difficulty with) vowels. What consonant sounds has Ben learned since March? Letter-name spellers break words into phonemes and represent the phonemes with letters of the alphabet (e.g., sound of long *e* in *porcepin*).

Transitional spelling is the last stage before conventional spelling. At this stage, children tend to spell words in a hyper-correct manner, including all sounds (e.g., *daysees* for *daisies*). Since they can read, transitional spellers also use visual memory of how words should look as a spelling aid. Figure 15.4 summarizes stages of spelling development and offers a few instructional suggestions for each stage.

Spelling and English Language Learners

Research-Based Strategies

English Language Learners

English language learners (ELLs), who are often new to important sound-symbol aspects of English, may encounter particular challenges related to developing alphabetic and word knowledge. In a study of more than 4,000 ELLs, grades 1 through adult, Helman and Bear (2007) found that stages of spelling development hold, but that ELLs lag behind their native-English-speaking counterparts in spelling development. In fact, "more than 50% of Spanish-speaking English learners in first through third grade are not meeting benchmark levels" (Helman 2005, p. 670), compared to 18 to 22 percent of English-only children.

Knowledge of the alphabetic systems of children's native languages can help teachers support ELL children's spelling development. In Spanish, for example, vowels have single sounds, which differ from

Figure 15.4 Stages of Spelling Development (Gentry and Gillet 1993; Henderson 1990)

Stage	Characteristics	Instructional Ideas
Prephonetic (Precommunicative)	■ Know some letters but not how to make them work ■ Random letters or letter-like forms ■ No sound-letter correspondences	■ Practice phonemic segmentation (syllable claps) ■ Practice letter-sound correspondence (picture sorts) ■ Write a lot
Early Phonemic (Semiphonetic)	■ Know that letters represent sounds ■ Often begin words with one letter (usually a consonant) followed by a random collection of other letters ■ Know left-to-right progression but do not yet have stable concept of word	■ Develop concept of word ■ Use big books or other enlarged texts ■ Practice voice-pointing ■ Write a lot
Letter Name (Phonetic)	■ More sounds represented ■ May not represent vowel sounds ■ Usually have stable concept of word ■ Spell words like they sound ■ May use letter names as spelling strategy	■ Encourage inventions through demonstration ■ Word hunts, picture sorts ■ Riddles or other guessing games (e.g., I start like *happy* and rhyme with *dill*. What am I?) ■ Write a lot
Transitional	■ May over-apply rules ■ Spell by attending to sounds and visual memory	■ Begin formal spelling instruction ■ Word searches, word sorts, games (e.g., Concentration) ■ Teach strategy for word learning: look, cover, write, check ■ Write a lot

their pronunciations in English. Moreover, "the short vowels in English can be quite difficult for Spanish speakers because most of these sounds do not exist in Spanish" (Helman 2005, p. 671). Additional challenges for ELL spellers include the various and sometimes confusing sounds for letters or letter combinations in English. For example, consider the child who said *W* made the *duh* sound (say the letter and you'll understand the child's logic) (Meier 2004). Accurately determining ELL children's development of alphabetic knowledge, then, relies on an understanding of the similarities and differences in sound-symbol relationships in English and Spanish. Charting letter-sound knowledge, as shown in Figure 15.5, can help teachers discover what children have learned through writing that can apply to their reading.

Many of the instructional recommendations provided in Figure 15.4 apply to ELL students. In addition, teaching contrasts, most explicit first, between first language and English may prove beneficial (Helman

Figure 15.5 Charting Children's Letter-Sound Knowledge

	Ben	Kathy	Juan
January			
February			
March	D, G, K, M, T, W		
April	B, E, F, H, L, N, P, R, S, V		
May			

and Bear 2007). In a series of case studies of 4- and 5-year-old biliterate (Spanish and English) children, Reyes and Azuara (2008) found that children developed metalinguistic knowledge and knowledge about print in both languages, so children's first-language knowledge can serve as a platform for learning to spell in English.

Supporting Young Writers

Perhaps the most important aspect of support for young writers is the classroom atmosphere itself. Children must learn to believe in themselves as writers and to develop confidence in their ability to share what they have to say with others through writing.

Young children, who ordinarily come to school expecting to learn to read and write, may need little more than the suggestion to write. Older children, however, may not take the teacher up on invitations to write. They may have learned negative lessons, such as "I can't write" or "Writing is boring" from their previous experiences in school. The teacher's patience, passion, and persistence are critical in order for these negative lessons to be unlearned; so we advise teachers to continue to invite children to write, to praise their attempts, and to establish the expectations that everyone can write and everyone will.

First efforts from all writers, especially young ones, may be drawings rather than writing, but letters and words soon appear. Some children seem to use drawing as a way to think up or refine ideas for their writing. Other children use drawing as a sort of note-taking tool; they sketch the things they want to remember to write about. Whatever its purpose, drawing seems to facilitate writing for many children.

Opportunities to talk and listen are important. Graves (1983) describes several ways children use oral language when writing. They sometimes plan their writing by talking to themselves or others. They may also read parts of drafts to themselves, as if to get a running start on what should come next. Some children compose aloud and then translate their speech into writing. Children may also talk themselves through writing by making procedural comments such as "There! Now I need to write 'The End.'" And of course, children read drafts of their work to others, either to help solve problems they've encountered or to get more general feedback.

Children also need teacher support. Some of this support is mundane, such as having necessary supplies readily available. Children need access to many kinds of paper, lined and unlined, and a variety of writing instruments, which can be collected in the classroom writing center. Time to write is another aspect of support. Children need predictable chunks of time every week to write and to share their efforts with interested others.

Other aspects of support, especially the encouragement of spelling efforts, appear to be critical. Teachers who accept invented spellings allow their students to be precise in their use of language and true to their own meanings because they can write what they want to say, not just what they know how to spell. More important, these opportunities to manipulate words and discover spelling principles clarify phonological relationships for children.

So how can teachers support this experimentation with print? In response to a child's question about how to spell a word, for example, the teacher might ask the child to say the word, and then ask, "What sound do you hear at the beginning? What letter would that be? Good. Write it down. Now say the word again. What sound do you hear at the end?" and so on. This strategy talks children through the speech-to-print connection and encourages them to develop independence as spellers. Listening for sounds and then representing them with letters supports children's efforts at phonemic segmentation, or separating words into their component sounds.

Mini-lessons for groups or the entire class about ways to handle spelling challenges can also be worthwhile (Williams and Phillips-Birdsong 2006). For example, the teacher can

Research-Based Strategies

- Encourage children to think about words or word parts that rhyme with a word they want to spell
- Help children see how "chunking" a longer unfamiliar word can unlock secrets about its spelling
- Tell children to stretch the unfamiliar word out, to say it very slowly and to think about its component sounds
- Help children see the resources available to them: peers, the classroom word wall, a personal dictionary, environmental print, and so on

Other classroom activities that focus on sounds and words are also useful for supporting children's invented spellings. Teachers can add a brief comment about spelling when engaging children in phonemic awareness word play, for example (see Chapter 6): "So if you wanted to write a word that begins like *baby* or *ball*, what letter would you use first?" Gentle reminders to use what they know about reading and sounds as they write will help children develop proficiency as spellers.

When children have reached the transitional stage of spelling development, some more formal attention to spelling is beneficial. The words chosen for focus should be few—perhaps 10 or 12 per week. The words should reflect spelling features and patterns that children use but confuse; that is, they should be developmentally appropriate for children (Gentry and Gillet 1993; Templeton and Morris 1999). Many teachers prepare groups of words at different levels of difficulty that represent the same letter-sound patterns so that instruction can be differentiated for children of varying spelling abilities while the entire class focuses on the pattern of interest (Fresch and Wheaton 1997). Other teachers rely on diagnostic spelling tests (see, for example, Bear et al. 2012) to create spelling groups, which may differ from guided reading groups. This diagnostic assessment is helpful for all children but seems to be especially important for ELL children (Helman 2005). Regardless of how the classroom spelling program is organized, teachers will need to make a conscious effort to help children transfer their new spelling knowledge to their writing and reading. Williams and Phillips-Birdsong (2006) found that effective word study programs build on children's strengths, help them use what they already know, and increase their confidence in using this knowledge.

In a review of research about spelling instruction, Templeton and Morris (1999) comment,

> Of the few methodological studies that have been conducted, none answers to everyone's satisfaction the question of whether spelling is learned primarily through reading and writing or primarily through the systematic examination of words. . . . What does emerge from the research is the suggestion that *some* examination of words is necessary for most students. (p. 108)

The ideal spelling program, then, is a balanced combination of writing for authentic purposes and focused word study.

Many primary grade teachers struggle with the issue of standard spelling. They express concern that words be spelled correctly if

Research-Based Strategies

Research-Based Strategies

the child's written work will be read by others. As children become more conscious of standard spelling, they too may express concern about their spelling efforts. Then teachers should help them deal with these concerns. Jane Davidson suggests that teachers should reply to students' queries in their initial drafts of "Is it right?" with a statement like this: "It's good enough for now. You can read it, and I can read it. We both know what you're saying here. Later, we can change some things, if you'd like, to make them look like they do in other books." These comments help lessen concern about spelling when students are generating ideas, yet assure them that their efforts will receive the polish they deserve.

Technology

When children's spelling is fairly well developed, perhaps grade 3 or beyond, spell-checkers on word-processing programs can be useful. (At earlier stages, the program can't recognize many approximations because they bear so little resemblance to the correct spellings.) Some teachers express concern that spell-checkers might become a crutch. This may be, but they're also an aspect of modern life and likely to be even more influential in the future. To ignore their potential does students a disservice. Instead, teachers may want to reserve their use for the final draft stage of writing, when the spell-checker can do what teachers have done for decades—identify misspelled words. Unlike teachers' circles of "sp" notations, however, the spell-checker also provides options for correcting the error, which promotes independence and the development of visual memory.

To support a young writer, the teacher needs to understand both the child's current thinking about written language and the stages through which spelling knowledge develops. In addition, children need opportunities to write for reasons they deem important. All this, and a consistently positive "you can do it" attitude from the teacher, will yield remarkable results.

Parents and the Spelling Program

Spelling, particularly invented spelling, concerns many parents. Approximations may look like errors to parents; they may wonder why these errors are not corrected. Through communication and information sharing, teachers can help parents see the value in invented spellings and the role that writing plays in their children's development as readers.

Parents should be informed about the merits of frequent writing and the integrity of their children's attempts at spelling. They may also need to think about what counts as writing in an early literacy classroom. Indeed, it's quite likely that parents themselves didn't write much as young schoolchildren. They may have copied letters and words, but they probably didn't write. So they may need to understand that learning to write is a more complex process than learning to make letters.

Many teachers compare written and oral language development to help parents see the developmental nature of writing and spelling growth, the importance of children's early efforts to put their ideas in writing, and the critical role of adults' support and encouragement. They ask parents to recall how they celebrated children's first attempts at talking and paid much more attention to what children were trying to say than how they were saying it. And, in fact, they didn't worry that a child would say "Boo Boo" for *Grandma* forever; they simply rejoiced in the child's ability to communicate. In other words, parents need to see that the support, encouragement, and acceptance they provided as their children learned to talk also apply to learning to write and spell.

Some parents may wish to learn about the stages of spelling development; others may worry that their children will never learn to value correct spelling. Simple charts can be shared with parents to help them learn about both of these issues (Rosencrans 1998). A chart depicting the stages of spelling development, for example, might list characteristics of stages and ideas for supporting children's learning at home. This brief example shows how information might be shared about the prephonemic stage of spelling development.

Prephonemic Spellers	Parents Can
Know how writing looks but not how it works	Read to children often
Use random letters and symbols	Play rhyming games
May know their letters but haven't figured out sounds	Encourage writing at home

Similarly, a chart can help parents see the role that accurate spelling plays in the classroom:

Levels of Accuracy	Examples
Ideas only	Notes, drafts
Readable	Journals, personal writing, assignments
Good copy	Writing to be displayed and read by others

Home-school communication can take several forms. At meetings early in the school year, teachers can use writing examples from the previous year's students to explain how writing develops and show parents the progressive growth in sound-symbol relationships that results from consistent opportunities to write. Letters or newsletters can serve the same purpose. Dialogue journals between parents and children with or without entries from the teacher are another great way to foster home-school communication (Shockley, Michalove, and Allen 1995).

Parent conferences also offer valuable sharing opportunities. Using dated samples of children's writing, teachers can show parents concrete examples of children's growth in word learning as evidenced by changes in their invented spellings. Early efforts at writing can seem quite peculiar from a parent's perspective, so helping parents understand instructional goals and children's development as spellers is important. Communication and information sharing should focus on how support and encouragement from interested adults, both at home and in school, will foster word learning that children can apply to both writing and reading.

In Conclusion

Learning to spell is more than just a memory task (Henderson 1990); it is also, and more important for our purposes in this book, "a process of coming to understand how words work—the conventions that govern their structure and how their structure signals sound and meaning" (Templeton and Morris 1999, p. 103). The process of writing words draws on the same underlying word knowledge as the process of reading words. This is why unaided writing supports students' phonics and word recognition development; this is also why opportunities to write and spell should be part of word-learning programs.

References

Bear, D., Invernizzi, M., Templeton, S., and Johnston, F. (2012). *Words their way: Word study for phonics, vocabulary, and spelling instruction* (5th ed.). Upper Saddle River, NJ: Pearson Education.

Fresch, M. J. and Wheaton, A. (1997). Sort, search, and discover: Spelling in the child-centered classroom. *The Reading Teacher, 51*, 20–23.

Ganske, K. (2000). *Word journeys: Assessment-guided phonics, spelling, and vocabulary instruction.* New York: Guilford.

Gentry, R. and Gillet, J. (1993). *Teaching kids to spell.* Portsmouth, NH: Heinemann.

Graves, D. (1983). *Writing: Teachers and children at work.* Portsmouth, NH: Heinemann.

Harste, J., Woodward, V., and Burke, C. (1984). *Language stories and literacy lessons.* Portsmouth, NH: Heinemann.

Heald-Taylor, B. G. (1998). Three paradigms of spelling instruction in grades 3–6. *The Reading Teacher, 51*, 404–413.

Helman, L. (2005). Using literacy assessment results to improve teaching for English-language learners. *The Reading Teacher, 58*, 668–677.

Helman, L. and Bear, D. (2007). Does an established model of orthographic development hold true for English learners? In D. Rowe, R. Jimenez, D. Compton, D. Dickinson, Y. Kim, K. Leander, and V. Risko (Eds.), *56th yearbook of the National Reading Conference* (pp. 266–280). Oak Creek, WI: National Reading Conference.

Henderson, E. H. (1990). *Teaching spelling* (2nd ed.). Boston: Houghton Mifflin.

Invernizzi, M. and Hayes, L. (2004). Developmental spelling research: A systematic imperative. *Reading Research Quarterly, 51*, 404–413.

Meier, D. (2004). *The young child's memory for words.* New York: Teachers College Press.

Read, C. (1971). Pre-school children's knowledge of English phonology. *Harvard Educational Review, 41*, 1–34.

Reyes, I. and Azuara, P. (2008). Emergent biliteracy in young Mexican American immigrant children. *Reading Research Quarterly, 43*, 374–398.

Rosencrans, G. (1998). *The spelling book.* Newark, DE: International Reading Association.

Shockley, B., Michalove, B., and Allen, J. B. (1995). *Engaging families.* Portsmouth, NH: Heinemann.

Templeton, S. and Morris, D. (1999). Questions teachers ask about spelling. *Reading Research Quarterly, 34*, 102–112.

Williams, C. and Phillips-Birdsong, C. (2006). Word study and second-grade children's independent writing. *Journal of Literacy Research, 38*, 427–465.

16

Beyond Word Study

Reading Fluency

Harry, a third-grade teacher in an urban school, has some interesting observations about his students.

Some of my students are still struggling with decoding words. Others however have gotten this down pretty well—they can decode most of the words they come across while reading. But even these more advanced readers, when reading aloud for me, read without any expression. Much of their reading tends to be word-by-word, sometimes even syllable-by-syllable. It's clear to me that even though they can decode, they are not yet proficient readers. They are focusing their attention so much on saying the words, they have little energy left over for making sense of or enjoying what they read. In short, they are readers, but they are not fluent readers yet.

Fortunately Harry uses some instructional time for developing students' reading fluency.

I like to read poetry to my class, and I try to get my students to read and appreciate poetry themselves. So throughout the school year students choose poems, practice them, sign up for performing them during our poetry breaks, and then read them to the class. I insist that students read their poems with expression, so they have to practice them a lot before they are ready to perform. Sometimes two, three, or even four kids will do a poem together. It's neat to see these students orchestrate and practice their performance so that it is a fun experience for them and their audience.

Harry also does a lot with readers theater. "I think readers theater is one of those special activities that all teachers should know about."

Harry has prewritten scripts that groups of students choose, practice, and perform in readers theater style (no memorization, physical movement, costumes, or scenery)—students stand in front of their audience and read their scripts with expression and fluency. He reads to his students every day and occasionally shows his students how their favorite stories can be transformed into scripts to be performed as readers theater.

> This is the best part for me, to watch these kids turn the class into a writers' workshop as they take a story they like and recast it into a script. Often they have to adapt it for readers theater by cutting out some characters, adding others, adding and deleting lines, making the script work for them. I keep telling them that I am going to send some of their best scripts to Hollywood to be turned into a movie or television show.

> Harry's students' poetry and script performances have impressive results: "Not only do my students become more fluent in their reading—in *all* their reading—over the year, but their word recognition improves and so does their comprehension." As Harry has noticed, fluency is associated with overall proficiency in reading (Pinnell et al. 1995). Moreover, lack of fluency is a problem for many struggling readers (Rasinski and Padak 1998). Since fluency is such an important part of reading, it must be taught and nurtured at the elementary and middle school levels. In this chapter, we define fluency, explain its importance, summarize the essentials of effective fluency instruction, and offer resources for fluency instruction and practice.

What Is Fluency?

Think about the last time you heard a very fluent speaker. Most likely, the speaker didn't bungle the words, but other aspects of the speaking—not just the spoken words—also helped you understand the message. The person probably spoke in chunks or phrases that made it easy to follow her or him. Perhaps the rate of speaking was helpful—neither too slow nor too quick. Perhaps the speaker paused or used his or her voice for emphasis. A fluent speaker helps listeners understand or comprehend the spoken message. Fluency in speaking is a multidimensional concept.

Reading fluency is also a multidimensional concept (Kuhn and Stahl 2000; National Reading Panel 2000). Fluency is like a bridge that connects word decoding to comprehension. This bridge consists of automatizing word recognition so that readers can pay attention to constructing meaning rather than word decoding. It also consists of interpretive and prosodic reading with appropriate expression and rate. Let's take a closer look at these elements.

Decoding is part of fluent reading. Clearly, someone who is unable to decode the words on a page isn't really reading, fluently or not. But mere decoding accuracy is not enough. Proficient and fluent reading requires effortless, automatic decoding. Readers need to expend as little effort as possible in the decoding aspect of reading so that their finite cognitive resources can be used for constructing meaning (LaBerge and Samuels 1974). Consider your own reading, for example; how often do you stop to analyze a word in order to decode it? Probably rarely. Like most adult readers, since you recognize the vast majority of the words you encounter instantly and automatically, you can think instead about making sense of the text—making predictions, asking questions, creating mental images. So now the fluency "bridge" has two supports: accurate decoding and automatic decoding, or automaticity in reading.

The third support for the fluency bridge involves parsing or chunking the text into syntactically and semantically appropriate units and interpreting the text by reading with appropriate expression, what linguists call prosodic reading or the melodic aspects of oral reading (Schreiber 1991). When a reader reads with appropriate phrasing and expressively, emphasizing certain words, making extended pauses at certain points, speeding up in some sections and deliberately slowing down at others, active meaning construction and interpretation is evident. Indeed, one must comprehend the text in order to decide about where to chunk text and how to read it expressively.

Fluency is the ability to read expressively and meaningfully, as well as accurately and with appropriate speed. Successful reading requires readers to process the surface level of the text in order to comprehend. The goal of reading is comprehension, of course, but proficiently processing the surface level allows the reader to direct his or her attention to meaning. Reading fluency enables control over this surface-level text processing (Rasinski 2010).

Why Is Fluency Important?

Part of the answer to this question should be evident in the definition just provided: Fluency is important because it builds a bridge that enables comprehension. In fact, research into repeated readings indicates that reading a particular passage several times, a common fluency instructional activity, leads not only to improvement on that text but also to improvements in decoding, reading rate, prosodic reading, and comprehension on unfamiliar texts (Dowhower 1987, 1997; Herman 1985; Koskinen and Blum 1984, 1986; Kuhn and Stahl 2000; National Reading Panel 2000; Rasinski, Reutzel, Chard, and Linan-Thompson 2011). The reading practice transfers to new, unread text. So fluency is important because it affects comprehension.

Research-Based Strategies

Unfortunately, significant numbers of students are not fluent readers. The large-scale National Assessment of Educational Progress study (Pinnell et al. 1995), for example, concluded that nearly half of U.S. fourth-graders read below minimally acceptable fluency levels, and only 13 percent of them read at the highest fluency level. From these results, then, we can assume fluency difficulties among approximately half of the primary-level population. We can also assume that nearly all primary-level students will benefit from fluency instruction. Thus, fluency deserves emphasis in your reading curriculum. Next we offer some research-based ways to accomplish this.

Helping Students Become Fluent Readers

The first step in planning a fluency component for your reading program involves time. About 15 to 20 minutes each day should be devoted to fluency instruction, and students should have additional opportunities within each school day to practice fluent reading. Here are brief descriptions of several activities you can use to provide the basis for your fluency instruction.

Model Fluent Reading

Some students are unaware that they are not fluent readers, and even more have never thought metacognitively about fluency—what a speaker does to enhance understanding. These students need to hear expressive reading. They need to hear how fluent readers read, and they need the opportunity to talk about the nature of fluent reading.

Teacher read-alouds can accomplish both of these goals. Most teachers read aloud to students each day. Transforming these read-aloud sessions into fluency development opportunities is easy. First, since the read-alouds must be as fluent as possible, you may need to practice beforehand. Second, vary the types of texts you select for read-alouds. Find poetry, drama, and speeches; don't just read storybooks. The variety in text types will help students develop a more elaborate notion of fluent reading.

Finally, find ways to draw students' attention to the ways you use your voice to promote fluent reading. In brief postreading conversations ask questions such as:

- What did you notice about my voice?
- How did my voice help you pay attention or understand?
- How did I use my voice to show happiness or excitement or anger or some other emotion?

These brief conversations can help students develop and refine their abstract concepts about fluency.

You might also want to experiment by reading a short passage in several ways—fluently, in a word-by-word laborious manner, too quickly, and so on. Ask students to compare the renditions, to tell which one was most effective at communicating the author's message and why. This practice, too, helps develop self-awareness about fluency. In all, teacher read-alouds, especially when supplemented with brief conversations about fluency, aid students' thinking about the nature of fully fluent reading.

Provide Fluency Assistance (Scaffolding) for Students

Hearing fluent reading is not the same as being a fluent reader. Thus, assisted reading, another method associated with fluency improvements (Kuhn and Stahl 2000; National Reading Panel 2000), is an important component of a fluency program.

Several methods for assisted reading show promise. One is a simple routine that begins with your reading a short text to students. This is followed by an invitation for students to follow along silently as you read aloud again. Group reading is next. Choral reading, antiphonal reading (dividing the class into groups), even choral reading in silly voices (e.g., like a robot, like a baby) are all effective and enjoyable assisted reading methods. This routine provides good models of fluent reading and unobtrusive assistance for children who may need it.

Paired reading, which may involve pairs of students' choice or pairings of more fluent and struggling readers, provides another excellent scaffold for children (Eldredge 1990; Eldredge and Butterfield 1986; Eldredge and Quinn 1988; Topping 1987a, 1987b, 1989, 1995). Partners spend 5 or 10 minutes several times each week reading together. One child reads while the other listens and follows along silently. The listener offers positive comments about the reader's fluency. Then the pairs switch roles. Paired reading can also involve two readers reading the same text aloud simultaneously.

Teacher coaching or feedback is another form of assistance. As students are reading, stroll around the room to listen. Talk with students about what you hear:

- You got all the words right, but you read so fast! It was hard for me to follow you.

- I really like how you paused between sentences. This gave me a chance to think about the author's message.

- I loved how you used your voice in this section! You really sounded angry.

This sort of assistance helps students become aware of their own interpretations and also provides a good model for children's own responses to partners.

Listening to prerecorded books while reading them silently is yet another way to provide assistance (Carbo 1978a, 1978b, 1981; Chomsky 1976; Pluck 1995). This is a good choice for a listening center activity. It may also provide another authentic audience for practice—students can create their own recorded books for others to enjoy. Assisted reading of this sort has been found to be a powerful strategy for improving fluency and comprehension.

Captioned television (see Chapter 18) is an interesting way to support students' reading. When students watch television with the captioning on and the volume low, they must focus on the printed words in order to understand the program. The video often provides the support students need to read successfully (Koskinen et al. 1993; Postlethwaite and Ross 1992). In addition, videos of favorite children's songs from animated musicals, with the lyrics presented in a captioned format, are available at stores and in public libraries. From our own observations, young children love watching, singing, and reading these video texts.

Encourage Repeated Readings

Practice leads to fluency in reading in the same way it does in other areas, such as driving a car, for example, or playing a musical instrument. As we have noted, repeated readings (Rasinski et al. 2011; Samuels 1979/1997) have been found to improve reading both on the practice passages and on unfamiliar texts.

Repeated readings works best when students have authentic and engaging reasons for practice. Performance can supply this motivation. The invitation to perform gives students a natural reason for practicing a passage repeatedly (otherwise known as rehearsal). Moreover, comparing different oral renditions of the same text often provides opportunities for students to consider fluency abstractly. For example, discussions with students might focus on questions such as:

- How was your second (or third or fourth) reading of this text better?
- What did you do differently with your voice? How did this change make the reading better?
- What will you do with your voice the next time to make the reading even better?

Of course, if students are asked to practice a text for performance, they also need performance opportunities. Many teachers we know have "fluency Fridays"; they devote some time, usually on Friday afternoons, for students to perform texts that they have rehearsed throughout the week. Some teachers convert their classrooms into poetry cafés. In Darlene's third-grade class, for example, Poetry Club happens every other week.

Students select poems or scripts, practice them throughout the week, and perform for classmates and parents on Friday afternoon. Students love the authenticity that comes from reading with expression for an audience. Darlene adds to the authentic atmosphere by turning off the overhead lights in her classroom and placing a reading lamp near a stool that students can use. Refreshments such as hot apple cider and popcorn complete the coffeehouse setting. Students in Darlene's class have even learned to snap their fingers (as a less noisy and much "cooler" alternative to clapping) to express their appreciation for each reading.

Other teachers have readers theater festivals. Readers theater involves the performance of a script without costumes, props, movement, scenery, or memorization of lines. Performers simply stand in front of the audience and read the script to the audience. Readers theater is very similar to the dramas and comedies broadcast over the radio in the 1930s through '50s. The actors simply stood around a microphone, without costumes, scenery, props, or movement, and read from a script. Of course, in order for the script to have any impact on the audience it needs to be read with expression— hence readers theater is a superb activity for promoting practiced or repeated readings.

Nearly any script can be used for readers theater. Some of our favorites are listed in Figures 16.1 and 16.2. However, we have found

Figure 16.1   Resources for Readers Theater

Technology

Online Scripts

www.storiestogrowby.com/script.html

www.aaronshep.com/rt/

http://storycart.com

http://www.teachingheart.net/readerstheater.htm

http://www.readinglady.com/index.php?module=documents&JAS
_DocumentManager_op=categories&category=15

http://www.timelessteacherstuff.com/

Print Resources for Readers Theater

Barchers, S. (1993). *Reader's theatre for beginning readers.*
Portsmouth, NH: Teacher Ideas Press.

Barchers, S. I. (2001). *From Atalanta to Zeus: Readers theatre from Greek mythology.* Portsmouth, NH: Teacher Ideas Press.

Barnes, J. W. (2004). *Sea songs: Readers theatre from the South Pacific.* Portsmouth, NH: Teacher Ideas Press.

Bauer, C. F. (1991). *Presenting reader's theatre.* New York: H. H. Wilson.

Blau, L. (2000). *The best of reader's theater* (Vols. 1 and 2). Bellevue, WA: One from the Heart.

(Continued)

Figure 16.1 (*Continued*)

Braun, W. (2000). *A reader's theatre treasury of stories.* Calgary, Alberta, Canada: Braun and Braun.

Fredericks, A. D. (1993). *Frantic frogs and other frankly fractured folktales for readers theatre.* Portsmouth, NH: Teacher Ideas Press.

Fredericks, A. D. (1997). *Tadpole tales and other totally terrific treats for readers theatre.* Portsmouth, NY: Teacher Ideas Press.

Fredericks, A. D. (2000). *Silly salamanders and other slightly stupid stuff for readers theatre.* Portsmouth, NH: Teacher Ideas Press.

Fredericks, A. D. (2001). *Readers theatre for American history.* Portsmouth, NH: Teacher Ideas Press.

Fredericks, A. D. (2002). *Science fiction readers theatre.* Portsmouth, NH: Teacher Ideas Press.

McBride-Smith, B. (2001). *Tell it together: Foolproof scripts for story theatre.* Atlanta, GA: August House Publishers.

Rasinski, T. and Bagert, B. (2010). *Poems for building reading skills* (Grades 4, 5, 6). Huntington Beach, CA: Shell Educational Publishing.

Rasinski, T. and Brothers, K. (2010). *Poems for building reading skills* (Grades 1, 2, 3). Huntington Beach, CA: Shell Educational Publishing.

Rasinski, T. and Griffith, L. (2005). *Texts for fluency practice* (Levels A, B, C). Huntington Beach, CA: Shell Educational Publishing.

Rasinski, T. and Griffith, L. (2008). *Building fluency through practice and performance* (Grades 1 through 6). Huntington Beach, CA: Shell Educational Publishing.

Ratliff, G. L. (1999). *Introduction to readers theatre: A guide to classroom performance.* Colorado Springs, CO: Meriwether.

Shepard, A. (2004). *Readers on stage: Resources for reader's theater.* Olympia, WA: Shepard Publications.

Sierra, J. (1996). *Multicultural folktales for the feltboard and readers' theater.* Phoenix, AZ: Oryx Press.

Sloyer, S. (2003). *From the page to the stage: The educator's complete guide to readers' theatre.* Portsmouth, NH: Teacher Ideas Press/ Libraries Unlimited.

Books Already Written in Script Format

Fleischman, P. (1989). *I am phoenix.* New York: Harper Trophy.

Fleischman, P. (1994). *Bull Run.* New York: Harper.

Fleischman, P. (2004). *Joyful noise.* New York: Harper Trophy.

Fleischman, P. (2004). *Seedfolks.* New York: Harper Trophy.

Fleischman, P. (2008). *Big talk: Poems for four voices.* New York: Candlewick.

Hall, D. (1994). *I am the dog, I am the cat.* New York: Dial. (The form of the book can also be used for students to write their own books that compare and contrast characters, events, or things—e.g., I am a Democrat, I am a Republican.)

Hoberman, M. (2001). *You read to me, I'll read to you: Very short stories to read together.* Boston: Little, Brown.

Hoberman, M. (2004). *You read to me, I'll read to you: Very short fairy tales to read together.* Boston: Little, Brown.

Hoberman, M. (2005). *You read to me, I'll read to you: Mother Goose tales to read together.* Boston: Little, Brown.

Hoose, P. and Hoose, H. (1998). *Hey, little ant.* Berkeley, CA: Tricycle Press.

Johnson, A. (1989). *Tell me a story, Mama.* New York: Orchard.

Raschka, C. (1993). *Yo! Yes?* New York: Orchard.

Rasinski, T., Harrison, D., and Fawcett, G. (2009). *Partner poems for building fluency.* New York: Scholastic.

Easy Books for Recasting as Scripts

Brett, J. (2000). *Hedgie's surprise.* New York: Penguin Group.

Carpenter, S. (1998). *The three billy goats gruff.* New York: HarperFestival.

Cronin, D. (2000). *Click, clack, moo: Cows that type.* New York: Simon and Schuster.

(Continued)

Figure 16.2 (*Continued*)

Fox, M. (1987). *Hattie and the fox*. New York: Bradbury.

Kellogg, S. (1987). *Chicken Little*. New York: HarperCollins.

Lester, H. (1990). *Tacky the penguin*. New York: Sandpiper.

Lobel, A. (1979). *Frog and toad are friends*. New York: Harper Trophy. (All the Frog and Toad books are good for recasting as scripts.)

Lobel, A. (1983). *Fables*. New York: HarperCollins.

Martin, B. (1983). *Brown bear, brown bear, what do you see?* New York: Henry Holt.

Schachner, J. (2003). *Skippyjon Jones*. New York: Scholastic.

Seuss, Dr. (1960). *Green eggs and ham*. New York: Random House.

Trivizas, E. (1993). *The three little wolves and the big bad pig*. New York: Scholastic.

Challenging Books for Recasting as Scripts

Blume, J. (1974). *The pain and the great one*. New York: Bradbury.

Brown, M. (1992). *Arthur babysits*. Boston: Little, Brown. (All the Arthur books are good candidates for recasting as scripts.)

Caseley, J. (1991). *Dear Annie*. New York: Greenwillow.

Champion, J. (1993). *Emily and Alice again*. San Diego: Harcourt, Brace.

Henkes, K. (1996). *Chrysanthemum.* New York: Mulberry.

Henkes, K. (2010). *Wembley worried*. New York: Greenwillow.

Karlin, B. (1992). *Cinderella*. Boston: Little, Brown.

Kimmel, E. A. (1994). *Anansi and the talking melon*. New York: Holiday House.

Rylant, C. (2007). *Gooseberry Park*. New York: Sandpiper.

Steig, W. (1982). *Dr. De Soto*. New York: Farrar, Straus and Giroux.

that scripts students write are often the best (Young and Rasinski 2011). Writing a script gives students a sense of ownership of the text. To make a script, students simply find a favorite short story or story segment and recast it in the form of a script, deleting unneeded parts and adding parts and lines that will contribute to the script. Usually a four- to five-page (double-spaced) script will result in a 10- to 15-minute performance. This is also a great way to encourage reluctant writers—script writing from an existing story provides plenty of support. It allows students to examine the story being scripted from the point of view of the author—what did the original author do to make the story worth publishing?

Martinez, Roser, and Strecker (1999) describe a weekly classroom routine in which second-graders formed into repertory groups. On Mondays, the teacher would read the stories on which their scripts were based. Students then worked on their scripts throughout the week and performed their scripts before an audience on Fridays. In just 10 weeks of doing readers theater, the second-graders made reading rate increases that were 2.5 times greater than two similar classes of second-graders who did not do readers theater. Other measures of reading, including informal reading inventories, also demonstrated significant gains for the readers theater students. Mrs. Carter, one of the second-grade teachers, said that readers theater helped her students in two ways: "The first is comprehension that results from having to become the characters and understand their feelings, and the second is the repetition and practice" (p. 333). A growing body of research supports the use of readers theater to promote fluency and reading achievement in the primary (Young and Rasinski 2009) and intermediate (Griffith and Rasinski 2004) grades.

An interesting twist on readers theater makes use of technology—more specifically, podcasting (Vasinda and McLeod 2011). Podcasting allows a computer to be turned into an audio-recording device. (Free audio-recording software is available online from Audacity, at http://audacity.sourceforge.net/.) The audio recording, or podcast, is an electronic audio file, rather than a physical cassette tape that is easily lost or broken. The beauty of podcasting is that podcast recordings can easily be stored and organized on a computer; they can also be electronically transported to other locations (students' homes, other classrooms and schools) as well as posted on websites for instant access by others. In essence, podcasting is a simple way for students to perform and publish the scripts (and other texts) that they have rehearsed.

Research-Based
Strategies

Technology

In a readers theater–podcast study (Vasinda and McLeod, 2011) struggling second- and third-grade students, working in small heterogeneous groups, spent 10 to 15 minutes Monday through Thursday rehearsing a different script each week. During these rehearsal days, the teacher would monitor and assist groups of students as they practiced, model expressive reading, and meet with small groups for targeted instruction. On Fridays each group recorded its script as a podcast. Later students listened to their own and their classmates' voice recordings. Results of a 10-week study indicate that students in the readers theater–podcast routine made, on average, over a year's growth in reading comprehension. Moreover, both students and teachers noted that the instructional routine was challenging, but also satisfying, and an authentic use of repeated readings.

Another approach to repeated reading is to encourage students to practice so that they can read to buddies in a lower grade-level class. Students love being able to perform for their younger buddies and help them in reading. The younger students, also, are motivated to read by the example their older buddies demonstrate. Gregg's fourth-graders have a date once a week with Lisa's first-graders. They alternate classrooms for their visits and bring blankets, pillows, and stuffed animals for their literary rendezvous. The fourth-graders practice their reading throughout the week so that the first-graders will hear fluent and meaningful presentations of their stories. Both groups of students love their meetings and even correspond on classroom email about books to be read.

Older students can also create recorded books for their younger buddies to read and listen to when time is available. The use of technology (i.e., podcasting) makes recording books and other texts easier than ever. Before recording, older students will need to practice reading the texts several times so that the recorded reading is read with expression, meaning, and minimal word recognition errors. Older students love to insert personal introductions, sound effects and audible cues for page turns into their tapes. The younger students benefit from a growing library of favorite recorded books.

Prerecorded books also have superb potential for use with ELL (English language learner) students. Pat Koskinen and colleagues (1993) found that having ELL students take home prerecorded books for reading practice resulted in increased reading achievement and interest as well as greater self-confidence in students. Those children who were the least proficient readers reported practicing their reading more often than their more proficient classmates. Koskinen and colleagues created two readings for each story on each tape. The first reading was a slower, more deliberate presentation, and the second was a faster, more fluent rendition. This permitted students to move from an initial focus on words and phrases to a more fluent presentation of the stories.

Many students are motivated by the opportunity to read with friends. Pat Koskinen and Irene Blum (1984, 1986) found that repeated readings work very well in what they called paired repeated reading. Each student reads a passage to a partner several times. The partner's role is to provide positive feedback and assistance. After several readings, the roles are reversed. Koskinen and Blum found that students enjoyed the alternative format and demonstrated strong gains in fluency, word recognition, and comprehension doing the paired repeated reading as little as 15 minutes three times per week for a little over a month.

Focus on Phrases and Phrase Boundaries

An important part of reading fluency is the ability to read in phrases, as opposed to word-by-word reading (Schreiber 1980, 1991). Consider the following sentences:

> The principal said the teacher was very helpful.
>
> Woman without her man is nothing.

Depending on how you phrase the first sentence, the principal or the teacher is helpful. And in the second, either woman or man could be interpreted to "be nothing." Punctuation within sentences sometimes helps readers phrase the text properly. More often, readers must separate the meaningful elements of a sentence without the help of punctuation. This is not an easy task for some readers. Many younger readers, especially those who have developed a word-by-word reading habit, may have difficulty in seeing that phrases, more than individual words, carry meaning.

All the activities we have described in this chapter, along with wide reading, will help students develop sensitivity to phrase boundaries. As readers read or listen to fluent reading they need to attend to the phrasing in the reading. Another approach to developing phrasing is to mark or highlight phrase boundaries in the text itself, using a slash mark, vertical line, or other marking to specify the boundary (see Figure 16.3). Marking phrase boundaries can improve fluency, reading performance, and comprehension, especially with less able readers (Rasinski 1990; Rasinski, Yildirim, and Nageldinger, in press).

When marking, keep the text reasonably short—no more than two pages at a time. Have students read the text once or twice in one day. On the following day have students read the same text without the phrase markings. This will give students repeated reading practice and help them transfer their syntactic understandings of text phrasing to unmarked texts.

Word recognition practice can also take on a phrased nature. Rather than always presenting sight words or word bank words in isolation, they can occasionally be taught in the form of phrases.

In the car

My old dog

When it rains

By the river

Inside the house

This adds variety to word recognition practice and emphasizes the notion that words are almost always read in the context of phrases and sentences.

Figure 16.3 Example of Phrase-Cued Text

Simply embedding slash marks into a passage / at phrase and sentence junctures / can have a positive effect / on students' own phrasing, / fluency, / and comprehension. For students who do not have a good understanding / of how sentences are phrased or chunked /, the slash marks provide direct visual cues / that enable students' own phrased reading.

Choose Texts Carefully

The texts students read can help or hinder their fluency. We all become less fluent when asked to read difficult or unfamiliar text. Often, students with fluency difficulties attempt to read texts that are too difficult. Such texts ensure a lack of fluency, perpetuating the students' self-images as poor readers.

If we accept the idea of performance providing the motivation for repeated readings, then we need to consider the types of texts that lend themselves to performance. Texts meant to be read aloud, like poetry, scripts, speeches, monologues, dialogues, and jokes or riddles, are perfect for fluency development. Storybooks may be good choices for fluency practice too, especially if students will read them to a younger audience.

When teaching fluency, choose texts that are relatively easy in terms of word recognition and syntactic complexity. Reading easier texts helps students develop power and confidence in their reading.

More challenging texts may also be appropriate for fluency instruction when practice and support is provided. Stahl and Heubach (2005) found that children can read more difficult material very successfully (and accelerate their reading growth) if the teacher provides adequate scaffolding in the form of repeated, assisted, or guided reading. So if the text is difficult, be sure to provide sufficient support before and during reading to ensure student success.

Research-Based Strategies

Material with a strong sense of voice works well for fluency instruction. When students reread such material, their practice is aimed at re-creating the author's voice. Poetry, speeches, songs, narratives, dialogues, monologues, journal entries, letters, and jokes generally have a greater sense of textual voice than informational text that is often presented in a dismembered, third-person voice. Figure 16.4 lists resources for finding songs to read and sing.

Predictable or patterned text (see Chapter 5), as found in poetry (see Chapter 7), is particularly well suited to helping students develop fluent reading. Their distinct and easily detected patterns make them not only easy to read but also require readers to attend to the pattern through phrasing and expression. Patterned or predictable texts are easy to memorize. Although students may take justifiable pride in memorizing a text, from a reading standpoint this is a concern. Memorized texts do not have to be examined visually (or read), so the visual representations

Figure 16.4 Websites for Finding Songs to Read and Sing

http://judyanddavid.com/cma.html

www.bussongs.com/

http://www.theteachersguide.com/ChildrensSongs.htm/

www.niehs.nih.gov/kids/music.htm

http://www.scoutsongs.com/

of words do not find a way into students' memories. Thus, when using patterned texts, pull words out of the context (you choose some and have students choose some), write them on the class word wall or in individual word banks, practice reading and chanting them in isolation, sort and analyze them for particular features, and play games with them so that students find themselves visually analyzing the words deeply and fully.

Poetry and song lyrics for children are especially well suited for fluency instruction (Wilfong 2008). These patterned texts have the advantage of being short, rhythmic, easy to learn, and are meant to be performed for an audience, thus lending themselves to repeated readings while appealing to many grade levels. Every elementary teacher should have several poetry anthologies in order to celebrate poetry every day of the school year. (See Figure 16.5 for online poetry

Figure 16.5 Children's Poetry Online

A Rhyme a Week: http://curry.virginia.edu/go/wil/rimes_and_rhymes.htm

Poetry4kids: http://poetry4kids.com

Children's Poetry: www.poetry-online.org/childrens_poetry_resource
_index.htm

Classic Poetry for Children: http://www.storyit.com/Classics/JustPoems/
index.htm

Jump Rope Rhymes: http://www.gameskidsplay.net/jump_rope_ryhmes/
index.htm

Figure 16.6 Websites for Speeches

Inaugural Addresses of U.S. Presidents: www.bartleby.com/124

History Channel: Great Speeches: www.historychannel.com/
broadband/ (search on speeches for videos of notable speeches)

The History Place, Great Speeches Collection: www.historyplace.com/
speeches/previous.htm

Gifts of Speech: Women's Speeches from Around the World: http://gos
.sbc.edu

Famous American Speeches: Americanrhetoric.com

Notable American Speeches: http://artofmanliness.com/2008/08/01/
the-35-greatest-speeches-in-history/

Technology

resources.) Teachers and children can also compose original verse or verse modeled after favorite poems, which can be put together into class collections.

Speeches are also wonderful sources for fluency instruction. Like drama, speeches are meant to be performed and heard by others rather than read silently. Using speeches from history is a great way to incorporate fluency instruction and practice into social studies. Figure 16.6 offers online sites where you can find great speeches for fluency work.

Synergistic Instruction—The Fluency Development Lesson

The most potent fluency instruction incorporates multiple components in a synergistic manner (by synergy we mean that the instruction that combines effective components is more effective that the sum of those components taught separately). The Fluency Development Lesson (FDL) (Rasinski, Padak, Sturtevant, and Linek 1994; Zimmerman and Rasinski, in press), which we developed and have tested, is a good example of this synergy. We originally devised the FDL for teachers who work with primary-grade children experiencing difficulty in achieving even initial stages of fluent reading. It combines several aspects of

**Research-Based
Strategies**

effective fluency instruction in a way that maximizes students' reading in a relatively short period of time (10 to 15 minutes) and is intended as a supplement to the regular reading curriculum. We have found the beginning of each day is a good time to do the FDL, as a sort of warm-up for school. Teachers make copies of brief passages, usually poems of 50 to 200 words, for each child.

A typical daily Fluency Development Lesson looks like this:

1. The teacher distributes copies of the text.

2. The teacher reads and rereads the text orally to the class while students follow along silently with their own copies.

3. The teacher and students discuss text content as well as the prosodic quality of the teacher's reading.

4. The entire class reads the text chorally several times. The teacher creates variety by having students read different verses or portions of the text in groups.

5. The class divides into pairs. Each pair finds a quiet spot, and one student reads the text to a partner three times. The partner's job is to follow along in the text, provide help when needed, and give positive feedback to the reader. Next, the roles are switched. The partner becomes the reader and reads the text three times as well.

6. Students regroup, and the teacher asks for volunteers to perform the text. Individuals, pairs, and groups of up to four perform the reading for the class. Students may also perform for the school principal, secretary, custodian, and other teachers and classes. The performing students are lavished with praise. Performances may also be recorded as podcasts.

7. Students and teachers choose words from the text for closer examination and study (e.g., rhyming words) and addition to word banks. Words can be practiced and sorted at various times throughout the school day.

8. Students take a copy of the text home to read to their parents and other relatives. Parents are asked to listen and to praise their child's efforts.

Our experience with the FDL indicates that, when employed three to four times a week over several months, it is easily implemented by teachers and parents, enjoyed by students, and leads to significant improvements in students' fluency and overall reading, considerably beyond their previous progress. The FDL is the core lesson in the Kent State University reading clinic where students routinely make progress in word recognition, fluency, and comprehension well beyond what would normally be expected (Zimmerman and Rasinski, in press). We have also found that the FDL can be adapted for a variety of grade levels in the elementary and middle school.

Our goal in describing the FDL is to help you see what can happen when a lesson format is created using informed practices as building blocks. Thus, we challenge you to adapt the FDL for use in your own classroom, with whatever modifications fit your students' needs.

In Conclusion

If reading instruction is to be successful, fluency must become a critical goal of the reading curriculum. It is not enough for students to become proficient in word decoding. They need to read *with* meaning, not just read *for* meaning. And reading with meaning is what reading fluency is all about. Fluent reading is accurate, quick, expressive, and above all, meaningful. Fluency is indeed the bridge between word recognition and comprehension.

Effective fluency instruction reflects three important principles:

- Children need to hear models of fluent reading.
- Children need support to develop fluency. This can take the form of teacher coaching, assisted reading, or both. Children also benefit from opportunities to think and talk metacognitively about fluency.
- Children need regular opportunities to practice texts—widely and repeatedly. Repeated reading works best when performance is the reason for the practice.

The activities we have described in this chapter share a common purpose: to help students develop the ability to read fluently. Fluency instruction should be woven seamlessly into other areas of the reading and school curriculum—it should not be turned into a skill-and-drill activity. This chapter provides a starting place for making fluency instruction an integral part of your reading curriculum. The next chapter asks you to think critically about the methods and materials for your fluency and word study instruction.

References

Carbo, M. (1978a). Teaching reading with talking books. *The Reading Teacher, 32,* 267–273.

Carbo, M. (1978b). A word imprinting technique for children with severe memory disorders. *Teaching Exceptional Children, 11,* 3–5.

Carbo, M. (1981). Making books talk to children. *The Reading Teacher, 35,* 186–189.

Chomsky, C. (1976). After decoding: What? *Language Arts, 53,* 288–296.

Dowhower, S. L. (1987). Effects of repeated reading on second-grade transitional readers' fluency and comprehension. *Reading Research Quarterly, 22,* 389–407.

Dowhower, S. (1997). Introduction to "The Method of Repeated Readings." *The Reading Teacher, 50,* 376.

Eldredge, J. L. (1990). Increasing reading performance of poor readers in the third grade by using a group assisted strategy. *Journal of Educational Research, 84,* 69–77.

Eldredge, J. L. and Butterfield, D. D. (1986). Alternatives to traditional reading instruction. *The Reading Teacher, 40,* 32–37.

Eldredge, J. L. and Quinn, W. (1988). Increasing reading performance of low-achieving second graders by using dyad reading groups. *Journal of Educational Research, 82,* 40–46.

Griffith, L. W. and Rasinski, T. V. (2004). A focus on fluency: How one teacher incorporated fluency with her reading curriculum. *The Reading Teacher, 58,* 126–137.

Herman, P. A. (1985). The effect of repeated readings on reading rate, speech pauses, and word recognition accuracy. *Reading Research Quarterly, 20,* 553–564.

Koskinen, P. S. and Blum, I. H. (1984). Repeated oral reading and the acquisition of fluency. In J. A. Niles and L. A. Harris (Eds.), *Changing perspectives on research in reading/language processing and instruction, 33rd Yearbook of the National Reading Conference* (pp. 183–187). Rochester, NY: National Reading Conference.

Koskinen, P. S. and Blum, I. H. (1986). Paired repeated reading: A classroom strategy for developing fluent reading. *The Reading Teacher, 40,* 70–75.

Koskinen, P. S., et al. (1993). Captioned video and vocabulary learning: An innovative practice in literacy instruction. *The Reading Teacher, 47,* 36–43.

Kuhn, M. R. and Stahl, S. (2000). *Fluency: A review of developmental and remedial practices* (CIERA Rep. No. 2-008). Ann Arbor, MI: Center for the Improvement of Early Reading Achievement.

LaBerge, D. and Samuels, S. J. (1974). Toward a theory of automatic information processing in reading. *Cognitive Psychology, 6,* 293–323.

Martinez, M., Roser, N. L., and Strecker, S. (1999). "I never thought I could be a star": A readers theater ticket to fluency. *The Reading Teacher, 52,* 326–334.

National Reading Panel. (2000). *Report of the National Reading Panel: Teaching children to read. Report of the subgroups*. Washington, DC: U.S. Department of Health and Human Services, National Institutes of Health.

Pinnell, G. S., Pikulski, J., Wixon, K., Campbell, J., Gough, P., and Beatty, S. (1995). *Listening to children read aloud: Data from NAEP's integrated reading performance record at grade 4*. Washington, DC: U.S. Department of Education, Office of Educational Research and Instruction.

Pluck, M. (1995). Rainbow Reading Programme: Using taped stories. *Reading Forum, 1*, 25–29.

Postlethwaite, T. N. and Ross, K. N. (1992). *Effective schools in reading: Implications for educational planners*. The Hague: International Association for the Evaluation of Educational Achievement.

Rasinski, T. V. (1990). *The effects of cued phrase boundaries in texts*. Bloomington, IN: ERIC Clearinghouse on Reading and Communication Skills (ED 313 689).

Rasinski, T. V. (2010). *The fluent reader: Oral and silent reading strategies for building word recognition, fluency, and comprehension* (2nd ed.). New York: Scholastic.

Rasinski, T. V. and Padak, N. D. (1998). How elementary students referred for compensatory reading instruction perform on school-based measures of word recognition, fluency, and comprehension. *Reading Psychology: An International Quarterly, 19*, 185–216.

Rasinski, T. V., Padak, N., Sturtevant, E., and Linek, W. (1994). Effects of fluency development on urban second-grade readers. *Journal of Educational Research, 87*, 158–165.

Rasinski, T. V., Reutzel, C. R., Chard, D., and Linan-Thompson, S. (2011). Reading fluency. In M. L. Kamil, P. D. Pearson, B. Moje, and P. Afflerbach E. (Eds.), *Handbook of reading research* (Vol. 4, pp. 286–319). New York: Routledge.

Rasinski, T., Yildirim, K., and Nageldinger, J. (in press). Building fluency through the phrased text lesson. *The Reading Teacher*.

Samuels, S. J. (1997). The method of repeated readings. *The Reading Teacher, 50*, 376–381. (Reprinted from *The Reading Teacher*, 1979, 32, 403–408.)

Schreiber, P. A. (1980). On the acquisition of reading fluency. *Journal of Reading Behavior, 12*, 177–186.

Schreiber, P. A. (1991). Understanding prosody's role in reading acquisition. *Theory into Practice, 30*, 158–164.

Stahl, S. and Heubach, K. (2005). Fluency-oriented reading instruction. *Journal of Literacy Research, 37*, 25–60.

Topping, K. (1987a). Paired reading: A powerful technique for parent use. *The Reading Teacher, 40*, 604–614.

Topping, K. (1987b). Peer tutored paired reading: Outcome data from ten projects. *Educational Psychology, 7*, 133–145.

Topping, K. (1989). Peer tutoring and paired reading: Combining two powerful techniques. *The Reading Teacher, 42,* 488–494.

Topping, K. (1995). *Paired reading, spelling, and writing.* New York: Cassell.

Vasinda, S. and McLeod, J. (2011). Extending readers theatre: A powerful and purposeful match with podcasting. *The Reading Teacher, 64,* 486–497.

Wilfong, L.G. (2008). Building fluency, word-recognition ability, and confidence in struggling readers: The poetry academy. *The Reading Teacher, 62,* 4–13.

Young, C. and Rasinski, T. (2009). Implementing readers theatre as an approach to classroom fluency instruction. *The Reading Teacher, 63,* 4–13.

Young, C. and Rasinski, T. (2011). Enhancing author's voice through scripting. *The Reading Teacher, 65,* 24–28.

Zimmerman, B. and Rasinski, T. (in press). The fluency development lesson: A model of authentic and effective fluency instruction. In T. Rasinski, C. Blachowicz, and K. Lems (Eds.), *Fluency Instruction* (2nd ed.). New York: Guilford.

17

Teaching Phonics and Fluency

Making Critical Choices for Authentic and Effective Instruction

Compare and contrast the following scenes. In a school we visited not long ago we found two dedicated and hardworking second-grade teachers who were doing their best to help students with the critical components of reading that are the focus of this book—words and fluency. However, the teachers approached their task in decidedly different ways.

Margaret, a veteran teacher with more than 10 years of classroom experience, spent a considerable amount of time on word recognition. Every day her students chanted the words on the classroom word wall; they said each word three times: "ladder, ladder, ladder, listen, listen, listen, forest, forest, forest, sparkle, sparkle, sparkle . . ." Then Margaret added three new words to the list. She defined the words and gave some cues about how to sound them out. The students then wrote each word three times in their word journals, followed by the definition, while Margaret wrote the words on the classroom word wall. The daily additions to the word wall meant that the daily chanting routine took more time with each passing day. When we visited the class in November, the students were chanting well over 100 words per day—a process that took close to 10 minutes to complete. Since students chanted the words in the same order each day, many students had memorized the words and were looking at the ceiling or a friend while chanting. The chant itself was done with little enthusiasm—students were merely reading the words in a staccato-like fashion, as if they were word recitation machines.

Throughout the word study component, students did a fair number of commercially prepared worksheets; they matched words to illustrations, divided words into syllables, and wrote sentences that contained targeted words. The same words were used for spelling, so students were expected to memorize the spelling of each word in a 15-word list for Friday's spelling test. Spelling bees, spell downs, and reading the words on flashcards were also common practices.

Recognizing its importance, Margaret reserved approximately 20 minutes of her daily reading period for fluency instruction. During this time, students repeatedly read passages on their own or while listening to a recorded version of the text. The passages tended to be informational texts on topics appropriate to second grade—the water cycle, forest animals, electricity, transportation, and so on. The students' primary goal was to read the passage more quickly than the day before. Indeed, before moving on to another passage, students read the passages to Margaret or an aide who timed the reading and asked some comprehension questions. Students' reading rates were recorded and eventually put on a graph to display their progress in "reading fluency." Students were proud to show us these bar graphs that demonstrated ever-increasing reading rates. We noted that when reading orally, students tended not to read with much expression. In fact, their solitary goal was to get through the passage as quickly as possible, with little attention to meaning, phrasing, or punctuation.

Two doors down the hallway resided another second-grade teacher, Kimberly, who was in her fourth year of teaching. She was very appreciative of the help that her mentor, Margaret, had given her in getting her teaching career off the ground. Kim also recognized that word recognition and fluency were absolutely critical to her students' growth in reading. She spent approximately the same amount of time teaching words and fluency as Margaret, focused on many of the same skills, and used some of the same general methods. Yet, the nature of the instruction was considerably different.

Kim also had a word wall and added new words to it daily. Kim chose high-frequency sight words or words that contained a particular pattern. Her students also chose words that they thought were interesting from their own independent and school reading or from a current event in the school, community, or nation. As new words were added to the word wall, other words were removed, or "retired" as Kim and her students called it. The retired words were put on another chart, added to word cards, and saved on a PowerPoint file for future games and practice. Students chanted the words too—first in order, one word at a time, but later Kim randomly pointed to words for students (or individuals) to read. We found students to be excited and visually attentive during this word wall routine.

Like Margaret, Kim also defined the new words for students; however, she also pointed out key features about the word, provided mnemonic clues to decoding or meaning, made reference to words with similar patterns or meaning, and, if possible, told a story that she had learned about the word from a word website or a book on word etymologies that she had open on her desk.

Rather than keeping the words in a word journal, Kim's students kept their words in personal word bank (see Chapter 11). At the bottom of each word card, students wrote the meaning of the word, drew a small illustrative picture, or wrote a sentence using the word. Kim's students practiced the words as flashcards with partners. Sometimes they practiced reading their word banks quickly and sometimes they read their word banks slowly, paying visual attention to the array of letters that made up the words.

The word banks were also used for word sort activities. Kim called out categories, and students worked with partners to sort the words— for example, words with and without consonant blends, words with and without prefixes, words that are/are not actions a person can do, and so on. Kim and her students also used the word banks for various games, from Wordo, to Word Match, to Word War, and many others.

Kim used worksheets with her students; most she made herself. Making and Writing Words, and Word Ladders (see Chapter 10) seemed to be daily activities. Kim also made cloze activities that featured sentences with key words missing. She often copied a page from a story that the students were reading, used a marker to delete words that she felt could be determined from the context, and copied this sheet for every student. Sometimes she would delete all but the first or last letter(s) in a word to give students additional clues. When correcting the cloze worksheets, she and students discussed strategies for "figuring out" the missing words. Sometimes the clue came from an illustration or the length of the deleted word. Sometimes the clue was the first letter or word order—students knew that the words *the*, *an*, and *a* were usually followed with a noun or a word that describes a noun. Sometimes words or sentences located before or after the deleted word gave clues to the missing word.

In Kim's class we saw students writing the targeted words for instruction. Generally, however, the words were not written in isolation or in lists, but in the context of sentences, paragraphs, poems, and stories the students composed.

Kim taught fluency for about the same amount of time each day as Margaret—20 minutes. And she focused on repeated readings. However, the instruction differed in purpose. Rather than reading to increase reading rate, Kim's students practiced or rehearsed reading their passages with expression and meaning because they performed them, usually on Friday. Speed does not normally help a reader or listener make meaning of the written word, so Kim's students did not focus primarily on speed.

The passages were also qualitatively different in the two classrooms. In Margaret's class students practiced informational texts that reflected topics of study in grade 2. Informational texts, however, do not generally lend themselves well to expressive reading and performance (e.g., try performing an explanation of "evaporation" for an audience). Poetry, scripts, and songs are meant to be performed, so these are the types of texts that Kim's students practiced. Even poems and scripts students wrote were used for fluency practice and performance. During the practice period, we saw Kim modeling the reading of certain texts for students, giving them formative feedback, encouraging and motivating students, giving hints to make a performance more dramatic or meaningful, and constantly focusing students' attention on "making meaning with your voice." Students were encouraged to take their passages home to rehearse in front of their parents. On Fridays Kim's class celebrated their readings with a poetry café, a songfest, a readers theater festival, or some combination of these.

Kim tested her students about once a month. She checked their reading rates, but she also rated students' appropriate expression, volume, phrasing, and emphasis. If she thought that students were attempting to read at a breakneck pace, she stopped them, reminded them that their best (not fastest) reading was expected, and asked them to begin reading again.

Both of these teachers taught words and fluency. And students made good progress in word recognition and reading fluency in both classrooms. Yet, which classroom do you think was more engaging? In what classroom were students learning to take delight and wonderment in words and language? In what classroom were students learning that reading was a matter of making and accessing meaning from the written words? In what classroom would you rather be a student or the teacher? We hope you chose Kim's classroom. We admire our colleague Margaret and her dedication to teaching and children, but we think that Kim's approach to instruction is more authentic, engaging, and ultimately more effective in growing competent and lifelong readers.

Our Orientation for This Book

Embedded throughout this book is the underlying belief that instruction is more effective when it is fun, when it is real, and when the learner can see the forest from the trees—the big picture when it comes to learning. Phonics or word recognition is important for all readers, but it can be taught in ways that are more than mere repetition of words on cards, more than completing worksheets that the teacher or students feel little ownership of, and more than the teacher and students simply following a script written by some disembodied author who supposedly knows students better than the teacher does.

As you have read our book, we hope you have been able to sense this important teaching orientation. Just because word recognition and reading fluency may be thought of as the mechanics of reading, they do not need to be taught in a mechanical manner. Throughout these chapters we have presented word study and fluency instruction that children and teachers will find fun, worthwhile, and connected to the real purpose for reading—to gain understanding of the world through print.

We hope that as you develop your own word recognition and reading fluency curricula and instructional routines, you will keep this philosophy in mind. Teaching involves choices. Our purpose in writing this book is not only to present you with evidence-based strategies for teaching words and fluency; we also hope that you will make informed instructional choices in order to develop the most effective and engaging curricula in word study and fluency for your students.

Select instructional activities that will lead students to love words and word study and that will motivate them to practice reading to make their voices, whether in oral or silent reading, help express the author's meaning.

The Sad Reality

Making word recognition and fluency instruction engaging and authentic may be easier said than done. You might think that commercially prepared instructional methods and materials for word recognition and fluency would naturally reflect principles of engagement and authenticity. The reality, in our opinion, is often far from this ideal. We see classrooms around the country that are more like Margaret's than Kim's. We believe that this is the result of the desire for products that manifest these features: mass-produced quick fixes, one-size-fits-all, and teacher proof. To get to the market first, publishers may allow products to be developed without sufficient thought and review from the profession. When a product supposedly meets the needs of all, or a large number of children, its potential market is huge. However, students are different, and it is very unlikely that one method or product can meet all needs. Instructional products or methods that can be implemented simply by having the teacher "follow the recipe and read the script" can be very appealing to some school administrators—they eliminate the teacher quality factor and minimize the need to hire highly trained and motivated teachers and provide professional development support.

As a result, many instructional materials and methods are questionable. Reading curricula have been reduced to specific instructional elements (skills, strategies, standards) that are taught in isolation, with little regard for the higher purpose for the particular element in authentic literacy activity. The instruction is often highly controlled by giving teachers specific directions and even scripts to read. Student involvement often comes in the form of rote drill and practice. The culminating activity usually entails an assessment or test in which students are asked to demonstrate mastery in a format that mirrors the instructional activity in which students were previously engaged. (In reality, the instructional activity is often designed to mirror the assessment.) If students do well, they move on to another instructional element or a more challenging lesson on the existing element. Those who perform poorly are often recycled through the same or similar instructional routine. All instruction seems to be aimed not so much at genuine learning, but on passing the high-stakes assessment—students' progress in school and teachers' careers may hang in the balance. In reality, instruction that is driven by such high-stakes assessment is "ineffective in achieving their intended purposes," and results in "unintended negative effects, as well" (Berliner 2006, p. 949).

Thus, in the area of phonics and word study we sometimes see instruction that involves the recitation and practice of words in an ever-growing list developed by authors of the instructional program. The practice often involves little thinking and certainly not much fun. Few words are read in real context; if students are provided with a "story" to read, it is often a decodable passage designed to provide practice with particular words or word elements. What do you think students are practicing with the following texts?

> Thad Smith and Seth Thorton had a sleep-over. After they had taken their baths and brushed their teeth, they threw pillows at Thad's sister Cathy.
>
> Mr. Mag had a dog named Tag. Mr. Mag gave Tag a dog treat from a bag. Tag's tail began to wag and his belly began to sag.

Clearly, these stories are meant to provide practice with the consonant digraph *th* and the word family *ag*. However, these highly contrived texts do not provide an authentic or engaging reading experience. Students may eventually master those particular elements, but at what cost? There are many unintended and negative consequences that result from such approaches to instruction.

Fluency Too

Regrettably, we see a similar trend occurring in some commercially developed fluency instruction. The research supports the use of repeated oral readings and assisted readings as keys to students' growth in fluency. The research also has demonstrated that reading rate is a valid and easy-to-administer measure of word recognition automaticity, a key component of reading fluency. Based on these understandings, we now see classrooms in which fluency instruction amounts to students' repeated reading of texts, sometimes on their own and sometimes while listening to a prerecorded and fluent reading of the text. The goal of the practice is to read the passage at a predetermined rate. The passages are often informational texts, as this is viewed as an opportunity to provide students with important information appropriate for their grade level. Often the passages have highly controlled vocabulary—mostly words from the 1,000 most frequently used words (Hiebert 2006) and few rare or difficult words. The practice cycle concludes when the teacher or an aide tests to see if the student has achieved the desired reading speed. If they have, they move on to the next, slightly more challenging passage and repeat the process.

Although such instruction is well meaning and research-based, we worry about some unintended and unresearched consequences. Here is what we see happening in many of the classrooms we have recently visited:

■ Teachers implore students to read their passages faster today than yesterday.

■ At the end of the "fluency instruction period," students chart their reading rate on a bar chart or graph.

■ Students time each other's reading; they compete to read faster than their partners.

■ Students read without expression, ignore punctuation, and have little understanding of what they read. Prosodic or expressive reading, another aspect of fluency that connects fluency to comprehension, is often largely ignored.

■ Students show little interest in reading for pleasure after engaging in the fluency instruction.

At our most recent diagnostic reading clinic in which graduate students working on their reading specialization credentials assess children with reading problems, we worked with six elementary-grade students. The clinicians administered a diagnostic informal reading inventory (IRI) in which the children read and answered questions about graded passages. When beginning the IRI, three children asked clinicians if they should read the passage "as fast as I can." Just a few years ago we never heard such a comment from children; now, unfortunately, we hear it with increasing regularity.

In our visits to schools, we often interview children and ask them to nominate someone in their class who is a good reader. Then we ask why they think the nominated student is a good reader. More often than not, it seems, the answer is "because they read fast." Children learn what we teach them, and if we convey to them, tacitly or directly, that the goal of reading is to do it quickly, they will develop the understanding that fast reading is good reading.

Sadly, this quest for speed does not necessarily result in better overall reading. We recently heard from a reading coach in Florida where a third-grade teacher zealously promoted the practice of students increasing their reading rate. Daily fluency time was specifically directed at improving reading rate. Although the students made significant rate improvements, they performed very poorly on silent reading comprehension (although they finished the assessment quickly), well below the norms for third grade.

Even more tragic, however, are the unintended consequences of such an approach to fluency instruction. Students see little authentic purpose and get little satisfaction from reading. Reading for the sake of enjoying a story or learning something new or communicating with another person is less likely to happen. Paraphrasing Mark Twain, those who know how to read but choose not to do it have no advantage over those who do not know how to read.

Choose Wisely

We hope that this book has convinced you that word study and reading fluency are critical components in effective reading instruction. However, a 2009 survey of reading scholars (Cassidy and Cassidy 2010) determined that both phonics and reading fluency were no longer "hot" topics for reading instruction. A similar survey done the following year again found that phonics and fluency are not "hot." Moreover, these experts felt that the designation of "not hot" was justified (Cassidy, Ortlieb, and Shettel 2011). We feel that phonics and fluency have lost their importance among experts not because they are not important, but because of the way that they are presented to teachers and students in many classrooms in the United States and around the world. So many of the commercial programs for teaching these important competencies treat phonics and fluency as skills that are best taught through dull, mindless activities that are not enjoyable and that do not reflect the kind of reading that happens outside of the classroom in real life.

Our goal for this chapter is to encourage you to be an informed and critical chooser of educational products and methods for teaching phonics, words, and reading fluency. We hope that you will be able to find and develop materials and instructional routines on your own. However, we realize that, for a variety of reasons, you may have to rely on commercial products and methodologies. In either case, we hope that your work will reflect our orientation in this book. Our orientation is echoed in the words of the great educational philosopher John Dewey over a century ago. Dewey urged that schools become "an embryonic community life, active with types of occupations that reflect the life of the larger society, and permeated throughout with the spirit of art, history, and science" (1907, p. 44). We interpret these words to mean that what we ask students to do in school should reflect the life that exists outside of schools in the larger community. Our charge, then, is to create instruction in reading that reflects outside-of-school reading experiences. If an instructional practice seems divorced from what we might see outside of school, then we need to questions its ultimate value for students.

In the area of phonics and word study you will, of course, have to involve students in practicing words and word elements. But that practice can be engaging and thoughtful. Look for activities that are game-like in nature—Wordo, Word Ladders, Go Fish, and Word War are just a few. Create activities that require students to think deeply and analytically about words and word parts in the same way that scientists analyze their fields of study. Have students sort words into various categories. Have students read the words you are teaching in real contexts. Have them use word meaning and passage meaning, as well as the word structure, to determine an unknown word—cloze activities work well here. Try to find more authentic texts that allow students to practice targeted words or word parts. Wouldn't a rhyme such as "Star Light, Star Bright" be an effective, engaging, and authentic way to provide practice the *ight* word family? We have found that students enjoy the rhymes we ourselves write and the ones they write as well. We enjoyed writing the following rhyme as an alternative text for the study of the *ag* word family.

> Diddle diddle dumpling my dog Tag
> Likes to chew on a dirty old rag
> Give him a treat and his tail will wag
> But his big old belly will begin to sag!

Such approaches to phonics and words will not only improve students' knowledge and ability in word decoding and determining word meanings, but they will also help students see that words are important in the big picture of reading—making meaning from print. Students will also learn to appreciate words and take delight in learning new words throughout their lives.

For fluency instruction we readily acknowledge that guided repeated and assisted reading, complemented with plenty of wide reading, are proven methods for improving students' reading fluency. However, rather than use informational texts that tend to dominate most commercially available programs for teaching fluency, we recommend that you use texts that incorporate voice and that lend themselves to performance. Students who work with these texts practice them not for the purpose of reading quickly but for recreating the author's voice. That is, the practice is aimed not simply at increasing reading rate, but at making meaning through one's voice. Reading speed will increase on its own, without emphasizing it. Rhythmical texts lend themselves to voice and/or performance: narrative, poetry, readers theater, dialogues, monologues, song lyrics, speech and oratory, letters, journals, and diary entries. Not only will practice on these texts lead to greater fluency, but they will also lead to unintended consequences that, in this case, are positive.

Practice with rhythmical texts leads to improved fluency and more (Pierce 2011)—students develop an appreciation and understanding of a greater variety of text types and genres, including some not often emphasized in conventional instruction. These texts are likely to lead students to a greater love of and appreciation for the literary qualities of the English language. Love of language comes from reciting well-written rhythmical texts; it comes from developing an awareness of the rhythm, rhyme, sound play, emphasis, phrasing, and other literary and prosodic qualities embedded in these texts. Moreover, such texts make it easy for students to see connections with other areas of the curriculum. Reading about the Civil War in a textbook is one thing. Reading, performing, analyzing, and responding to the speeches, songs, poems, quotes, letters, and diaries of people who lived through and wrote about the Civil War can lead to a different (and deeper) understanding. Rhythmical texts offer writing opportunities as well. Optimal texts for fluency instruction allow the reader to hear the author's voice in the text. Readers practice with the purpose of re-creating this voice, not of reading fast. One of the best ways to learn to write with voice is to first learn to read with voice. Thus, when students write their own scripts, dialogues, monologues, poems, songs, and other texts, they are challenged to write in genres that require a strong sense of voice—genre and text types that are not typically emphasized in conventional writing instruction (Young and Rasinski 2011).

Rhythmical texts lead to greater group cohesion among students. Patriotic songs, military service songs, and civil rights era songs were written to develop common purpose and cooperation, qualities also desired in classrooms. Thus, using rhythmical texts may lead to greater cooperation and teamwork among students.

Finally, rhythmical texts can lead to aesthetic reading responses that cannot be easily evoked from informational and expository texts. Nearly everyone we know has a favorite poem, song, speech, or other rhythmical text that, when read or heard, evokes an emotional response. We think that students need more opportunities to respond to what they read aesthetically. Rhythmical texts allow such responses to happen.

In Conclusion

Phonics, word study, and fluency instruction are absolutely crucial to students' reading development. However, instruction in phonics, word study, and fluency does not have to be unauthentic—nor do the materials used in teaching them need to be mechanistically applied. Rather, instruction and materials for these critical areas can and should be engaging and authentic. If we become critical and thoughtful developers and consumers of engaging and authentic instructional materials for phonics, word study, and fluency, we will go a long way in not only developing readers who are good decoders, have large vocabularies, and are fluent and expressive readers but who also love reading and have a love of and appreciation for the power of this wonderful language of ours.

References

Berliner, D. C. (2006). Our impoverished view of educational research. *Teachers College Record, 108*, 949–995.

Cassidy, J. and Cassidy, D. (2010). What's hot for 2010. *Reading Today, 26*(4), 1, 8, 9.

Cassidy, J., Ortlieb, E., and Shettel, J. (2011). What's hot for 2011. *Reading Today, 28*(3), 1, 6, 7, 8.

Dewey, J. (1907). *The school and society*. Chicago: University of Chicago Press.

Hiebert, E. (2006). Becoming fluent: Repeated reading with scaffolded texts. *PsychINFO*, 204–226.

Pierce, L. (2011). *Repeated readings in poetry versus prose: Fluency and enjoyment for second graders* (Unpublished doctoral dissertation). University of Toledo, Toledo, OH.

Young, C. J. and Rasinski, T. V. (2011). Enhancing author's voice through scripting. *The Reading Teacher, 65*, 24–28.

18

Involving Parents in Word Study and Reading Fluency Instruction

Maureen is a second-grade teacher in an urban school who has worked hard over the years to involve parents in their children's reading. We caught up with her after a long school day and her first response when asked to tell us about parental involvement was "It's hard! It is really hard!" But after a few seconds she added, "But you know, it's worth the effort. Of all the things I have done to help kids learn to read over the years, I think the most important and powerful has been to get parents involved." Maureen told us about a variety of programs, some just aimed at getting parents to read with their children and others that have been more directive, such as having parents of children who struggle do Paired Reading daily. "Sometimes I have had great success, and sometimes the program has fallen flat on its face."

We asked Maureen what was most effective in promoting active parental involvement. Her response was immediate:

> You've got to have patience and persistence. Look at parental involvement as a long-term process; continue to make improvements on the program that you use. When I first started my Paired Reading program only a few parents showed up for my training session, and only about half of them did the Paired Reading for the suggested three months. But every year the program seems to get better. The second year I had about 25 percent participation, and today it's more like

75 percent. I don't know what it is—word of mouth that the program really works, the improvements I have made in the program, or just the fact that I have learned to become more comfortable working with parents over time. Whatever the reason, I will tell you this—getting parents involved does work. Those kids whose . . . parents read to and with them are the kids who make the most progress in reading each year. If I were a school principal, I would insist that we have a schoolwide parent-child reading program.

In many ways parents and home involvement are the secret weapon in learning to read. Research over the past several decades has demonstrated empirically what Maureen has found: home involvement invariably improves students' school performance (Epstein 1984, 1987; Henderson 1987, 1988). More specifically, two international studies of students' reading achievement found that parental involvement and cooperation and the amount of reading students do at home are powerful variables associated with achievement (Mullis, Martin, Kennedy, and Foy 2007; Postlethwaite and Ross 1992). Any exemplary reading program must include a parent/home involvement component.

Research-Based Strategies

Advising Parents

Most families read and write. It's natural, and it varies between and among families. Aside from picking up the value of reading and writing from their families, children are motivated to read and write when their interests are tapped and when family members share the joy of their reading and writing efforts. Families plant the seeds of literacy well before children come to us in school and continue to play a critical role in young children's literacy development.

To develop effective partnerships with parents, we must acknowledge their importance in children's literacy efforts, during and well beyond their preschool years. We wish to communicate with and advise parents on how they can help their children progress in reading, but this communication must be grounded in respect for each family's home culture and literacy practices. This stance is important for developing successful partnerships with all families but especially with English language learner (ELL) families. A study of young biliterate children (Spanish and English) showed a variety of family literacy

practices—what families did, how they did it, and in what language
(Reyes and Azura 2008).

In addition to underscoring their importance in their children's
literacy development, we need to advise parents about materials for
reading and how to use these materials to help their children read.
That's what this chapter is all about.

Literacy at Home

**Research-Based
Strategies**

Learning to read takes time—time, especially, for reading. And with
the school day already crowded, we must look at the time after the
school day when students can read and receive additional support
in their learning to read. We know that simply reading is associated
with higher levels of reading achievement. We also know that reading
provides students with practice in recognizing words and helps develop
students' sight vocabulary. Thus, one of most important things we can
do to improve students' reading and word recognition is to develop a
program to promote reading at home. In one study, just 20 minutes of
reading outside school each day was associated with above-average
reading performance (Anderson, Wilson, and Fielding 1988). Promoting
20 minutes or more of reading at home will go a long way to promote
reading growth (Rasinski and Padak 2011).

We have several examples of schools that have developed successful
home-reading programs involving parents (Baumann 1995; O'Masta
and Wolf 1991; Shanahan, Wojciechowski, and Rubik 1998). In these
schools, teachers agree at the beginning of the school year that parental
and family involvement in reading is their goal. They want parents to
ensure that children read for pleasure at home for a specified period of
time (usually 20 minutes per day at home). Parents can read aloud to
children who are not yet reading conventionally.

The school year then becomes a campaign to encourage reading at
home. The school year begins with a school assembly to introduce the
home-reading campaign. The principal and teachers challenge students
to read, as a school community, a specific number of minutes over the
course of the school year. An impressive goal is one million minutes of
reading (a school of 300 students would accumulate 1,080,000 minutes
of reading if each student read 20 minutes, five days a week, over a
36-week school year). Parents are invited to the assembly as well as
to an informational session, early in the school year, in which the

home-reading campaign is explained. Information is also sent home to parents periodically throughout the school year.

Beginning with the first week of school, each student takes home a weekly log sheet for recording the number of minutes read each day (see Figure 18.1). Students return these log sheets every Monday, and an aide or parent volunteer tallies them, often using a spreadsheet computer program to summarize data about each student's home-reading progress. Classroom, grade level, and school updates are also made in order to give students a sense of the school's progress and to encourage friendly rivalries between classrooms and grade levels.

Visitors to the school are greeted by a large chart that explains the home-reading campaign and provides a progress update. (In one school a huge cardboard thermometer displayed the school's progress as the mercury rose during the school year.) Periodic assemblies to promote reading, book fairs, author studies and visits, posters placed throughout the school reminding students to read, and personal notes and words of encouragement from teachers and the school principal help many students catch the reading habit and bootstrap themselves to proficient reading. With such wonderful support from the school staff, the school will reach and surpass its goal. Ultimate attainment of the reading goal is celebrated with a school parade, author visit, picnic, ice cream social, or some other special event.

Reading to Children

We know that reading to students can have a dramatically positive effect on various aspects of students' reading achievement. One of the first scholars to note the importance of parents reading to children, Dolores Durkin (1966), found that children who learned to read before beginning formal schooling had parents who read to them in such a way that their children could see the text, could follow their parents' reading, and could ask and answer questions about the words encountered in the reading. These actions seemed to help children begin to develop a sight vocabulary and examine the spelling and structure of words. More important, perhaps, is that they were picking up the reading habit.

When we remind parents to read to their children, we might add that they should read in such a way that their child can see what they are reading. Furthermore, we need to encourage parents to direct their children's eyes toward the text by pointing and informally asking

Research-Based
Strategies

Figure 18.1   Weekly Reading Log

Name _____   School _____

Please return this log to your child's teacher at the beginning of the week.

Day of Week	Date	Time Spent Reading (minutes)	Names of Passages Read	Other Reading Activities Done	Comments
Mon.					
Tue.					
Wed.					
Thu.					
Fri.					
Sat.					
Sun.					

questions about a few words. This is in no way meant to imply that parents turn the very effective and bonding activity of reading to their children into a reading lesson. Nonetheless, informal chats about the text may help children develop more quickly as readers and learn to recognize and analyze words.

Read-alouds can also help children develop phonemic awareness and other beginning reading skills (see Chapter 6). In 2006 Monique Sénéchal did a meta-analysis of a number of experimental studies that looked at the effects of three kinds of parent involvement on children's reading growth—parents reading to children, parents listening to children read, and parents following either of these up with word play or "literacy skills." Nearly 1,200 families were studied. Sénéchal found that the addition of word play or other "literacy skills" was two times more effective than having parents simply listen to their children read and six times more effective than when parents simply read to their children. Thus, we want to encourage word play as part of families' read-aloud routines.

Encourage parents to read, tell, or sing children's stories, songs, rhymes, or other texts that have a strong language-sound component. The books we listed in Chapter 6 are excellent choices for parents. Familiar songs printed for parent and child use are another great choice. Some of the best texts for phonemic awareness development are nursery rhymes. Encouraging parents to read and reread nursery rhymes with children will inevitably lead to wonderful discussions about sounds and will support children's development in sound awareness.

Since traditional nursery rhymes are in the public domain, they can be copied freely for parents. In an attempt to get young children on the right track in reading, the Ravenna, Ohio, Even Start program, a family literacy program connected to the local public schools, has made its own nursery rhyme book, complete with illustrations. It is given to parents of young children in the hopes that they will begin reading to their children early in life, which will help children develop abilities critical to their growth in phonics and word recognition.

Technology has expanded the possibilities for literacy learning and parent involvement. The Internet is another superb source of parent-child reading material. Parents and children can together explore the Web, parents working at the keyboard and children in control of the mouse. As they visit different sites, parents can read

Research-Based Strategies

Technology

when requested, and parents and children can read together when appropriate.

Writing at Home

Engaging in invented or phonemic spelling allows children to apply their emerging phonics knowledge in their own writing (see Chapter 15). Parents can foster their children's writing development and their phonics knowledge by encouraging their children to write at home (Rasinski and Padak 2009). Usually, this means using writing at play to make recipes, create menus, and make lists. Journal or diary writing, also, is an exceptional and authentic way for children to write at home.

Dialogue journals are particularly well suited for parental involvement and for developing students' writing and word knowledge. A dialogue journal is a conversation between parent and child that takes place in writing. One person writes in it one day, asking questions or making observations, and then passes the journal to his or her partner. The partner writes in the same journal on the following day, replying to the questions and comments, and then adding questions, comments, or observations for the first writer. Over time, the journal is an exceptional way to learn about the other person and to communicate in ways that are often difficult or superficial when done orally, for instance, offering explanations for one's behavior or making apologies. In addition, the more proficient writer provides an immediate model for the child, who begins to emulate the parent's writing.

Tim began a dialogue journal with his son, Mike, in April. It was Mike's seventh birthday. The journal passed between Tim and Mike a couple of times a week when they first began. Mike's early written entries were at an emergent level. Mike and Tim kept their journal going over the summer months. By September, Mike's written entries were longer and significantly more conventional. This was due mainly to the writing and modeling that took place during the summer—no formal instruction took place. His writing became much more conventional in format, and his knowledge of how words are spelled grew greatly as he responded to his dad's writing by using the words his dad used. Parents and teachers never know just how much they influence their children's development. Mike is now an adult, but his love for writing has not ceased. In college, he was the basketball team beat writer, and sports and assistant managing editor for the *Kent Stater*, Kent State University's daily newspaper.

Captioned Television

Reading researchers have been looking into the effects of captioned television on children's reading development; what they have found is very promising. Captioned television has been found to help children learn words and increase the reading performance of readers who struggle (Adler 1985; Koskinen et al. 1987; Koskinen et al. 1993; Neuman and Koskinen 1992). As children watch the visual image on the screen and hear the words spoken, they also see the words printed on the screen. The dual presentation of words, in visual and oral formats, helps children develop their sight vocabulary and decoding skills as they read the screen. Moreover, parents have to do little to make this work.

Teachers who want to encourage parents to turn their children on to reading through captioned television might send home a letter

Figure 18.2 Letter to Parents Explaining Captioned Television

September 15

Dear Parents:

Now that the school year is under way, I'd like to inform you of an exciting and easy way to help your child in reading. Recent research has shown that children who watch TV with captions improve their word learning as well as their overall reading. Seeing the words on the screen while listening to them helps readers learn to recognize words and read with fluency.

Please make sure that the captioning option is turned on when your child watches television. Actually, it would be a good idea to have the captioning on all the time. Talk to your child about how paying attention to the captions will improve reading. Encourage your child to "read the screen" as he or she watches TV.

Your family may find the captions a bit distracting at first. This will only last a few days until you and your child become comfortable

(Continued)

Figure 18.2 (*Continued*)

> with captioned television. It won't take long before the captions become an accepted part of the television experience.
>
> Captioned television is a very easy way to help your child in reading! The amount of reading he or she does will increase significantly just from the addition of captioned TV. And, the more students read, the better readers they will become.
>
> Please feel free to call me if you have any questions. Thank you for your assistance in helping your child become a better reader.
>
> Sincerely,
> Mr. Rasinski

explaining the potential and encouraging parents to enable captioning on the television their child watches (see Figure 18.2). Remind parents to discuss the reasons for captioning with their children. Although children may find the captions bothersome for the first few days, it won't be long before it becomes a natural part of children's television experience.

All teachers, preschool through grade 6, should recommend to parents the activities we have described. For most children, especially those experiencing difficulty in reading, more directed activities at home may provide essential reinforcement to the word recognition instruction they receive at school. The remainder of this chapter examines more specific ways in which parents can help their children learn how words work.

More Home Activities for Improving Word Recognition

Often teachers give students lists of words to learn to spell or read. If these lists are sent home, parents can work with their children on the words: practice reading the words, spelling the words, or playing word games that the teacher has introduced to children and parents (see Chapter 14). Indeed, many of the phonemic awareness, word recognition, and reading fluency activities can easily be adapted for home use. Many parents would jump at the chance to help their children in these more directed ways.

Two weeks prior to the end of summer vacation in the years that Tim's children's were entering first and second grades, the teachers mailed home a list of 10 to 20 words that children would encounter during the initial weeks of school. Tim and his wife, Kathy, were glad to get the words and to briefly introduce them to their children for 10 to 15 minutes a day on those waning days of summer. Their mini word studies eased the transition from vacation to school and helped children learn what to expect in their new classrooms. Of course, Tim and Kathy also continued to read to and write with their children daily.

In Chapter 7 we described a classroom routine in which students learn about rimes and phonograms by writing poems that feature a particular rime. As you will recall, children brainstorm words belonging to a particular rime pattern, read poems and other texts containing the targeted rime, and are then encouraged to make a short poem of their own featuring the rime. Although students can do this final writing task on their own, with classmates, or with an older reading buddy, we have found that the activity works best when parents work with their children to make the short poems. Not only does this give children expert help (even low-literate parents can be quite successful with the activity), it demonstrates to children that their parents are readers and writers also and that they should emulate their parents' writing. Later, when children read their poems in school, parents can occasionally be invited to share the spotlight with their children.

Paired Reading (see Chapter 16) is a direct way to improve students' word recognition and overall fluency. Topping's (1987) original application of Paired Reading was as a parent tutorial. Parents of elementary students attended a brief training session in which Paired Reading was described and modeled. The activity is simple—a parent and a child sit side by side and simultaneously read aloud a text of the child's choosing, with either the parent or child pointing to the text as it is read. When the child experiences difficulty with a word, the parent supplies the word and the partners continue reading. When ready to try reading without assistance, the child signals the parent, who then either follows the text silently or reads in a very soft voice, following the child's reading.

Topping (1987) found that about 10 minutes a day of this sort of parent-child activity could accelerate children's reading progress significantly. We know of many teachers and schools that have developed Paired Reading as a parent involvement program with great success and wide participation.

Research-Based Strategies

Family Workshops

Periodic family literacy workshops are very effective ways to communicate the importance of literacy involvement at home and ways that parents can support their children at home. At these monthly, quarterly, or biannual workshops, parents are given specific information on how to help their children become better readers and love reading.

In their Family Fluency Program, Morrow, Kuhn, and Schwanenflugel (2007) describe a set of family workshops in which parents were informed about simple fluency activities that could be done at home, such as partner reading, choral reading, echo reading, and repeated reading. The Family Fluency Program was an integral part of a larger fluency study that found that students receiving fluency instruction made greater gains in reading than students not receiving such instruction. Also, parents in the Family Fluency Program were more likely to engage in fluency and other literacy-related activities at home than a control group of children not involved in Family Fluency.

This study shows that family-oriented workshops can be effective, especially if we focus those workshops on what matters for young readers—lots of reading, writing, word study, and fluency.

Systematic Routines

One of the best ways for teachers to involve parents in their children's word recognition learning is to develop a systematic word recognition and fluency routine for the home. A systematic routine is simply a set of learning activities designed to be regularly implemented in a preordained sequence. We have worked with many schools and teachers in our local area to develop and implement such routines with parents. One is called Fast Start (Rasinski 1995), and it is based on research indicating the potential of parents reading to their children, reading with their children, and then listening to their children read on their own.

In the Fast Start routine, teachers provide parents with texts to be read and practiced each evening, usually five per week. Along with the pack of texts (see Figure 18.3), which are often rhymes, poetry, or other short passages of no more than 200 words, is a weekly log sheet (see Figure 18.4) that is to be placed on the refrigerator at home as a reminder for parents and children to do the routine daily. For younger children, short poems, jokes, and nursery rhymes may be most

Figure 18.3 Fast Start Text

Pease-porridge hot,

Pease-porridge cold,

Pease-porridge in the pot,

Nine days old.

Some like it hot,

Some like it cold,

Some like it in the pot,

Nine days old.

Dear Parents:

1. Read the poem to your chid several times; point to the text as you read.

2. Read the poem with your child several times.

3. Listen to your child read the rhyme to you several times.

4. Point to and read individual words in the text.

5. Identify rhyming words (e.g., *hot, pot*) and write out several other words that follow the same rhyme pattern on this sheet.

Figure 18.4 Fast Start Monthly Reading Log

Date	Time Spent on Lesson	Name of New Passage Introduced	Other Reading Activities
Name			
11-1			
11-2			
11-3			
11-4			
11-5			

appropriate. For older students, more sophisticated poetry and other genres may work best. Each lesson takes approximately 15 minutes and goes like this:

1. Parents read the text to their children, one to three times.

2. Parents chat with their children about the passage and how it was read.

3. Parents and children read the text together orally. Again, this may be done several times until the child feels comfortable and confident in reading it.

4. When ready, the child reads the passage independently with the parent providing support and encouragement. Again, the child can read the text several times, perhaps to different listeners each time.

5. After having read the passage several times through, the parent and child can engage in some word-learning activities. These can involve adding words from the text to a home word bank and doing word bank activities such as word sorts, flash cards, and word games (see Chapters 11 and 14), or finding words from the text that belong to a particular word family (rime group) and brainstorming and practicing other words that fit into the word family (see Figure 18.5).

6. To make a good connection to the school, teachers can ask students to perform the passage at school the next day. The topic of the original text may lead to other passages on a similar topic or theme at school.

Fast Start is inexpensive, easy for parents to learn, and quick for them to implement. Parents report that they and their children enjoy the quick-paced activities. We have also found that the Fast Start program,

Figure 18.5   Fast Start Text with Word Study

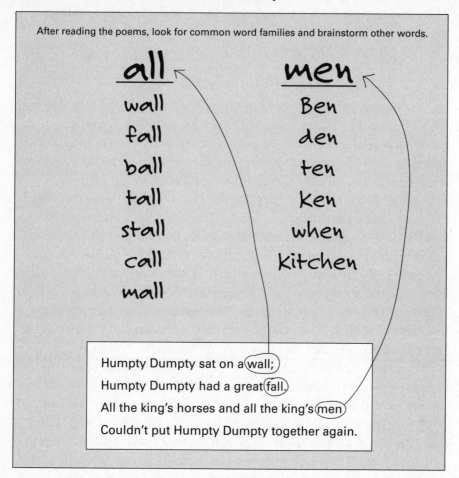

After reading the poems, look for common word families and brainstorm other words.

all	**men**
wall	Ben
fall	den
ball	ten
tall	Ken
stall	when
call	Kitchen
mall	

Humpty Dumpty sat on a (wall;)
Humpty Dumpty had a great (fall.)
All the king's horses and all the king's (men)
Couldn't put Humpty Dumpty together again.

implemented at several grade levels and with parents whose children attend our reading center clinic, results in significant improvements in word learning and overall reading proficiency (Rasinski 1995).

More recent research into Fast Start (Padak and Rasinski 2004a, 2004b) has shown it to be very effective and, as important, very enjoyable for parents and children. For example, a two-year study in 18 elementary schools showed that kindergarten children who participated in Fast Start learned letters and concepts about print faster and developed more extensive writing vocabularies than children who did not participate. Moreover, first-grade children who participated in Fast Start outperformed their non–Fast Start peers on published tests

**Research-Based
Strategies**

of general reading achievement. An astonishing 91 percent of children in these studies said they enjoyed Fast Start, and 98 percent said they thought Fast Start made them better readers. Their parents agreed: Eighty-three percent believed that Fast Start sessions with their children represented time well spent. It's clear that this relatively simple routine has power to affect children's achievement as readers.

Another study of beginning first-grade students found that the most at-risk beginning readers using the Fast Start routine at home with their parents made nearly 50 percent greater progress in word recognition and more than 100 percent greater gain in reading fluency (words in context read correctly per minute) than a matched group of at-risk first-graders who were not using Fast Start at home but were receiving the same reading instruction in school (Rasinski and Stevenson 2005). Clearly, well-designed instructional routines for parents can have a dramatic impact on student reading growth and achievement. Frances Imperato (2009) has employed Fast Start in the kindergarten classrooms in her school for several years with excellent results. She notes, "Without doubt, this family instructional routine, as well as others that involve real reading and word play between parents and children, have had a positive influence for literacy in my school."

We originally intended Fast Start as a program for parents of beginning readers (Padak and Rasinski 2005). However, the instructional routine around which Fast Start was developed (parents read to, read with, listen to their child read to them, then do a bit of word study) can easily be adapted for children at any age (and for use in school as well as in the home). The major adaptation for home use with older children would be the selection of text for the parent and child to read—instead of a nursery rhyme, it could be a more age-appropriate poem, a newspaper article, a famous speech, a section from a familiar story, a letter, or many other text forms. The nature of the word study component would also likely change. Instead of a focus on sight words and word families, a greater focus on word meanings, synonyms, antonyms, and word derivations might be more appropriate.

Fast Start is a good example of the kind of program that can be designed at any grade level to help students become better at word recognition and reading at home. Although we have no hesitation in recommending it for any elementary classroom, we encourage you to develop your own systematic routine, or an adaptation of Fast Start, for your own students and parents that will maximize their learning.

In Conclusion

The home is a wonderful place to support children's literacy learning, and teachers and schools should support parents in helping their children become readers and writers. But, in our efforts to encourage home reading, we need to remember that home is not school, nor should it be turned into school. When we ask parents to read to and with their children or to engage in activities such as Fast Start, we must emphasize the importance of the ambiance that parents create around the activity. Home reading should be natural and enjoyable for children and parents. Parents and children should feel at ease throughout their reading and writing. We need to remind parents to praise their children lavishly for their reading efforts and to focus attention on children's success. And we need to help parents understand that parent-child learning can be emotionally taxing for both parent and child and that any parent-child reading activity should stop at the first sign of frustration.

Parents are absolutely necessary to children's reading development. In addition, effective parent involvement can take a variety of forms— from a fairly explicit type of intervention like Fast Start, to simply encouraging children to read 20 to 30 minutes at home every day for pleasure. Either way, students get more exposure to, and practice with, the written word. The extra reading students do at home will help them significantly in becoming proficient readers. If achieved early in children's education, parental involvement leads to reading success and ongoing support for schools and teachers. Getting parents involved may be a tough nut to crack for some teachers, but if you are truly interested in maximizing your students' development in decoding, fluency, and overall reading, it is essential that you get parents involved in their children's reading.

References

Adler, R. (1985). Using closed-captioned television in the classroom. In L. Gambrell and E. McLaughlin (Eds.), *New directions in reading: Research and practice: Yearbook of the State of Maryland International Reading Association* (pp. 11–18). Silver Spring, MD: State of Maryland International Reading Association.

Anderson, R. C., Wilson, P., and Fielding, L. (1988). Growth in reading and how children spend their time outside of school. *Reading Research Quarterly, 23,* 285–303.

Baumann, N. (1995). Reading millionaires—It works! *The Reading Teacher, 48,* 730.

Durkin, D. (1966). *Children who read early.* New York: Teachers College Press.

Epstein, J. (1984). School policy and parent involvement: Research results. *Educational Horizons, 62,* 70–72.

Epstein, J. (1987). Parent involvement: What research says to administrators. *Education and Urban Society, 19,* 119–133.

Henderson, A. T. (1987). *The evidence continues to grow: Parent involvement improves student achievement.* Columbia, MD: National Committee for Citizens in Education.

Henderson, A. T. (1988). Parents are a school's best friend. *Phi Delta Kappan, 70,* 148–153.

Imperato, F. (2009). Getting parents and children off to a strong start in reading. *The Reading Teacher, 63,* 342–344.

Koskinen, P. S., et al. (1987). *Using the technology of closed-captioned television to teach reading to handicapped students.* Performance Report, United States Department of Education Grant No. G–00–84–30067. Falls Church, VA: National Captioning Institute.

Koskinen, P. S., et al. (1993). Captioned video and vocabulary learning: An innovative practice in literacy education. *The Reading Teacher, 47,* 36–43.

Morrow, L. M., Kuhn, M. R., and Schwanenflugel, P. L. (2007). The family fluency program. *The Reading Teacher, 60,* 322–333.

Mullis, I. V. S., Martin, M. O., Kennedy, A. M., and Foy, P. (2007). *IEA's Progress in International Reading Literacy Study in primary school in 40 countries.* Chestnut Hill, MA: TIMSS and PIRLS International Study Center, Boston College.

Neuman, S. B. and Koskinen, P. S. (1992). Captioned television as comprehensible input: Effects of incidental word learning in context for language minority students. *Reading Research Quarterly, 27,* 95–106.

O'Masta, G. A. and Wolf, J. A. (1991). Encouraging independent reading through the reading millionaires project. *The Reading Teacher, 44,* 656–662.

Padak, N. and Rasinski, T. (2004a). Fast Start: A promising practice for family literacy programs. *Family Literacy Forum, 3*(2), 3–9.

Padak, N. and Rasinski, T. (2004b). Fast Start: Successful literacy instruction that connects homes and schools. In J. Dugan, P. Linder, M. B. Sampson, B. Brancato, and L. Elish-Piper (Eds.), *Celebrating the power of literacy, 2004 College Reading Association Yearbook* (pp. 11–23). Logan, UT: College Reading Association.

Padak, N. and Rasinski, T. (2005). *Fast Start for early readers: A research-based, send-home literacy program.* New York: Scholastic.

Postlethwaite, T. N. and Ross, K. N. (1992). *Effective schools in reading: Implications for educational planners.* The Hague: International Association for the Evaluation of Educational Achievement.

Rasinski, T. V. (1995). *Fast Start: A parental involvement reading program for primary grade students.* In W. Linek and E. Sturtevant (Eds.), *Generations of literacy. Seventeenth*

Yearbook of the College Reading Association (pp. 301–312). Harrisonburg, VA: College Reading Association.

Rasinski, T. V. and Padak, N. (2009). Write soon! *The Reading Teacher, 62,* 618–620.

Rasinski, T. V. and Padak, N. (2011). Who wants to be a (reading) millionaire? *The Reading Teacher, 64,* 553–555.

Rasinski, T. V. and Stevenson, B. (2005). The effects of Fast Start Reading, a fluency based home involvement reading program, on the reading achievement of beginning readers. *Reading Psychology: An International Quarterly, 26,* 109–125.

Reyes, I. and Azuara, P. (2008). Emergent biliteracy in young Mexican American immigrant children. *Reading Research Quarterly, 43,* 374–398.

Sénéchal, M. (2006). *The effect of family literacy interventions on children's acquisition of reading.* Portsmouth, NH: RMC Research Corp.

Shanahan, S., Wojciechowski, J., and Rubik, G. (1998). A celebration of reading: How our school read for one million minutes. *The Reading Teacher, 52,* 93–96.

Topping, K. (1987). Paired reading: A powerful technique for parent use. *The Reading Teacher, 40,* 608–614.

Appendix A

Common Rimes
(Phonograms or Word Families)

ab: tab, drab
ace: race, place
ack: lack, track
act: fact, pact
ad: bad, glad
ade: made, shade
aft: raft, craft
ag: bag, shag
age: page, stage
aid: maid, braid
ail: mail, snail
air: hair, stair
ain: rain, train
ait: bait, trait
ake: take, brake
alk: talk, chalk
all: ball, squall
am: ham, swam
ame: name, blame
amp: camp, clamp
an: man, span
ance: dance, glance
and: land, gland
ane: plane, cane
ang: bang, sprang
ank: bank, plank
ant: pant, chant
ap: nap, snap
ape: tape, drape
ar: car, star
ard: hard, card
are: care, glare

ark: dark, spark
arm: harm, charm
arn: barn, yarn
arp: carp, harp
art: part, start
ase: base, case
ash: cash, flash
ask: mask, task
ass: lass, mass
at: fat, scat
atch: hatch, catch
ate: gate, plate
aught: caught, taught
ave: gave, shave
aw: saw, draw
awn: lawn, fawn
ay: hay, clay
ax: wax, sax
aze: haze, maze
ead: head, bread
eak: leak, sneak
eal: real, squeal
eam: team, stream
ean: mean, lean
eap: heap, leap
ear: year, spear
eat: beat, cheat
eck: peck, check
ed: bed, shed
ee: tee, tree
eed: need, speed

eek: leek, seek
eel: feel, kneel
eem: deem, seem
een: seen, screen
eep: keep, sheep
eer: peer, steer
eet: meet, sleet
eg: leg, beg
eigh: weigh, sleigh
eight: weight, freight
ell: fell, swell
elt: felt, belt
en: Ben, when
end: tend, blend
ent: sent, spent
ess: less, bless
est: rest, chest
et: get, jet
ew: flew, chew
ib: bib, crib
ibe: bribe, tribe
ice: rice, splice
ick: kick, stick
id: hid, slid
ide: wide, pride
ie: die, pie
ief: thief, chief
ife: wife, knife
iff: cliff, whiff
ift: gift, sift
ig: pig, twig
ight: tight, bright

ike: Mike, spike
ile: mile, tile
ill: fill, chill
ilt: kilt, quilt
im: him, trim
in: tin, spin
ince: since, prince
ind: kind, blind
ine: mine, spine
ing: sing, string
ink: sink, shrink
ip: hip, flip
ipe: ripe, swipe
ire: tire, sire
irt: dirt, shirt
ise: rise, wise
ish: dish, swish
isk: disk, risk
iss: kiss, Swiss
ist: mist, wrist
it: hit, quit
itch: ditch, witch
ite: bite, write
ive: five, hive
ix: fix, six
o: do, to, who
o: go, no, so
oach: coach, poach
oad: road, toad
oak: soak, cloak
oal: coal, goal
oam: foam, roam
oan: Joan, loan
oar: boar, roar
oast: boast, coast
oat: boat, float
ob: job, throb
obe: robe, globe
ock: lock, stock
od: rod, sod

ode: code, rode
og: fog, clog
oil: boil, broil
oin: coin, join
oke: woke, spoke
old: gold, scold
ole: hole, stole
oll: roll, droll
ome: dome, home
one: cone, phone
ong: long, wrong
oo: too, zoo
ood: good, hood
ood: food, mood
ook: cook, took
ool: cool, fool
oom: room, bloom
oon: moon, spoon
oop: hoop, snoop
oot: boot, shoot
op: top, chop
ope: hope, slope
orch: porch, torch
ore: bore, snore
ork: cork, fork
orn: horn, thorn
ort: fort, short
ose: rose, close
oss: boss, gloss
ost: cost, lost
ost: host, most
ot: got, trot
otch: notch, blotch
ote: note, quote
ough: rough, tough
ought: bought,
  brought
ould: could, would
ounce: bounce, pounce
ound: bound, found

ouse: house, mouse
out: pout, about
outh: mouth, south
ove: cove, grove
ove: dove, love
ow: how, chow
ow: slow, throw
owl: howl, growl
own: down, town
own: known, grown
ox: fox, pox
oy: boy, ploy
ub: cub, shrub
uck: duck, stuck
ud: mud, thud
ude: dude, rude
udge: fudge, judge
ue: sue, blue
uff: puff, stuff
ug: dug, plug
ule: rule, mule
ull: dull, gull
um: sum, chum
umb: numb, thumb
ump: bump, plump
un: run, spun
unch: bunch, hunch
une: June, tune
ung: hung, flung
unk: sunk, chunk
unt: bunt, hunt
ur: fur, blur
urn: burn, churn
urse: curse, nurse
us: bus, plus
ush: mush, crush
ust: dust, trust
ut: but, shut
ute: lute, flute
y: my, dry

Appendix B

Fry Instant Word List

These are the Fry 600 most often used words in reading and writing. The first 300 words represent about two-thirds of all the words students encounter in their reading. Students should be able to recognize these words instantly and accurately (i.e., become part of their sight vocabularies) in order to read with fluency. We recommend, as a rule of thumb, that the first 100 words be mastered by the end of first grade and each succeeding group of 100 mastered by the end of each succeeding grade (i.e., by the end of grade 6 all 600 words should be part of students' sight vocabularies).

First 100 Instant Words

the	are	but	which
of	as	not	she
and	with	what	do
a	his	all	how
to	they	were	will
in	I	we	up
is	at	when	other
you	be	your	about
that	this	can	out
it	or	said	many
he	one	there	then
was	had	use	them
for	by	an	these
on	words	each	so
some	more	been	get
her	write	called	come
would	number	who	made
make	no	oil	have

Source: From Fry, E., Kress, J., and Fountoukidis, D.L. (2000), *The Reading Teacher's Book of Lists,* Fourth edition. Englewood Cliffs, NJ: Prentice-Hall. Reprinted with the permission of the Fry family.

like	way	sit	from
him	could	now	their
into	people	find	if
time	my	long	go
has	than	down	see
look	first	day	may
two	water	did	part

Second 100 Instant Words

over	say	set	try
new	great	put	kind
sound	where	end	hand
take	help	does	picture
only	through	another	again
little	much	well	change
work	before	large	off
know	line	must	play
place	right	big	spell
years	too	even	air
live	means	such	away
me	old	because	animals
back	any	turned	house
give	same	here	point
most	tell	why	page
very	boy	asked	letters
after	following	went	mother
things	came	men	answer
our	want	read	found
just	show	need	study
name	also	land	still
good	around	different	learn
sentence	form	home	should
man	three	us	American
think	small	move	world

Third 100 Instant Words

high	saw	important	miss
every	left	until	idea
near	don't	children	enough
add	few	side	eat
food	while	feet	face
between	along	car	watch
own	might	miles	far
below	close	night	Indians

country	something	walked	really
plants	seemed	white	almost
last	next	sea	let
school	hard	began	above
father	open	grow	girl
keep	example	took	sometimes
trees	beginning	river	mountains
never	life	four	cut
started	always	carry	young
city	those	state	talk
earth	both	once	soon
eyes	paper	book	list
light	together	hear	song
thought	got	stop	being
head	group	without	leave
under	often	second	family
story	run	later	it's

Fourth 100 Instant Words

body	dog	piece	door
music	horse	told	sure
color	birds	usually	become
stand	problem	didn't	top
sun	compete	friends	ship
questions	room	easy	across
fish	knew	heard	today
area	since	order	during
mark	ever	red	short
better	rock	pattern	south
best	space	numeral	sing
however	covered	table	war
low	fast	north	ground
hours	several	slowly	king
black	hold	money	fall
products	himself	map	town
happened	toward	farm	I'll
whole	five	pulled	unit
measure	step	draw	figure
remember	morning	voice	certain
early	passed	seen	field
waves	vowel	cold	travel
reached	true	cried	wood
listen	hundred	plan	fire
wind	against	notice	upon

Fifth 100 Instant Words

done	front	stay	warm
English	feel	green	common
road	fact	known	bring
half	inches	island	explain
ten	street	week	dry
fly	decided	less	though
gave	contain	machine	language
box	course	base	shape
finally	surface	ago	deep
wait	produce	stood	thousands
correct	building	plane	yes
oh	ocean	system	clear
quickly	class	behind	equation
person	note	ran	yet
became	nothing	round	government
shown	rest	boat	filled
minutes	carefully	game	heat
strong	scientists	force	full
verb	inside	brought	hot
stars	wheels	understand	check
object	power	dark	fine
am	cannot	ball	pair
rule	able	material	circle
among	six	special	include
noun	size	heavy	built

Sixth 100 Instant Words

can't	picked	legs	beside
matter	simple	sat	gone
square	cells	main	sky
syllables	paint	winter	glass
perhaps	mind	side	million
bill	love	written	west
felt	cause	length	lay
suddenly	rain	reason	weather
test	exercise	kept	root
direction	eggs	interest	instruments
center	train	arms	meet
farmers	blue	brother	third
ready	wish	race	months
anything	drop	present	paragraph
divided	developed	beautiful	raised
general	window	store	represent

energy	difference	job	soft
subject	distance	edge	whether
Europe	heart	past	clothes
moon	sit	sign	flowers
region	sum	record	shall
return	summer	finished	teacher
believe	wall	discovered	held
dance	forest	wild	describe
members	probably	happy	drive

Prefixes

Letter patterns added to the beginning of words that change the word's meaning.

Prefix	Meaning	Example
after-	after	afternoon
ambi-	both, around	ambidextrous
amphi-	both, around	amphibian
ante-	before	antebellum
anti-	against	antiwar
auto-	self	automatic, automobile
bene-	good	benefit
bi-	two	bicycle
by-	near, aside	bystander
cent-	hundred	century
circu-	around	circulate
co-	together	coauthor
col-	with	collaborate
contra-	against	contraband
de-	from, down	decay
dec-, deci-	ten	decade, decimal
di-	two	digraph
dia-	through, across	diameter
dis-	opposite	disagree
re-	back, do again	recall, rewrite
semi-	half	semicircle
sept-	seven	September
sub-	under	submerge
super-	more than, over	supernatural, supervisor
syn-	together	synonym
tele-	distant	telephone
trans-	across	transcontinental
tri-	three	tricycle
ultra-	beyond	ultramodern
un-	not, opposite	unhappy, unable
under-	below, less than	underground, underage
uni-	one	unicorn

Appendix D

Suffixes

Letter patterns added to the end of a word that change the word's meaning.

Suffix	Meaning	Example
-ance	state or quality of	repentance
-ancy	state or quality of	vacancy
-ant	one who	servant
-ar	one who	beggar
-arium	place for	aquarium
-ary	place for	library
-ation	state or quality of	inspiration
-cle	small	particle
-cule	small	miniscule
-cy	state or quality of	accuracy
-d	change of verb tense	baked
-dom	state or quality of	freedom
-ed	change of verb tense	talked
-en	change of verb tense	taken
-en	made of	golden
-ence	state or quality of	absence
-ency	state or quality of	frequency
-er	comparative	smaller
-er	one who	teacher
-ern	direction	eastern
-ery, -ry	state or quality of	bravery
-ery	trade or occupation	surgery
-ess	female	hostess
-ess	one who	actress
-est	comparative	smallest
-ette	small	cigarette
-eur	one who	chauffeur
-ful	full of	careful
-hood	state or quality of	childhood
-ier, -yer	one who	lawyer
-ily	in what manner	speedily

-ing	change of verb tense	singing
-ion	state or quality of	champion
-ism	state or quality of	heroism
-ist	one who practices	biologist
-itis	inflammation of	laryngitis
-ity	state or quality of	civility
-ization	state or quality of	civilization
-less	without	worthless
-let	small	islet
-ling	small	duckling
-ly	in what manner	strangely
-man	one who works with	craftsman
-ment	state or quality of	amazement
-most	comparative	innermost
-ness	state or quality of	kindness
-ology	study of	biology
-or	one who	doctor
-orium	place for	auditorium
-ory	place for	laboratory
-phobia	fear of	claustrophobia
-ry	trade or occupation	dentistry
-s	more than one	dogs
-ship	state or quality of	ownership
-ship	art or skill of	swordsmanship
-sion	state or quality of	tension
-t	change of verb tense	slept
-tion	state or quality of	fascination
-ty	state or quality of	loyalty
-ward	direction	backward
-wright	one who works with	playwright

Appendix E

Greek and Latin
Word Patterns

Root	Meaning	Examples
act	do	react
aero	air	aerate
agri	field	agriculture
alt	high	altitude
alter	other	alternate
ambul	walk, go	ambulance
amo, ami	love	amiable
ang	bend	angle
anim	life, spirit	animal
ann, enn	year	annual
anthr, anthro	man (people)	anthropology
aqua	water	aquarium
arch	chief	archbishop
archae, arche	ancient	archaeology
art	skill	artist
ast	star	astronaut
aud	hear	auditorium
belli	war	belligerent
biblio	book	bibliography
bio	life	biology
brev	short	brevity
cam, camp	field	campus
cap	head	captain
cardi	heart	cardiac
center, centr	center	egocentric
cert	sure	certain
chron	time	chronological
cide	cut, kill	suicide
cogn	know	recognize
common	common	community
corp	body	corporation

cosm	universe	cosmonaut
crat	rule	democrat
credit	believe	incredible
cycl	circle, ring	bicycle
dem	people	democracy
dict	speak	contradict
div	divide	divorce
doc	teach	indoctrinate
don, donat	give	pardon
dont, dent	tooth	orthodontist
dox	belief	orthodox
duct	lead	viaduct
esth	feeling	anesthetic
fac	make, do	factory
flex, flect	bend	reflex
form	shape	uniform
fract, frag	break	fracture
frater	brother	fraternity
fric	rub	friction
gam	marriage	polygamy
gen	birth, race	generation
geo	earth	geology
gon	angle	pentagon
grad	step	gradual
gram	letter, written	telegram
graph	write	telegraph
grat	pleasing	gratitude
homo, hom	man	homicide
hydr	water	hydrant
ject	throw	reject
junct	join	juncture
jud	law	judge
jur	law, swear	perjury
jus	law	justice
lab	work	labor
lat	side	collateral
liber	free	liberty
loc	place	location
log, logue	word	monologue
luc	light	elucidate
lum	light	illuminate
luna	moon	lunar
lust	shine	luster
man	hand	manual
mand	to order	command

Root	Meaning	Examples
mania	madness	maniac
mar	sea	marine
mater, matri	mother	maternity
max	greatest	maximum
mech	machine	mechanic
mem	mindful	remember
ment	mind	mental
meter	measure	thermometer
migr	move	migrate
min	small, lesser	minimize
miss	send	missionary
mob	move	automobile
morph	shape	polymorphous
mort	death	mortal
mot	move	motor
mut	change	commute
narr	tell	narrate
nat	born	innate
nav	ship	naval
neg	no	negative
neo	new	neoclassic
nov	new	novel
ocu	eye	binocular
opt	eye	optometrist
opt	best	optimal
onym, nym	name	pseudonym
orig	beginning	origin
ortho	straight, right	orthodontist
paed, ped	child	pediatrician
pater	father	paternal
path	feeling, suffer	sympathy
ped	foot	pedal
phil	love	philosophy
phob	fear	claustrophobia
phon	sound	phonograph
photo	light	photograph
phys	nature	physical
plur	more	plural
pod	foot	tripod
poli, polis	city	metropolis
pop	people	popular
port	carry	transport
pos	place	position

psych	mind, soul	psychology
pug	fight	repugnant
quer, ques	ask, seek	inquiry
rupt	break	bankrupt
scend	climb	ascend
sci	know	conscience
scop	see	microscope
scribe, script	write	inscribe
sect	cut	dissect
serv	save, keep	reservoir
sign	mark	insignia
sol	alone	solitary
son	sound	unison
soph	wise	philosopher
spec	see	inspect
spir	breathe	spirit
stell	star	constellation
strict	draw tight	restrict
struct	build	structure
sum	highest	summit
tact	touch	contact
temp	time	temporary
term	end	exterminate
terr	land	terrain
tex	weave	texture
the, theo	god	theology
therm	heat	thermos
tract	pull, drag	tractor
urb	city	suburb
vac	empty	vacant
vag	wander	vagrant
var	different	variety
ven	come	advent
ver	turn	convert
ver	truth	verify
vict, vine	conquer	victory
vid	see	video
viv, vit	live	survive
voc, vok	voice	vocal
void	empty	voided
volv	roll	revolver
vor	eat	voracious

Appendix F

Websites for Word Study

Kid Crosswords and Other Puzzles http://www.kidcrosswords.com
Crosswords, word searches, crostics, and other word games.

Vocabulary Can Be Fun! http://www.vocabulary.co.il
Vocabulary games.

The Lex Files http://www.lexfiles.info/
This site of Latin and Greek prefixes, suffixes, and root words includes lists of quotations, legal terms, medical words, prescription terms, religious expressions, and various abbreviations from Latin and Greek.

Puzzle Choice http://www.puzzlechoice.com/pc/Kids_Choicex.html
Lots of puzzles at this site—crosswords, word searches, word play, and more.

?uzzability: Current Puzzles http://www.puzzability.com/puzzles/
Word games of all sorts that change regularly.

Vocabulary.com http://vocabulary.com
All kinds of word games that provide vocabulary practice. Includes puzzles and other activities based on Latin and Greek roots. All puzzles change regularly.

A.Word.A.Day http://www.wordsmith.org/awad
Introduces a new word each day; provides interesting information about the word.

Word Games and Puzzles! http://mindfun.com/
Calls itself the "best place on the net to have fun with your mind." Students will find word scrambles, webs, crossword puzzles—even Boggle. Lots of word trivia too!

Word Central http://www.wordcentral.com/
Maintained by Merriam-Webster, this site has plenty of activities and information for students, as well as resources (including lesson plans) for teachers. You can even build your own dictionary.

Wordsmyth http://www.wordsmyth.net/
Online educational dictionary and thesaurus. Includes anagram and crossword puzzle help.